Buried Caesars, and Other Secrets of Italian American Writing

SUNY series in Italian/American Culture
Fred L. Gardaphe, editor

Buried Caesars, and Other Secrets of Italian American Writing

Robert Viscusi

STATE UNIVERSITY OF NEW YORK PRESS

Published by
State University of New York Press, Albany

For information, address State University of New York Press,
194 Washington Avenue, Suite 305, Albany, NY 12210-2384

Production by Judy Block
Marketing by Michael Campochiaro

Library of Congress Cataloging in Publication Data

Viscusi, Robert.
   Buried Caesars, and other secrets of Italian American writing / Robert Viscusi.
      p. cm. — (SUNY series in Italian/American culture)
   Includes bibliographical references.
   ISBN-10 0-7914-6633-7 (hardcover : alk. paper)
   ISBN-10 0-7914-6634-5 (pbk.: alk. paper)
   1. American literature—Italian American authors—History and criticism.
2. American literature—Italian influences. 3. Italian Americans—Intellectual
life. 4. Italian Americans in literature. I. Title. II. Series.

PS153.I8V57 2005
810.9'851—dc22

2005003758
ISBN-13 978-0-7914-6633-9 (hardcover : alk. paper) —
ISBN-13 978-0-7914-6634-6 (pbk.: alk. paper)

10 9 8 7 6 5 4 3 2 1

To the memory of my grandparents

Contents

Preface

"Italian America is an underworld empire where gangsters rule." Italian
Americans wonder why people believe this. They object. "I am a cardi-
ologist." "I am a gardener." "I am a poet." "I am a teacher."

They are right to wonder and to object. After all, the belief is false
and damaging. What is the secret of its amazing persistence? Why is the
gangster epic *the* Italian American story?

Yes, there are gangsters, but they do not rule.

Yet Italian America is indeed shaped by powers that lie deep in
darkness. Most of these hidden powers are not criminals, not even persons at all. Rather they are beliefs—lost causes and impossible loyalties.
These beliefs, and the conditions of their subsistence, are what give life
to the myth of Italian America as an underworld.

Italian America is like an iceberg. Most of its mass is invisible.

Italian America looks like Pizzaland. But it thinks with the mind
of a lost empire. Italian Americans are not always aware that they operate from the tacit assumptions of imperial subjects. By *tacit assumptions,* I mean beliefs that people share without exploring in detail where
they originate or what they imply. Many assumptions that govern Italian America are old pieces of Italian national propaganda deeply
embedded in Italian American culture: "Italy is not just a *country*. It is a
civilization—a *culture* admired and envied and imitated by the whole
world." "The Italian language was invented by Italy's national poet
Dante Alighieri." "The Italian family is eternal." "Italy is destined to
rule Africa." This brand of propaganda was beamed at Italians who
lived in the colonies for decades. The intensity of the beam grew greater
and greater until December 11, 1941, when it flat-out stopped. On that
day, Benito Mussolini, the Fascist dictator of Italy, declared war on the

United States, and all the fine fantasies about Italy that Italian Americans had been reading in their newspapers and hearing on the radio suddenly became enemy propaganda. This is no mere figure of speech. Those who had not become U.S. citizens—about 600,000 persons—had to register as enemy aliens. Hundreds of Italian Americans were interned in army camps all over the country, fifty-two thousand more lived under conditions of virtual house arrest. In Italian neighborhoods, posters everywhere commanded, "Don't Speak the Enemy's Language! Speak American!"[1]

Italian Americans stopped speaking Italian in the street. They no longer taught their children the language they themselves had grown up speaking. Many Italian-language publications went out of business.

This abrupt way of becoming American left Italian Americans with a large set of beliefs that they shared and continued to pass on to their children, beliefs that had no easy entry into the general American-language conversation. These beliefs are the Buried Caesars of my title. They survive in a half-light where they rarely become the subject of outright debate. They function as an unconscious imperialist faith. They are as powerful as they are hidden. When they surface, they usually take some distorted form. I will conduct a tour of many such forms. The most famous of these forms—the most glamorous, the most damnably attractive to Americans, who have their own imperialist dreams—are the ones that surface in the myth of the mob. That myth is both the glory and the curse of Italian American writing. It is a curse because it keeps Italian Americans in a state of suspended colonization. It is a glory because it is tremendously inventive, and because unpacking it, as we shall see when we come to the Imperial Sopranos, can teach us an enormous amount about what it means to tell an Italian American story.

Sightings

Caesars' ghosts are familiar apparitions in U.S. culture. Americans, it sometimes seems, go to Rome in a time machine. There they encounter, at the minimum, "a vague sense of ponderous remembrances." Nathaniel Hawthorne, one of the first analysts of this phenomenon, describes the experience as something uncanny, "a perception of such weight and density in a by-gone life, of which this spot was the center, that the present moment is crowded out, and our individual affairs are but half as real, here, as elsewhere."[2]

Italian Americans can taste this thrill without visiting Rome. Of course the dynamics are different. The Roman past touches them very near. It lives in their own bodies. Italian Americans know and recognize this, often without being ready to say why or how it is that they do. They suffer "the forgetting of history which history itself produces."[3] However, they can, and sometimes do, turn to the "ponderous remembrances" that they share. Italian American writers have worked to represent this encounter. Many have aimed to show how the forgotten and embodied past can surprise a person:

> Michael shifted uneasily in his chair. He looked at his older brother. He remembered Sonny as being sometimes casually brutal but essentially warmhearted. A nice guy. It seemed unnatural to hear him talking this way, it was chilling to see the names he had written down, men to be executed, as if he were some newly crowned Roman Emperor.[4]

Italian Americans have seen them at Sunday dinner, the bridges of those imperial noses, the curls of those familiar haircuts. And Roman totems, still today, are always heroes of spectacle. But they are not always heroes of thought. Indeed, for many Italian American writers, these figures evoke troubling reflections. They bristle with buried feelings of unutterable loss and unspeakable desire. The images of Caesars recall the very contradictions that made Italian America.

Contradictions

Memories of dominion look out from under their brows, reproaching Italy for its centuries of decline. A long time has passed since Caesars ruled in Rome. Italian immigrants of the late-nineteenth and early-twentieth centuries knew this. They had often heard that after the 1860s, the newly unified Italy of the Risorgimento was going to change the story. There would be a new empire. Not soon, however, as it turned out.

Singing Italy's glorious songs about itself, millions left in search of work. They could never forget the despair and hunger that had driven them out, nor could they forget the dead silence of the boundless ocean. Living in the United States, they would read Italian newspapers that liked to trumpet Italy's new national will to power, but they could readily see (even though many of them chose not to) that a more formidable will to power was shaping their lives in the United States. Italy had abandoned them when they lived there. That was why they left. Now it would abandon them all over again in the United States. Like hopeless lovers, many went on believing in Italy's greatness no matter how badly she treated them.

Love forgets injuries. Once Italian Americans grew accustomed to living in English, the memories of many unhappy contradictions went underground. Most Italian Americans nowadays have forgotten their origins as orphans of massive political catastrophes. Their writers can hardly avoid such knowledge, however. In Italian American writing, *Italy* is a word that means both "the homeland of desire" and "the empire that failed." Reading Italian American writing without encountering the hopeless dreams of glory that lie entombed in it is impossible. These dreams too are Buried Caesars. They shape the tormented mixture of pride and humiliation that gives this literature its emotional texture and appeal.

Method

The history of how Italian American literature came to use the English language has its moment of crisis in 1941, but it neither begins nor ends there. As soon as Italian immigrants were able to write in English, they began to do so. But language is a complex phenomenon, deeply intertwined with questions of power and identity. Consequently, the most difficult problem for Italian American writers and readers is language. For some, English is the enemy's language. As lately as the 1980s, a Sicilian American poet was calling English a cursèd tongue.[5] For most, however, it has been necessary both to accept English and at the same time to find a way of making it visibly Italian.

Italian American writers, when they want to present themselves as such, generally do so by finding ways to use Italian words when writing in English. This seems a simple enough procedure, but it presents many problems. On the one hand, Italian words establish place and filiation and pride, but on the other hand, the class systems of both Italy and the United States tell Italian Americans that their Italian is "only" a dialect—a sign of marginality. This opposition can be treated as a paradox, only a seeming contradiction. More frequent, however, is the attempt to resolve this contradiction by resorting to figures that seem large enough to contain both sides. Frank Sinatra might act like a thug, but he would also be known as the Chairman of the Board. Such characters are among the Caesars of Italian American ideology, deeply buried in ways of thinking and behaving. They resemble neurotic "solu-

tions"—hidden illusions we use to distance ourselves from the contradictions of our lives.[6] Such solutions are hard to get rid of, even when
we know where they are, because so many things depend on them.

Contradictions and solutions produce and reproduce one another
in a culture. This book shows how some writers—John Fante and Don
DeLillo, for example—have emphasized the contradictions. One can see
how Italian-American writing often plays two opposing hands at the
same time. This book also shows how other writers—Mario Puzo and
Gay Talese, for example—have dug up the Buried Caesars and placed
them on view, allowing the reader to see the intimate relationships
between deep conflicts and the mythic figures that appear to rise above
them.

This book follows the windings of political self-contradiction
through attention to the evolution of an Italian American literary language. This language is always the scene of conflict, always open to the
temptations of grandiose solutions, always susceptible to deflation and
revision.

Language presents us with the most visible structural evidence of
contradictions, especially when we bear in mind that language is never
merely the vehicle for personal beliefs. National languages, which
mingle on the page of Italian American writing, are intricately bound
with national literatures. And these present the student of literature
with serious issues of discernment.

All literatures are ideologies, but not all literatures are equal. A
national literature is an ideology that reflects the tastes and interests of
the people who dominate the nation. Other literatures have less concentrated force behind them. Italian American writing, the subject of this
book, arises from the history, thought, and beliefs of a people that has
not exercised dominion in any nation, a marginalized people forced to
leave its ancestral home in Italy, a people forced to abandon its inherited languages, a people that has long struggled to achieve social and
economic progress in the United States. To study Italian American literature means to engage that struggle—to engage in that struggle if the
student is an Italian American. The task that faces such a student is
daunting.

The first difficulty is to define an Italian American literature that
differs critically from those of both Italy and the United States. *Italian*
and *American* are both names for national projects, each of which has
its own imaginary and its own literature. These are well-constructed,
well-established, and forceful projects. They constitute overwhelming
presences in Italian American writing. Italian literature belongs to the

warriors, priests, and merchants who have ruled Italy for many centuries. American literature reflects the ideology of Western culture and territorial expansion that have guided the growth of this continental empire throughout the centuries of its career as an expansionist power. Each of these literatures looms infinitely larger than Italian American writing can possibly do, and each comes supplied with a large institutional force in the form of school textbooks, curricular requirements, histories, biographies, works of reference, libraries, editions, newspapers, reviews, publishing houses, endowed chairs in universities, national prizes, private patronage, and government support at many levels.

Because Italian American literature does not belong to a national project, it has no large established force of its own. Instead, it maintains relations—sometimes consciously, but always in a posture that is inevitably subordinate—with the agenda of fully articulated and fully institutionalized national ideologies. Thus, Italian American literature often engages in its own marginalization.

- Many Italian American writers boast thoughtlessly of Italy. Their texts repeat the Italian notions that *real* Italian culture is the metropolitan ideology of the great Italian cities and, correlatively, that immigrants are poor and uneducated persons, more interesting for their folklore and their cooking than for their philosophic or artistic contributions. This unconscious colonialism is often intensified under the old defensiveness that afflicts exponents of Italian metropolitan culture; these defenders live with a degree of self-doubt that has nothing to do with migration, but rather has its own deep roots in Italy's long history as a country, once great, that later suffered foreign dominion for many centuries before it became a nation, an old thirst for vindication that led directly to Italy's history of disastrous imperialism during the first half of the twentieth century.
- American literature still treats Italy as a conquered province. Americans see Italy as a pleasure colony of dubious virtue. And much Italian American literature works against its own interests by exploiting this attitude. In some Italian American writing, one sees reflected the American notion that Italians are people whose main contribution to life in the United States has been to charm and entertain Americans, while at the same time constituting an ineradicable criminal conspiracy—in short, a

people morally unequipped to enter civil life in the democratic paradise of the United States.

In neither case does Italian American literature have a clear and independent agenda. In both cases its position is colonial; that is, its own force is alienated from itself to strengthen claims that belong to one or another national project.

- Italian America stands to Italy in the relation of a captive market for Italian value-added goods; its history flows from its position in the market of cheap labor, of migrants who left Italy in search of salaries and then, for generations afterward, sent back money that kept Italy's balance of payments flourishing. Today, many Italian Americans not only continue to identify themselves with the nation that excluded them, but they also carry within them many of the leading themes of Italian national culture.
- Italian America stands to the United States in the relation of a colony-within, perpetually assigned certain historical tasks in the food, fashion, and entertainment industries. The default belief is that Italian Americans are a people not to be trusted past a certain point. Thus the myth of a vast underworld conspiracy. Its illegality serves as a constant ceiling to Italian American political and social ambitions.

The ideological effect of this doubly colonized position has been a double blindness.

- Italian Americans have forgotten why Italy matters in their lives. They have only the vaguest notion of how their position in the United States is affected by their relationship with Italy. They have forgotten why they no longer speak the Italian language; and with that language has gone the much effective notion of Italian history and thought, along with any sense of what the current political and economic interests of Italy may be, or any critical understanding of how these interests may affect Italian Americans.
- Italian Americans believe in a Hollywood version of their lives in the United States. Most Italian Americans have only a hazy idea of what their actual history in the United States has been.

Any precise knowledge of their real purposes, interests, struggles, or heroic leaders has been replaced by the ubiquitous
luminescent cloud of semidivine Mafia dons and movie stars—
that is to say, by the American ideology that permanently
assigns Italian Americans to life in a subaltern colony within
the United States. Political leaders such as Arturo Giovannitti
and Vito Marcantonio are infinitely less well known than Al
Capone and Lucky Luciano, or Frank Sinatra and John
Travolta.

Not all literary texts engage in self-subordination. This book
shows how Italian American writing has begun to develop a critical
sense of its own historical role. This is necessary work. Literary texts
that deal directly with colonial blindness are little known in Italian
America. Works that explore the paradoxes and difficulties of the Italian American position—works such as John Fante's *Ask the Dust* or
Helen Barolini's *Umbertina*—are still little read and less discussed
among Italian Americans. Today, Italian Americans go to college. They
learn to read the contradictions that give life to the novels of Herman
Melville and Virginia Woolf. But they have yet to acquire the habit of
paying the same kind of intellectual or political attention to the contradictions that animate the writings of Italian Americans.

This failing is most evident in the way that Italian American readers have received works such as *The Godfather* and The *Sopranos*.
Whereas critics from Rose Basile Green to Fred Gardaphe and Marianna DeMarco Torgovnik and Chris Messenger have analyzed these
works for what they have to tell us about the complexities of Italian
American culture and history, their approach has not dominated the
conversation. Many Italian American readers and organizations have
greeted these works as occasions for lament and for cries of discrimination. Such readers are correct to say that discrimination inevitably
accompanies and draws nourishment from works such as these. But
they make a fatal mistake when they stop there. *The Godfather* and *The
Sopranos* are the most widely influential works of narrative that Italian
America has yet produced. Their very successes call for the best critical
and historical understanding that critics can bring to bear on them.
Their enormous popularity and prestige does not rest simply on an
uncritical use of criminal stereotypes (and indeed, these stereotypes are
themselves complex historical facts that call for patient analysis and
unraveling). Stereotypes alone do not produce the impact that these nar-

ratives have had. *The Godfather* and *The Sopranos* are, for good or ill, works of art. To respond to them with less than full critical attention amounts to a serious failing, one that leaves Italian Americans unprepared to deal with the cultural situation they in fact occupy.

National literatures can confuse the issue for colonized persons. National literatures convey, or they reflect on, the national ideologies to which they belong. Colonized literatures convey, or they reflect on, the profoundly conflicted ideologies that constitute them. Colonized persons have a special need of literature because it helps them to clarify and to make conscious the unspoken contradictions that hold them in thrall to their historical condition. A critical understanding of Italian American literature can allow Italian Americans to see and to understand the ideological double bind that constitutes their condition. Thus, this book has two steady themes:

1. How Italian American literature embodies Italian nationalist and imperialist ideology, often unconsciously, at the level of language and rhetoric, as well as in moral standards and visionary imagination. This ideology is the source of the Buried Caesars in the book's title, the powerful meanings that come, often unannounced, with the very name *Italian*.
2. How Italian American writing embodies the American ideology. Acceptance, conscious and unconscious alike, of the Italian ideology has made escaping American ideology, which has class interests more in common with Italian national culture than with Italian immigrant culture, difficult for Italian Americans. This is why the Buried Caesars of Italian ideology emerge in the United States.

To the degree that Italian Americans achieve critical awareness of these inherited ideological burdens, they grow freer to invent an Italian American culture rather than to repeat one symptomatically.

This book examines the shape of a literary history that can call itself distinctly Italian American. But a literature does not begin with critical consciousness alone. Italian American writing, like other literatures, requires an institutional and economic base. Its very condition ensures that it lacks the institutional force of the national literatures that stand on either side of it. Italian American literature cannot thrive as such without coming to terms with its relationship to these national literatures. Italy's fortunes affect Italian America both directly and indirectly, and Italian American ideology needs to take account of this, needs to develop awareness that is much more conscious and to articulate a relationship with Italian ideology and with American notions of Italy.

Shakespeare's Mark Antony says, "I come to bury Caesar, not to praise him." Neither of these predictions is fulfilled. Antony does not avoid praising Caesar. Nor does Caesar remain buried. His ghost continues to play an important role long afterwards.

Italian Caesarism showed a similar resilience in Italian America after the lights went out in December 1941, recurring everywhere in the form of unacknowledged and misunderstood allegiances to dead ideals. These allegiances became the colonial phantasms that still return in the shapes of Don Corleone and (for that matter) Frank Sinatra.

Italian America, if it is ever to stop reliving its ancient dependency, needs a new vision of its American past and of its relationship to Italy. This need alone is reason enough to examine the dreams and purposes that move under the surface of Italian American writing.

Acknowledgments

When I began working on this subject in 1979, little of the institutional discourse that makes a collection of texts into the body of a literature existed. A rising generation of scholars and writers, however, was interested in supplying what was lacking, and this work has been conducted, as it were, in their midst. When a field is forming, the most important discussions are often not the ones printed in books. The writings of Italians in America, their use of English and of Italian, have been the themes of many debates during the time I have been working on this book. My interlocutors have included the following persons—some professionally interested in the subject and some simply willing to discuss it with someone who needed to talk about it: Steven Acunto, Theresa Aiello-Gerber, Flavia Alaya, Stefano Albertini, Carole Bonomo Albright, Bruno Arcudi, Patrizia Ardizzone, Joseph Arleo, Stanley Aronowitz, Louis Asekoff, Ignazio Baldelli, Luigi Ballerini, Franco Bagnolini, Helen Barolini, Regina Barreca, Luigi Barzini, Thomas Belmonte, Jean Béranger, Adria Bernardi, Steen Boatti, William Boelhower, Mary Jo Bona, Luigi Bonaffini, Jerome Bongiorno, Marylou Bongiorno, Vittore Branca, Marina Cacioppo, John D. Calandra, Sal Cannavo, Philip V. Cannistraro, Vincenzo Cappelletti, Rocco Caporale, Betty Boyd Caroli, Alessandro Carrera, Santa Casciani, Robert Casillo, Frank Cavaioli, Diana Cavallo, Teresa Cerasuola, Mark Ciabattari, Edward M. Cifelli, Gaetano Cipolla, Raffaele Cocchi, Furio Colombo, Terri Colpi, Francesco Corrias, George Cunningham, Matilda Raffa Cuomo, Pellegrino D'Acierno, Rosetta D'Angelo, Robert D'Attilio, Alexander De Conde, Don De Lillo, Tony De Nonno, Louise De Salvo, Dona De Sanctis, Bénédicte Deschamps, Mario Diacono, Bill Di Biasi, Jeanne Dickey, Pietro di Donato, Elvira Di Fabio, Cesare di Montezomolo, Robert Di Pietro, Diane Di Prima, Giuseppe Di Scipio, Lawrence Di Stasi,

Francesco Durante, Connie Egelman, William Egelman, Gil Fagiani, Michele Fazio, Francis X. Femmenella, Luigi Fontanella, Emilio Franzina, Vincent Fucillo, Dariel Gabriel, Richard Gambino, Fred Gardaphe, Eileen Gardiner, Maria Mazziotti Gillan, Dana Gioia, Paolo A. Giordano, Daniela Gioseffi, Fabio Girelli-Carasi, Edvige Giunta, Rose Basile Green, George Guida, Hermann Haller, Josephine Gattuso Hendin, Joanna Hermann, Robert L. Hess, Irene Impellizzeri, Natalia Indrimi, Lisa Interollo, Luciano Iorizzo, John T. Irwin, Matthew Frye Jacobson, Richard Juliani, Robert J. Kelly, Jerry Krase, Salvatore La Gumina, Gioacchino Lanza Tomasi, Marina La Palma, Valerie Lasciak, Michael La Sorte, Maria Laurino, Maria Lisella, Maristella Lorch, Francesco Loriggio, Stefano Luconi, Carmine Luisi, Sal Lumetta, Gianclaudio Macchiarella, Carolina Mancuso, Jerre Mangione, Silvana Mangione, Mary Ann Mannino, Martino Marazzi, Angela Marrantino, Sebastiano Martelli, Giuseppe Massara, Joseph Massaro, Carole Maso, Elizabeth Mathias, Sante Matteo, John Maynard, Elizabeth Messina, Gerald Meyer, Vicenzo Milione, Mario Mignone, Eugene Mirabelli, Franco Mulas, Adrienne Munich, Ronald Musto, Louise Napolitano, Kathryn Nocerino, Elizabeth Pallitto, Rocco Pallone, Michael Palma, Josephine Pane, Remigio Pane, Flavia Pankiewicz, Anne Paolucci, Henry Paolucci, Joseph Papaleo, Emanuele Papparella, Michael Parenti, Will Parinello, Masia Passaro, James Periconi, Sergio Perosa, Joseph Perricone, Carl Picco, Luciana Polney, Cristina Previtali, Giorgio Radicati, Roberto Ragone, Vittoria repetto, Andrew Rolle, Gianfausto Rosoli, Evelyn Rossetti, Fred Rotondaro, John Paul Russo, Edward Said, Barbara Sansone, Kenneth Scambray, Gloria Salerno, Joseph Scelsa, Neil Schaeffer, Joseph Sciorra, Paola Sensi-Isolani, Ilaria Serra, Lorraine Shea, Joann Sicoli, Graziella Sidoli, Paolo Spedicato, Adele LaBarre Starensier, Felix Stefanile, Victoria Surluiga, Gay Talese, Anthony Tamburri, Peter Taubman, Gioia Timpanelli,. Maddalena Tirabassi, Lydio Tomasi, Silvano Tomasi, Bill Tonelli, Ellen Tremper, Joseph Tursi, Joseph Tusiani, Mariana DeMarco Torgovnick, Bernard Toscani, Donald Tricarico, Anthony Valerio, Paolo Valesio, John Van Sickle, Pasquale Verdicchio, Gianni Viola, Justin Vitiello, Itala Vivan, Brooke Watkins, Fiorenza Weinapple, Ethyle R. Wolfe, Donez Xiques, Leo Zanderer, and Sharon Zukin.

The National Endowment for the Humanities, the John D. Calandra Italian American Institute, and Professional Staff Congress/City University of New York have all provided fellowship support. Among my most engaged interlocutors have been members of the American Italian Historical Association, the American Association for Italian

Studies, the American Italian Cultural Roundtable, the Italian American Writers Association, and students at Brooklyn College, New York University, and the City University of New York Graduate School. I have been fortunate in my family conversation. My sisters Linda Lentini and Carole Presti, my cousin Michael Di Marco, Marjorie Brescia, and Kip Viscusi have all taken part in this conversation, as did my grandparents, my parents, my aunts and uncles, and all my other cousins. Linda, in particular, was the first of our generation to learn Italian and to visit Italy. She gave us our first lessons in the Italian language. Her interest and support have been basic to this whole enterprise. The Brooklyn College Library has helped me at every step of the way, as have my colleagues at the Center for Italian American Studies, in the Department of English, and at the Ethyle R. Wolfe Institute for the Humanities—all at Brooklyn College. I owe an immeasurable debt of gratitude to my secretary and flawless proofreader Magdelibia Garcia. My wife, Nancy O'Shea, my children Robert Jr. and Victoria Ann, have been enthusiastic and engaged partners in the debate.

Some of the chapters of this book have had earlier lives, in somewhat different form, in the following places: "*De vulgari eloquentia*: An Approach to the Language of Italian American Fiction," *Yale Italian Studies*, I, no. 3 (1981): 1–28; "*Il caso della casa*: Stories of Houses in Italian America," in *The Family and Community Life of Italian Americans*, ed. Richard N. Juliani (New York: American Italian Historical Associaiton, 1983), pp. 1–9; "*Son of Italy*: Immigrant Ambition and American Literature," *MELUS: Multi-Ethnic Literature of the United States*, 28, no. 3 (Fall 2003): 41–54; "The Text in the Dust: Writing Italy across America," *Studi Emigrazione* (Marzo 1982): 123–30; "The Semiology of Semen: Questioning the Father," in *The Italian Americans through the Generations*, ed. Rocco Caporale (New York: American Italian Historical Association, 1986), pp. 185–96; "Circles of the Cyclopes: Schemes of Recognition in Italian American Discourse," in *Italian Americans: New Perspectives*, ed. Lydio Tomasi (New York: Center for Migration Studies, 1985), pp. 209–19; "A Literature Considering Itself: The Allegory of Italian America," in *From the Margin: Writings in Italian Americana*, ed. A. Tamburri, P. Giordano, and F. Gardaphe (West Lafayette, Ind.: Purdue University Press, 1991), pp. 263–81; a draft of chapter one served as keynote address at the October 1999 conference of the Semiotic Society of America in Pittsburgh.

My steadiest interlocutors have been the published texts of scholars who have addressed this theme, particularly Rose Basile Green, *The*

Italian American Novel: A Document of the Interaction of Two Cultures (1974); Lawrence DiStasi, *Malocchio: The Underside of Vision* (1981), *Dream Streets: The Big Book of Italian American Culture* (1989), and ed., *Una storia segreta The Secret History of Italian American Evacuation and Internment during World War II* (2001); William Boelhower, *Immigrant Autobiography: Four Versions of the Italian American Self* (1982): Helen Barolini, "Introduction," *The Dream Book: An Anthology of Writings by Italian-American Women* (1985); Giuseppe Massara, *Americani* (1986); Fred Gardaphe, Anthony Tamburri, and Paolo A. Giordano, "Introduction," *From the Margin; Writings in Italian Americana*; Fred Gardaphe, *Italian Signs, American Streets: The Evolution of Italian American Narrative* (1995), *Dagoes Read: Tradition and the Italian American Writer* (1996), and *Leaving Little Italy: Essaying Italian American Culture* (2004); Anthony Tamburri, *To Hyphenate or Not to Hyphenate* (1991), and *A Semiotic of Ethnicity* (1998); Antonio D'Alfonso, *Italics* (1996); Pasquale Verdicchio, *Bound by Distance: Rethinking Nationalism through the Italian Diaspora* (1997); Pellgrino D'Acierno, ed., *The Italian American Heritage* (1998); Mary Jo Bona, *Claiming a Tradition: Italian American Women Writers* (1999); Kenneth Scambray, *The North American Italian Renaissance* (2000); Francesco Durante, *Italoamericana* (2001); Edvige Giunta, *Writing with an Accent: Contemporary Italian American Women Writers* (2002); Martino Marazzi, *Voices of Italian America* (2004). These are some of the books that have mattered to me, but there are dozens of other works, all duly recorded in footnotes, to which I owe the pleasure and enlightenment that any student needs to keep going. These works have kept me company when I was writing, challenged me the most deeply, and rewarded my attention the most fully. My longest and most sustaining conversation has been with the philosophical poet and critic Peter Carravetta whose many essays and journal, *Differentia: Review of Italian Thought*, have kept me in dialogue with a transatlantic conversation of considerable breadth and of irreducible disparity with the kinds of things we were more likely to talk about here in Italian America. Carravetta took it on himself to provide a forum for Italian thought in the United States, which served to remind intellectuals in Italian America that they need no longer consider themselves alone on the planet.

Introduction

Secrets of Italian American Writing

Italian Americans have two problems, one they acknowledge and the other they keep secret, even from themselves.

The problem they acknowledge is the Mafia. They not only acknowledge this problem, but they never stop talking about it. People (I am one of them) who would like official Italian America to spend much more of its money supporting writers and scholars find this obsession with the Mafia frustrating. Its workings are familiar: in a game of blame tag, some Italian Americans make a lot of money on a Mafia movie, and other Italian Americans, especially large Italian American organizations, give the movie free publicity by loudly protesting it. Whether these protesters are insincere or just too angry to stop and think is hard to determine. On the one hand, they certainly mean what they say, and they write eloquent speeches and articles about their position, articles that would be more convincing if they had had any demonstrable effect. But thirty years of protesting *The Godfather,* often hailed as the greatest movie ever made, did not hamper *The Sopranos,* often hailed in its turn as the greatest television show ever made. Oscars and Emmys have rained down on the producers, directors, actors, screenwriters, composers, editors, set designers, and just about everyone else who has had anything to do with these productions. Such a result might lead the protesters to wonder if something might be wrong with their tactics or even with the case they are making. That something is their second problem, the one they do not acknowledge.

The second problem, the secret problem of Italian Americans, is Italy. This problem is a secret in two ways. First, plenty of Italian Americans have forgotten all about Italy. It has nothing to do with them, they suppose, even if they still keep their Italian names.[1] They are Americans pure and simple, and glad of it. Second, many Italian Americans, particularly the ones who protest the Mafia films, do not think of Italy as a problem but as a reason to boast. We painted the *Mona Lisa*. We discovered America. We invented the opera.

But Italy *is* a problem, and pretending that it is not is the main reason Italian Americans have never been able to dispel the Mafia stereotype. Let us look at how the ways of pretending that Italy is not a problem have confused the issue for Italian Americans.

The belief that Italy has nothing to do with Italian Americans. This amounts to a massive act of denial, comparable to a black person's pretending to be white. *Italian* is the difference-marker in the expression *Italian American*; and for a long series of reasons, Italy continues to play a role in giving that expression its meaning as a social and historical fact. A few cases in point:

- Anglo-Americans descend from a long history of not liking, wanting, or respecting Italians. During the Protestant Reformation, Italians became synonymous with the evil, double-dealing Catholic Church. In England, the spokesperson for Renaissance Italy was Niccolò Machiavelli, a political thinker so feared, hated, and secretly admired that the English began calling the devil Old Nick in his honor.
- Italy, long divided into many states, became a system of subordinate provinces and principalities after the Treaty of Cateau-Cambrésis in 1559. Dominated afterward for centuries by French, Spanish, and Austrian armies, Italy suffered the contempt that accompanies the condition of a dependency.
- The Risorgimento aimed to restore dignity to Italy and to Italians in the world, a worthy task that had only begun—and begun badly—during the years of the great Italian exodus, when millions of people decided that Italy's good fortunes were too far into the future for them. When they left, the name of Italians in the world was still not what they might have hoped.
- All of these factors came into play during the Great Migration to the United States. Millions of Italians poured into U.S. ports, while Nativist Americans looked at them through eyes narrowed by racial and religious bigotry and by the greed and class arrogance of people who were systematically exploiting the

Italians as cheap substitutes for slave labor. Italian immigrants suffered discrimination, hatred, and even lynchings.[2]

- During Prohibition, Italians became the designated guilt-bearers for American hypocrisy about liquor, gambling, and sex, forbidden pleasures that Italian gangsters supplied to them.
- Finally, during World War II, Italy was an enemy nation, and Italian Americans were interned in concentration camps and forbidden to speak their native language in the streets of their own neighborhoods.

In short, the history of Italian American stereotypes has everything to do with the history of Italy. Italy's long subjection to the other powers in Europe combined with American conditions to ensure that Italian Americans would live in a subaltern condition, a colony within. Italy's doomed adventurism in the years since the Risorgimento led to the wars of Fascism, whose policies first flattered Italian Americans with dreams of Italian glory, then left them, millions of them, to live with the memories of those dreams in a country where they had suddenly become enemy aliens.

The belief that Italy is a reason to boast. Would that this were true, but it is not. Italy is wonderful, no doubt. Too wonderful, in fact. Seen from Italian America, Italy represents a mountain of prestige that Italian Americans do not share.

- Italy expects Italian Americans to consume Italian manufactures: cheese, wine, textiles, clothing, leather goods, perfumes, and bottled water.
- Through its network of Italian Cultural Institutes in major U.S. cities, Italy supports the diffusion of Italian paintings, sculptures, films, operas, books, and programs of language instruction.
- Italy expects Italian Americans to be proud of Italy. Indeed, it needs them to be proud of Italy, which is still industriously at work overcoming the effects of political misadventures that have very long histories. Italy, indeed, still feels the need to improve its image in the world. Italian nationals can scarcely help bristling whenever anyone identifies them with Italian Americans, who still live in a colonial condition that Italians want to believe they themselves have overcome.

- Italy finds not colonizing Italian Americans difficult. Certainly, of course, Italy pays them attention. They are not only a colony but also a rich one—a large market driven by American prosperity, ambition, energy, and organizational power. Italian Americans function as distributors for Italian exports in the United States. The Northeast corridor alone, where so many Italian Americans live, constitutes a market for Italian luxury goods as large as the entire national market for those goods in Italy itself. Italian Americans are fit to import Italian goods and culture. But they remain in a colonial condition.
- Italy is slow to accept Italian Americans as equals in culture and intelligence. No Italian American Cultural Institutes exist in Italy. As a consequence, every time Italian Americans devote their time, money, energy, and will to boasting about Italy, they are reinforcing a colonial order of prestige that places them at the bottom of a very large, very old, and very heavy pyramid.

The Mafia is the myth of the Italian American colonial condition. The message is that Italian Americans cannot achieve cultural equality. They belong to Little Italy and can never escape. Getting rich does not help. Little Italy began its life as an informal colony of the Italian nation. Thanks to this arrangement, Italy, with its ancient woes and its intense interest in its own affairs, is always inclined, and often without much thinking about it, to reinstate Italian America in its colonial condition. "Just when I thought I was *out*," Michael Corleone complains in *The Godfather, Part III,* "they pull me back *in.*" That line is frequently quoted in *The Sopranos,* where Italian Americans still have their loyalties in the old neighborhoods, still operate outside the rules of the dominant culture, even after they move to the suburbs, even after they send their children to Ivy League schools. To be sure, this story belongs to the history of American culture. But it also has a powerful Italian context, not only in the past, but also in the present. Italian Americans descend from people Italy does not even want to remember. Italy still has no need to redeem them, even if it wanted, or were able, to do so. The Mafia fable dramatizes the truth that Italian Americans still secretly belong to the order of prestige established by Roman aristocrats thousands of years ago and never once seriously disturbed in all this time. Italy has never had a successful revolution. The Risorgimento, which pretended to be a revolution, ended by making rich people richer and by starving poor people, millions and millions of them, out of Italy altogether.

Italian Americans cannot forget Italy, even if they would like to. They must, however, learn to deal with it on their own terms and not those dictated by the Italian Trade Commission or the Ministry of Foreign Affairs. Like other colonials, Italian Americans must learn to see themselves at the center of their own world, not merely on the periphery of someone else's. This takes time, and it takes writers. Italian American writing, the subject of this book, grapples with the meaning of Italy in Italian America. The Italy of the mind is large and complicated. Its meanings in the lives of Italian Americans are many and not always easy to sort out—or even to discover. But writing does this necessary work, taking old meanings apart and using the pieces to assemble new ones.

In Italian America, writing finds the monumental display of a colonial mind. The Roman Caesars built altars to themselves throughout their military empire. Imperialist United Italy exported cheap labor, settled trading colonies, printed newspapers, inspired Columbus Day parades, and promoted the cult of its own greatness throughout its mercantile empire in the United States. The monuments of that empire are the fetish foods Italian Americans still import from Italy, as well as the beliefs, the heroes, and the attitudes that still shape their sense of themselves and of their history. These monuments do not usually carry labels. They do not even seem to be monuments. They are Buried Caesars.

What are Buried Caesars?

In Italy, a *Caesar* is not just a person, but also a category.

A Caesar is, first, a leader who arises out of a deadly stalemate.[3] Italian history has been rich in such violent oppositions, so Italians have found it useful to have a name for what happens when the situation becomes serious and neither side wishes to risk extinction. The opponents compromise on a figure that, characteristically, glows with an impossible glamour for as long as he lasts and then afterward makes a bad end. Outside of Julius Caesar himself, some examples of such figures are Mussolini, whom they hung naked by his heels in the public square; Cesare Borgia, who was found with twenty-seven stab wounds in his body; and the great Roman rabble-rouser of the middle ages Cola di Rienzo, whom the Romans tore to ribbons, then hanged upside down naked before burning him to ashes in front of the Mausoleum of Augustus.

Italian culture, we may say, also has many Caesars who are not persons but monuments to persons. Marble Italy is littered with portrait busts and colossal fists and broken temples that commemorate Caesars. In Italian America, the statues are not as numerous, but the Caesars are everywhere.

In Italian America, the Caesars include impossible ideals and exaggerated claims to which Italian Americans still give their devotion: the notion that Rome was noble; the belief that the Family is sacred; the axiom that Italians discovered America. As with Caesars themselves, such claims and ideals, arising out of impossible conflicts between one set of interests and another, can seem necessary to social and civil survival. American realities were in harsh conflict with Italian dreams. Emigrants departing Italy did not always leave their heroic phantoms behind. Indeed, a faith in such ghosts would remain basic to their sense of themselves as Italians. Beliefs that Italy's emigrants carried away with them have found their lodging places in what emigrants and their descendants have written in new countries and new languages.

Many Caesars lie buried in Italian American writing, as do many themes of Italian politics and culture. Most such themes are secret, not because they are hidden but because readers do not recognize them as what they are. Like other elements of the old Italian ideology, they are the sources of profound conflict in the colonial imagination. Reading Italian American writing well means understanding its secret themes, where they come from, how they work, and what they accomplish.

Where They Come From (Resurrecting Rome)

This story begins in Italy.

In Italy, people do not worship the dead, but they consult with them. Often, it is an intimate conversation. Come Saturday morning, under the cypress trees just outside any small town, people are changing candles and flowers at family tombs and telling their departed the week's news. It is also a public ritual. The Patriarch of Venice addresses the remains of Saint Mark. The pope talks to Saint Peter at his tomb on the Vatican Hill where the apostles laid him to rest. And the dead reply. On the graves of grandparents, children in Sicily find sweets and toys. Saints send dreams and miracles. The dead fill the audience chamber where we hear the lines of Italy's great poets.

Italians learn from the dead. This process is basic to the way that Italians reinvent themselves, century after century. They follow the sun that emerges from the underworld. They are experts in raising the dead. Christian religion preaches the resurrection of the body. This has its precise parallel in Italian ideology. In the fourteenth century, when the popes were forced to live at Avignon under the protection of the King of France, the poet Francesco Petrarca and the notary Cola di Rienzo began preaching the need to restore the authority of the Eternal City. The resurrection of Rome has been a steady element in Italian national ideology ever since.

The Renaissance or Rebirth (1400–1600) grew out of a centuries-long dialogue in which medieval Italians learned from the shades of ancient Romans. Poets contended with Virgil and Ovid. Lawyers took lessons from Cicero and Quintilian. Political scientists quibbled over Livy and Tacitus. Architects measured the Pantheon and the baths of Diocletian. Painters competed with frescoes they found on the walls of imperial villas. Generals would imitate Caesar; popes would ape Caligula. Out of all this copying and rivalry with the mighty dead, Renaissance Italians developed a style of spectacle that has left many reminiscences of itself along the streets of Rome and Florence, Naples, and Milan.

The Risorgimento or Reawakening (1815–1870) grew out of the same conversation, this time concentrating on questions of empire. That is, medieval trade and Renaissance spectacle had long since collaborated to make Italy a rich prize, but the prize had afterward fallen mostly into the hands of non-Italians. The French, the Spanish, the Austrians, and the Papacy had divided the opulent territories of Italy among themselves. The Risorgimento addressed this situation, and it imagined itself reviving the heroes who had once made Rome a great power. The Risorgimento's marching song begins with these words:

Fratelli d'Italia,
l'Italia s`è desta;
dell'elmo di Scipio
s`è cinta la testa.

Brothers of Italy,
Italy has risen now,
with Scipio's helmet
has belted her brow.[4]

The grandeur that was Rome: Scipio Africanus, the Roman general who defeated Carthage, scored the definitive victory that gave Rome its *imperium* or empire in the Mediterranean. Invoking Scipio, the Risorgimento foreshadowed its aim to build what it would come to call the Third Rome—third after those of the emperors and the popes.

The habit of constructing tomorrow in competition with yesterday runs deep in Italian culture.

Italians did not leave this habit behind when they moved into the English language. But resurrecting Rome in a country where there was no ancient Rome has had an odd effect.

How They Work (Visionary Supplements)

In America, Italians became colonials, and, like all colonials, they became visionaries. These colonials needed to make Italian sense out of the American world.

Italy supplied them with its long-elaborated notion of itself: the story of its past greatness that it asserted would become its future greatness. Italy had long filled the contradictory space between its reality and its ambitions with its narrative of empire, thus merging an imperfectly remembered past, rumored to be glorious, with an imperfectly understood present, known to be less than glorious. Italy sent its emigrants into the world carrying the dream of the colonial empire it hoped to construct: the emigrants, as a consequence, possessed the trappings and pretence of world dominion, but not the military, political, or diplomatic institutions that could make colonialist visions into fact and substance. Such contrasts between pretence and reality are humiliating, and often enough the response to such comedowns is to ratchet up the pretence a little higher.

Immigrants to the United States from Italy during the period of the Great Migration (1880–1924) needed Caesars to dream of. These people had little but imagination to guide them, arriving in the United States with hardly any practical idea of what they would find there. Of course, they all expected the ordinary uncertainties of life, and most knew something of the hardships they could expect to endure on the ocean. But Italian immigrants found America itself a huge puzzle. They could attempt to solve this puzzle with tales they had heard from their *paesani*, or they could refer to promises labor contractors had made to them.[5] But such scraps of advance information scarcely met the needs of the situation. And the United States, once they reached its shores, continued to confound them. Indeed, as they struggled with its language, laws, markets, and customs, and as they began to measure with their own eyes the planetary blankness of its open plains and mountain ranges, they found that America's enigmas grew deeper and wider. When America supplied them with explanations of itself, Italians often found themselves more offended than enlightened. Settlement-house missionaries who planted themselves in the Italian colonies preached Baptist and Methodist virtues as essentials of American life, but it was hard for Italians to accept that they ought never to drink wine, smoke cigars, or dance at weddings. At such moments, they learned to consult their own ideas of who they were and what they were doing in the United States.

These ideas had come with them from Italy. Italy for them was not what it later came to seem—a set of recipes, gestures, and other behaviors great and small, ready to be observed, catalogued, filmed, recounted, packaged, and sold as the formula of what it might mean to be Italian. For them, Italy resembled America in that it was a mystery that needed to be unraveled, full of intimate understandings and a desperate grandeur. Looking back, they saw their native land, one might say, under several distinct aspects, of which we can isolate three:

1. Home. Each migrant came from a *comune*, a city or a town somewhere in the peninsula or on the islands that belong to the nation called *Italia*—Sulmona, Agrigento, Anacapri, and thousands of smaller, lesser-known places. In practice, for many immigrants, one such place stood for Italy. When they spoke of Italy, this *comune* was the place they meant. Its people were the population they knew, its concerns were the ones they carried with them across the sea. This place was often anything but imperial. Indeed, each such place might be little more than a colony within the nationalist state. The local identities of Italian *comuni* survive in America in the myth of the Mafia, always attached to origins in towns of Sicily or Calabria or Campania, even when the commentators are themselves not Italian or knowledgeable about Italy. Mafia mythographers always emphasize that Italian Americans have a permanent connection with political subordination and linguistic exclusion. "They are all from Caltanissetta." "Castellammare del Golfo."

   The humble condition of such points of origin sometimes gives to Italian American thinking, living, and writing a powerful sense of connection with the preimperial and anti-imperial; but that effect is not simple, and its strength ought not be overestimated. It does not often become a clear political motive. For there is a countervailing force, and it is great. To the poor and the humble, Italian political traditions provide circus dreams of awesome display, and these too are things that immigrants see when they look back to Italy.

2. Nation. The Kingdom of Italy, its chamber of deputies, its min-istries, its elaborate and even impenetrable bureaucracies, had touched every one of these migrants. Not always lovingly. The immigrants carried away from Italy a bittersweet taste. They were proud to belong to a nation with a flag and a navy to fly it. They were thrilled to watch the *bersaglieri* in their feathered hats. But they were unhappy to leave their native places and families of origin behind, and they frequently carried resent-ments against a nation that had made earning a decent living in the places they were born impossible for them. This bitterness might have been enough to render them immune to the siren call of Italian imperialism and its hundred ways of reminding them of their own marginalization. But the Italian ideology had an appeal that actually increased when people left Italy.

3. Promised Land. Another Italy accompanied these Italians across the oceans and into the twentieth century. This was the visionary Italy that had appeared before the eyes of Giuseppe Verdi in 1841 as he began to compose an opera about the Babylonian captivity of the Hebrews. In that opera, named for the Babylonian king Nabucco (Nebuchadnezzar), the Hebrews sing an anthem in slavery that Italian patriots began to chant in the streets almost immediately after the opera's premiere in Milan in 1842[6]:

> *Va, pensiero, sull'ali dorate;*
> *va, ti posa sui clivi, sui colli*
> *ove olezzano tepide e molli*
> *l'aure dolci del suolo natal!*
> *Del Giordano le rive saluta,*
> *di Sionne le torri atterrate.*
> *Oh, mia patria sì bella e perduta!*
> *Oh, membranza sì cara e fatal!*
>
> Go, thought, on golden wings
> Go, rest on cliffs, on hills
> Where there are wafting the warm and gentle
> Sweet breezes of our native land!
> Greet the Jordan's banks,
> The fallen towers of Zion. . . .
> Oh, my fatherland—so beautiful and so lost!
> Oh, remembrance so dear, and fatal!

Italy the Promised Land. This song became, almost instantly, the rhapsody of the Risorgimento, and to this day people are still proposing it for the national anthem of the Italian state. Singing its trance melody, men and women through the decades of the Risorgimento faced down the French, the Austrians, and the Neapolitan Bourbons who sent armies against them, and they defied the popes who excommunicated them. To be sure, the vision of Italy that sustained the Risorgimento did not always suffice the Italians once Italy was made. But for those who left Italy afterward, the magic of distance raised this image into a perpetual niche of glory. "Oh, my fatherland—so beautiful and so lost! / Oh, remembrance so dear, and fatal!"

The visionary habit of mind was easily transferable to the United States, a nation that had its own imagery of land and promise, much of it derived from the same source in the chronicles of the ancient Hebrews. The United States would appear to Italians in a set of registers similar to those that characterized their relations with Italy:

1. Home. The house, the church, and the neighborhood became for many Italian Americans the *comune*, the encircled map of what they understood, the sacred space where they belonged— the place they would, if possible, never leave. Sometimes it was specifically attached to their towns of origin in Italy. But even when it was not so connected, it acquired its own rationale, its own spectacles of self-possession, its own rituals of permanent habitation. Immigrants called the Italian district *la colonia*, and it has retained this distinct political identity. Even though Italian neighborhoods have mostly dwindled, they are still recognizable protagonists in contemporary Mafia films, as if Italian Americans permanently retained a foreign identity and inhabited a colony regardless of where they went or what they did.
2. Nation. America as a civic enterprise differed from Italy in many respects but not in all. Many Italian immigrants found the process of entry humiliating. The laws of labor and property, as elsewhere, favored those already in possession of the means of production. The suspicion that years of poor government had taught the poor to practice in Italy often remained with them in their dealings with American officialdom. On the other hand, the Italian nation had a thriving propaganda industry, and it pursued the immigrants into other countries and

other languages, always reminding them of an Italian pride they
had often not felt at home and had certainly not needed there
the way they soon came to need it in the streets of places such
as Lawrence, Massachusetts, and Boulder, Colorado, where the
bosses housed them like cattle and the native populations
shunned them like plague germs.

3. Promised Land. The American program of Manifest Destiny
   was familiar to them as well. Often enough, that vision had
   been a factor in their choice of where to go when they left their
   hometowns. The United States was a place where Europeans
   had learned to expect that land would be secured for them to
   possess. Many Italian Americans were people who felt that the
   Italian promise had failed them, and they organized their lives
   as a sort of transatlantic Risorgimento, meaning to make at
   least the American promise real in their lives. Their way of
   doing this, as we shall see, had more to do with Italian habits
   and rituals of settlement than with American notions of biblical
   promise.

The present work belongs to one among many possible visionary
histories. In a time of nationalist and imperialist agenda and propaganda, numerous such histories are possible. I make this point by way
of a disclaimer. This is not, for example, the literary history of those
political visionaries, beginning in the days after the fall of the Roman
Republic in 1849, who came to the United States and started newspapers and wrote political tracts and published journals in Italian.[7] Nor is
it the literary history of Italian American women, which has its own
utopias and narratives of meaning.[8]

Rather, the essays in this book focus on the place where two
visionary systems meet and exchange meanings. Italian visionary
nationalism—the focus of the *patria*—remained a standard focus of ideology in both Italy and in its *colonie* from the end of the Risorgimento
(1870) until the period after World War I. But then it needed to meet
directly with American visionary nationalism, another repository of
dead Caesars, but with interests and directions very much its own.

From the 1920s forward, Italian visionary nationalism began to
move into crisis both in Italy and, for other reasons, in the United States
as well. Italy saw the doomed attempt to erect an actual Caesar: the
Fascist regime had come to power in Italy in 1923 and began its long
drive to realize the most ambitious and bloody of Italy's dreams of

glory. Eventually this movement was fated to dismantle most of those dreams. In the United States, Americans treated Italians in ways that increased the distance between reality and immigrant colonialism's notions of itself, driving those notions increasingly further into hiding where they would become the persistent phantoms this book examines. Immigrants more acutely felt the need to become fully acculturated English-speaking citizens after the McCarran-Walters Act of 1924 closed the Golden Door through which hundreds of thousands of Italians had been passing each year, placing a real barrier to return migration. This event blocked the circulation of travelers, "birds of passage," who had moved back and forth freely between communities of laboring poor in Italy and the United States alike. This turn of events would accelerate the acceptance of English as the main language—and, with it, acceptance of U.S. democracy as the dominant political ideology—in Italian America. In 1941 Italy declared war on the United States, and Italian Americans were left with the machinery of an Italian nationalist vision that no longer quite applied to any current situation.[9]

What They Accomplish (Shaping a Literature)

Italian American writing in English began to develop a distinct history in the period between World War I and World War II with its first important works appearing in the 1920s and its first masterpieces, *Ask the Dust* and *Christ in Concrete,* appearing in 1939 on the threshold of the war. After World War II, Italian Americans would need to negotiate the powers of an American identity machine that never quite forgot to repeat its subjugation of Italy. Italy had now become an American satellite. And that was but part of the challenge that faced writers who not only wished and needed to use Italian but also, implausibly, to do so in the English language. Italian Americans also had to negotiate the strenuous linguistic hegemony that had characterized Anglo-America since the nineteenth century when official U.S. culture had first set itself to suppress the cultures of its indigenous peoples and to absorb its variegated immigrants into the vaudeville of working-class American English.

One way of thinking about the work we will examine here is that most of it is written in English by writers close enough to the Italian language to feel it both as a presence and an absence. This is a world of words and feelings I can best suggest by telling a little about what it was like for a writer to grow up in it. I was born in 1941, just a few months before Italy declared war on the United States. Italian in all its many varieties had been the dominant language of the *colonia* with newspapers and radio stations and theaters to keep it alive, but it now began its long slide into American oblivion, beginning in enforced secrecy and ending in near silence. This produced conflicts that made themselves felt in every use of language, from the transactions of family life to the stylistic choices of prose fiction.

Italian as a presence. When I was a boy, Italian speech of every kind was around us most of the time at home. My parents gossiped with each other in their own mixtures of Abruzzese and Neapolitan. To us they spoke only English. My grandparents, all immigrants, spoke their native dialects with one another always, but English to us. Their English was broken with bits of Italian dialect—some of that broken, in its turn, with bits of English. They had developed a creole that people in their own native towns would have had trouble understanding. Their grandchildren could even speak their languages a little. By the time I was seven, I had learned from my mother's mother to say the Abruzzese for *Shut up and eat* and from my father's stepfather how to express in Neapolitan certain things I was not allowed to say in English. We commanded many such bits of everyday Italian, and we could use them to name countless pastas and other foods, from anchovies to fennel to sheep's brains. We knew how to say that a baby was beautiful.

Italian as an absence. But even the Italian we heard in those days signified a hole in our understanding. Most of the time, we could not decode what our parents were telling one another, much less our grandparents, who spoke more rapidly and in a lingo much farther from anything we could follow. From this grew the notion of Italian as a reserve of secret and higher knowledge, something available only to such masters of life as our grandparents and their *paesani*. A little later on, we came to learn of the much greater absence signified by another language, "the real Italian" itself, which our grandfather liked to tell us the poet Dante had invented long ago. A most powerful language, according to Grandpa, because it had achieved something magical: it had brought the Italian nation into being. This potent code grew more plainly absent to us as we grew up and came to understand that it was the medium of great poems that we could not read and great philosophers whom we could not understand.

From Grandpa we drew a sort of catechism that, it is plain enough to me now, mingled ancient Italian beliefs and practices with a sort of visionary gospel about what they meant—a nationalist ideology that immigrants of his generation had either carried away with them when they left Italy or found in the local newspapers when they arrived in America, a set of beliefs that guided their thinking about the wider and deeper implications of the risky enterprise that had shaped their lives. The elements of this ideology have not gone out of existence, but they have subsided from view. Either these Caesars are in fact buried, or else they are hidden by their very obviousness, surviving where everyone can see them but no one makes much of their importance. The chapters of this book examine what is in effect an archaeology of the colonial mind.

Buried Caesars provide Italian Americans with a shared historical and cultural point of view. A large, slightly obscure body of beliefs exists that Italian Americans share and that their writers confront when they sit down to explain the world. Judging from what one reads in the popular press, one would think that the secret inner life of Italian Americans had mostly to do with cooking, eating, singing, dancing, acting, painting, sculpting, and making love. True, all of these things are important, and no doubt there are styles of performance and practices of excellence for most of them that one can reasonably call *Italian*, *colonial*, or *Italian American*. But those cultural performances, although they are mostly produced in the face-to-face situations of ordinary life, are hardly secret nowadays if ever they were. No, the secret culture of Italian Americans, like that of Italy itself, has to do with their attachment to the myth of Italian greatness in all its manifestations large and small. Some of these are straightforwardly political: every other mob chieftain in Italian American history has cultivated comparison with the Caesars; on Columbus Day, Italian Americans fly the Italian flag and reenact Columbus's arrival in the Western Hemisphere as an occasion for flying the tricolor banner of Italy, a flag Columbus never saw. Other attachments are sources of a sense of superiority: to choose one example, Italian Americans like to remember that the Capitol building, in Washington, D.C., is designed to resemble the dome that Michelangelo built for Saint Peter's in Vatican City. Such attachments give a shape, a tone, to literary work. They amount to an unstated morality of power. Such morality has had deep effects on Italian American culture, particularly on literary history.

Chapter One: English as a Dialect of Italian

The Italian language is itself a Buried Caesar. Italian American writers often use English as if it were a dialect of Italian. They can scarcely help it. In the ideology of the Italian language, many modern languages are dialects of Italian. Here is a place where the Italian ideology offers something writers often find irresistible. It preaches that Italian is the first modern European language and in many ways the progenitor of the others.

The Risorgimento believed that Dante Alighieri had invented the Italian language. In a sense, he had, but that is not what he said he was doing. Dante claimed to be inventing a vulgar eloquence, a courtly language based on the everyday speech of people in Italy. To this impossible contradiction, Dante gave a perfect Caesarist name: he called it a New Latin. He meant to transfer the prestige of the ancient Romans to the speech of medieval Italians. This transfer found a permanent home in Italian ideology. Dante's language, according Grandpa, had divine powers. It had not only created Italy, but it had also been the medium of all the thinkers and artists and writers who were the glory of Italy. Niccolò Machiavelli. Leonardo da Vinci. Giacomo Leopardi. The Italian language spoke with the voices of the great Caesars of Rome on whose altars the ancient Italians had for centuries laid their burnt offerings.

Grandpa wanted me to know how this divine language sounded so that I would come to love it as he did and perhaps someday learn it myself. On Saturdays he bid me listen to the Metropolitan Opera on the radio, where heroes and heroines expressed human feelings in voices of such size and power they could only belong to superhuman beings. I think of these performances every time I hear the old Toscanini recording of Verdi's *Manzoni Requiem*. In the midst of the wild *Dies irae*, a loud chorus about the Last Judgment, one can hear the great conductor's voice shouting in Italian, sounding much like my grandfather in a bad moment, exhorting the booming timpani and trombones to a greater noise and terror, as if he were himself roaring out the final rage of God Almighty.

Underlying everything else in the visionary imagination of Italian American literature is the notion that the Italian language belongs to a higher order of understanding, that it connects Italians with the gods of their forefathers. In this respect, Italians of the Risorgimento very much resemble the founders of the Jewish state in Palestine who reconstructed and resurrected Hebrew as a language of national life and of daily commerce. A century earlier, Italian nationalists had done something similar in Italy, making the national tongue the official language of public communication.

Chapter Two: *De vulgari eloquentia:* Ordinary Eloquence in Italian America

Italian American writers transform English freely with Italian. The Risorgimento wanted to claim that Dante had foreseen its enterprise as far back as the end of the thirteenth century. But the nineteenth-century concept of a national language would have been foreign to this aristocratic poet, who devised his "illustrious, cardinal, courtly, and curial" Latin eloquence as useful to specific classes of clerks and politicians. Nonetheless, Dante's notion of a vulgar eloquence, a high language made out of the materials of common speech, had a plausibly modern ring to the nineteenth-century Risorgimento, which aimed to make the national language into a tool that could mold many disparate classes and places into a single people. Italian American writers came to the fashioning of English prose armed with a received belief, not necessarily conscious but nonetheless quite deeply rooted in their sense of how language operates in society. According to this belief, literary language is something that writers can invent, something that can reflect and unify the experiences of rich and poor alike. This belief shaped their approach to English when they came to use it to tell Italian stories.

Migration after all was an element of modernism in both Italy and the United States, and a belief in the power of invented languages is a basic modernist belief. After becoming a single nation in 1861, Italy began to promote a version of Dante's invented Italian as a way of overcoming differences among the many peoples who inhabited the Italic peninsula and islands. It has more than once been objected, most notably by Pier Paolo Pasolini, that this Italian language does not actually exist.[10] Faith in its powers nonetheless became basic to Italian national identity, both in Italy and abroad. Writers who grew up within this belief system tended to feel that a good part of their personal, even political, force rested on their closeness to this national language. Many in Anglo-America were reluctant to change their names. Italian became a fetish, a source of power and validation they needed to keep within reach. They found ways of writing English so that it would exhibit an Italian presence. They used the Italian in their English to orient themselves in historical time and space.

Chapter Three: *Il caso della casa:* Stories of Houses in Italian America

Italian American writers tell stories that make a place Italian. Stories of houses have a ritual shape. They enact the struggles of immigrants. Building houses, building neighborhoods, consecrating them to communal purposes are basic rituals in Italian America, and they give shape to some of its most powerful storytelling.

Italians have practices, many of them self-consciously Roman and even Etruscan in origin, of appropriating territories and houses, and of consecrating these places to their own purposes. Rites of settlement and of foundation belong to the Italian colonies, as does a sense that every act belongs to a long and coherent history of similar acts. Even in the humblest surroundings, this ancient gospel might express itself. Felix Stefanile writes of his "fierce remembrance" of his father's planting a fig tree in a backyard in Long Island City, New York, as if he were Virgil telling the story of Aeneas's migration from Troy:

> my father, moving slowly through the ruins,
> like Virgil in his baggy overalls,
> to aim his spade as if it were a spear,
> and kick, from a slum, the cold slags of Troy. . . .[11]

Aeneas carried his household gods from Troy and established them on the hostile plains of his Promised Land in Latium. When the *Società San Gennaro* lifts its fringed banners and leads the statue of its saint wobbling down Mulberry Street, the spectacle recalls rituals that ancient Italians were performing even before the rise of early Rome. Many such practices crossed the ocean with Italians. Immigrant shrines and processions, household altars and blessings are all ways of marking spaces and inhabiting them fully. These rituals insinuate themselves into the matter and manner of Italian American writing. This immigrant people has carried its saints through the streets as if it were writing long ornamental sentences, reenacting old stories of impossible journeys and miraculous arrivals. Its houses stand along the streets of Little Italys. Each house is the site of family feasts that are themselves rituals of challenge and survival. In these rites, immigrants and their descendants enact their trials, reconfirm their persistent ambitions, and consecrate their triumphs.

Chapter Four: Immigrant Ambitions and American Literature

Italian Americans identify with the grandeur of Italian ambitions.
Many Italians faced almost unimaginable reversals in the United States.
They lived under a system of contract labor that had in view many
things other than the welfare and prosperity of the people it employed.
They suffered class and race hatred. This harsh welcome that Italians
received tested their vision of American possibilities. Many judged the
United States a bad bet and went back to Italy. However, millions per-
sisted until they found ways to solve the riddle of how to enter the
American polity. The secret lay in accepting, even in glorifying, their
national origins in a way that was often quite new to them.

America called on immigrants from Italy to think of themselves
as Italians. Although these immigrants knew that their passports identified them this way, they often lacked a sense of themselves as actors
in the national drama of the *patria* they had left behind. Many had
come, indeed, to avoid military conscription there or to live more
freely as anarchists or socialists. Italy had not been in existence long
enough to make its national imaginary second nature to many of its
people. The Italy they returned to was a house, a clan, a town, a
region. The Great Italy was less vivid to them. They were Abruzzesi,
Napoletani, Siciliani. But Americans did not recognize these categories.
Furthermore, the vastness of America's presence and of its own ideological claims simply flattened the pretenses of an Italian region. This
was the age of nations, and before Calabrian and Sicilian immigrants
could become Americans, they needed to understand their place in that
age. They needed to find a way of becoming Italians. The task was
more demanding than one might at first suppose. The determined
Prime Minister Francesco Crispi (1818–1901) had tried a program of
wars and empires to stimulate national feeling among the inhabitants
of Italy's many towns and provinces. But this policy had not proved
universally effective. In fact, it had driven many poor people to emi-
grate rather than fight in Italy's wars. But what militarist propaganda
had failed to evoke in Italy the travails of assimilation now achieved in
America. The immigrants recognized that other Americans thought of
them as *Italians,* and they sought ways to make sense of that in their
lives. The paradox of their situation was that they could not safely
become Americans until they had found a way of knowing what it
meant to be Italians.

In Pascal D'Angelo's *Son of Italy* (1924), one sees an immigrant learning to enter the American *patria* by first learning to see himself as part of the Italian *patria*. He does it in many ways, but the critical moment occurs at a performance of *Aida*. The narrator, an Abruzzese peasant, finds himself suddenly identifying with the militarist poetry of this great Italian opera. This is a primal scene of nationalization. There is something deeply plausible about an opera as the site for such a transformation. Operatic performances were already thriving when Italian immigrants began to inundate U.S. cities. The opera initiated even the most naïve and uneducated immigrants into the mysteries of Italian national and imperial dreams, allowing them to see themselves as Italians in a way that was ideologically strong enough that it would not entirely disappear under the weight of American power.

Chapter Five: The Text in the Dust: Writing Italy across America

Italian Americans claim a place at the origin of the New World. The Risorgimento was careful to claim Columbus and Vespucci as national heroes, even though those men might more plausibly have been branded national enemies. There were perfectly good reasons that Spain and Portugal had sponsored such Italian adventurers. And perfectly good reasons why the Italian states had not done so. Why would Genoa or Venice have sought to open sea lanes that would destroy their monopoly of trade with the East? One might argue that the discovery of America, more than any other single factor, doomed the mercantile dominance that had supported the Italian Renaissance. Four centuries later, however, in the late nineteenth century, for many reasons, it now made sense to claim America as an Italian invention.

Italian immigrants in the United States made the most of this claim, erecting monuments to the Great Navigators to mark for themselves a place in the American imperial enterprise. Such practices led immigrants to feel themselves entitled to a position of honor in the New World empire, quite superior to the lowly status that had actually awaited them when they arrived at Ellis Island. Everyone knew that Spain and Portugal had sponsored Columbus and Vespucci specifically to compete with the Italian cities in trade. Thus, making these men Italian national heroes required an ideological leap, to say the least. Nor was this the only contradiction that needed to be resolved. The difference between the class position of most immigrants and that of state-sponsored captains such as Columbus and Vespucci was sharp. The difference was bound to create problems when identification with the great explorers brought the immigrants close to identification with the American imperial project. In that vicinity, there were factors that would cause considerable discomfort and self-contradiction—conditions that many Italian American writers, beginning with John Fante in the 1930s, have explored.

Chapter Six: The Semiology of Semen: Questioning the Father

Italian Americans claim an Italian genealogy. Breaking the line of filiation caused many immigrants their most lasting wound. Those who subscribe to the Ellis Island Restoration and those who visit the numerous genealogical Web sites are propelled by a motive that has never died in Italian America. The passionate elegy for a lost father that gives form and force to Pietro di Donato's 1939 masterpiece *Christ in Concrete* situates this text on the fault lines between *patriae*, nations, generations, and languages. Di Donato tells the story as a fable of class warfare, where immigrant culture struggles to overcome the rupture in human relations caused by industrial capital.

Chapter Seven: Circles of the Cyclopes: Concentric History

Italian Americans use figurative speech to perpetuate the colonial condition. Italian immigrants live inside a self-enclosed world. Italian literature, whether local or national, deploys a large repertory of figurative equipment: tropes, schemes, rhyming forms, debating rituals, insult competitions, as well as fables and folktales handed down through generations. Italian American literature draws freely on the libraries of ancient Greece and Rome and finds in them figurative precedents for the situations immigrants face in Italian America, using the old stories, many of them themselves profoundly related to questions of migration and isolation, to draw maps of their current conditions and to find ways of appropriating the resources they need. This is the literary map of the colonialist mind, counterposing its sense of enclosure with its ambition of universalist expansion.

Chapter Eight: A Literature Considering Itself: The Allegory of Italian America

Italian Americans use allegory to authorize their historical claims. In Christian scholarship, the Hebrew Bible becomes the "Old Testament," a sort of preface to the "New Testament," as the Christians call their Revelation. Christians accomplish this act of appropriation using allegory, which allows them to read everything in the Hebrew Bible as a foreshadowing of the life, death, and resurrection of Jesus Christ. From Augustine onward, Christian scholars refined the method of allegoresis, which basically allowed them to make things mean whatever suited them. The method economically wove together history, revelation, morality, and prophecy. A thousand years after Augustine, Dante Alighieri was using allegoresis as a method for constructing visionary poetry. Italian literature has so absorbed Dante that it employs allegory as part of its normal mode of operation. Italian American literature as well has adapted allegorical methods to its narratives of its own meanings and purposes. Italian American literature, in effect, constitutes a new chapter in the history of Italian rhetoric. It uses allegory as a way of naturalizing national and imperial myth in situating itself as an historical subject.

Chapter Nine: The Italian American Sign

Italian Americans aim to reappropriate the Renaissance. When the masses of Italians, most although not all of them poor and uneducated, arrived in the United States, they discovered that rich Americans had appropriated the Italian Renaissance to their own class purposes. In many arts—in music, architecture, painting, and sculpture—the so-called American Renaissance was a rebirth of nothing that was American but of a great deal that was Italian. The American Renaissance belonged to a bourgeois Anglo order of prestige that had a steady interest in excluding, devaluing, and dehumanizing the Italian immigrants. This chapter calls that system "the Italian American Sign" and analyzes the strategies that Italian American writers have used in their collective effort to undermine it and to overcome its effects on their lives and literary ambitions.

Chapter Ten: The Imperial Sopranos

A Caesar, as Gramsci teaches, expresses a conflict that cannot be resolved. Italian America has had many Caesars. The most famous of these, the standard-bearers of the Italian American narrative in popular art, have been gangsters. What conflict do gangsters express? The gangsters express the conflict between class identities of Italian Americans. No matter how successful they are, they live under the shadow of the Mafia. They are subordinated both in the United States and in Italy.

Americans regard them with suspicion, never forgetting the long history of criminality, illiteracy, and emotional dysfunction that Italian immigrants are supposed to have. No matter how adept Italian Americans become in the mysteries of Italian opera, painting, wine, or clothes, Italians regard them as barbarians who speak a laughable Italian and are hopelessly out of touch with contemporary Italy.

The Sopranos shows this conflict in operation, and it shows the role of the Buried Caesars in resolving it. The Italians in this series are aspiring upper-class Americans who buy big houses, big cars, big boats; they play golf and send their children to Ivy League schools. Nonetheless, they are supposed never to lose their regional identities or their dialectal speech: even when they live in posh suburbs, they speak the language of Little Italy. Their command of Italian culture is colonialist: they believe in the Renaissance, the opera, and imported wine and water. The heroes of this saga are obsessed with Caesarist posturing and Roman imagery.

Italian American Caesarism has a long history in the relation of Italian Americans with the American majority, which has its own Caesarist obsessions and finds the Italians a convenient screen for projecting them. Understanding the relationship between the Mafia and its American audience is a basic issue in *The Sopranos*, as it is in Italian American culture. Italian Americans remain dependent for a sense of their own self-worth on a nation that has never considered them as members of its commonwealth or as the voice of a culture worthy of serious attention. Italian Americans need to recognize what *The Sopranos* shows them. Not that they are gangsters, but that they are actors whose cultural style—inherited from the imperialist nation that died in the war—leads them unwittingly, unwillingly, to play the role of Shadow to the imperial culture of the United States. Italian America is a colony where Americans can see their own flaws in caricature, accompanied by good meals and good singing. The capital city of this playland is Las Vegas, where Italy has been reduced to the dimensions of gambling strip—Bellagio, Venice, Caesars Palace.

Many Italian American writers understand this reality. They outline it in blunt terms no one can ignore, and they explore its subtleties in ways that deploy the full richness of the rhetorical and narrative heritage they claim. Italian Americans need such writers if they are ever to overcome the prejudice and suspicion that have greeted them ever since poor Italians began to come to the United States to earn money. Italian American readers, rather than shooting the messenger, would do well to read the message with attention. "This is how Americans see you. Do

you inhabit your own position? Do you even know why you are in this
position?" The message begins to make sense only when one looks at
the outlines of the colonialist culture that Italian Americans have inherited, when one seeks an understanding of one's actual historical role.

CHAPTER 1

English as a Dialect of Italian

"We don't speak Italian," my mother used to say, "we speak dialect." Everything we spoke, English included, was a dialect of Italian. We had a clear sense that we did not speak any national language at all. As far as we were concerned, national standard Italian was exactly what Dante had meant it to be when he first proposed it: an imperial tongue—that is, a language whose speakers were by definition cosmopolitans. My grandparents were all immigrants, which means they were transnationals, to be sure, but no one would have called them *cosmopolitan*. National standard Italian was a language for them to respect, to talk about, to read in the Italian papers, to hear on the radio, to tell us to learn, but not for them to speak. And as for English, that was another imperial tongue, and still something to conquer. "Learn English!" My mother was determined that we should master this language as well as possible. It was not something she thought we could take for granted. As a girl in school, she had felt much as Maria Mazziotti Gillan remembers feeling:

> Miss Wilson's eyes, opaque
> As blue glass, fix on me:
> "We must speak English.
> We're in America now."
> I want to say, "I am American,"
> but the evidence is stacked against me.
>
> My mother scrubs my scalp raw, wraps
> My shining hair in white rags
> To make it curl. Miss Wilson
> drags me to the window, checks my hair
> for lice. My face wants to hide.

25

> At home, my words smooth in my mouth
> I chatter and am proud. In school,
> I am silent, grope for the right English
> words, fear the Italian word
> will sprout from my mouth like a rose,
> fear the progression of teachers
> in their sprigged dresses,
> their Anglo-Saxon faces.[1]

Neither English nor Italian belonged to us, although we belonged to them. They were signs that others had mastered us.

Italian, right from the start, has never been just a way of speaking. From the moment of its invention, Italian was a political act with international consequences. Dante Alighieri called it a New Latin.[2] He based it on the ordinary speech of living people (unlike Old Latin, which had become either the speech of dead people or else the exclusive living speech of privileged people such as priests and lawyers), but he nonetheless designed it to travel in wide circles. Italian dialects were not like that. The languages Italians called dialects were *local*, intensely local. The three thousand people in my mother's home town of Salle, provincia di Chieti, high in the Apennines of Abruzzi, spoke a tongue they could easily distinguish from the language the two thousand people who lived in San Tommaso, a few kilometers away, spoke. In short, each dialect was tied to a single place. It was the opposite of cosmopolitan. It marked its speakers by locale and by class as well. In the days before mass media, the educated people learned national Italian in school. Poor people generally left school too soon even to think of mastering it.

Like most Italian immigrants, my family came into the English language with the mental habit of people who have lived forever in a dialect. Their speech marked them geographically and tribally. It assigned them a low place in Italy's economic and cultural hierarchies. For the poor, to live in a dialect meant to live within narrow limits. The word *dialect* recurs in two distinct adjectival forms, *dialectal* and *dialectic. Dialectal* refers to attributes of a kind of speech that specify its physical and class location. It is a linguistic and social term, referring to phonemes and morphemes, marks of sound and of other physical features. *Dialectic* refers to verbal struggle. It is often used to describe historical process. In using it to refer to a form of speech, we make this adjective emphasize the protagonism implied in a dialect, its power to limit a person's life chances and to place a person in class relations

toward others. A dialect can be called *dialectic* because it assigns a
person a set of possibilities and positions in the process of history.

In a relatively static social arrangement such as the one the
migrant Italians left behind them, the dialectic aspect of their linguistic
situation was little more than an implication, a possible meaning that
only rarely could show itself in action. But in the life of the Great
Migration, the immigrants perceived themselves to be confronted continually by the challenges of social change. They were forced daily to
assess the meaning of their class location, which they experienced in the
social implications of how they spoke.

> When I was a little girl,
> I thought everyone was Italian,
> and that was good. We visited
> our aunts and uncles,
> and they visited us.
> The Italian language smooth
> and sweet in my mouth.
>
> In kindergarten, English words fell on me,
> thick and sharp as hail. I grew silent,
> the Italian word balanced on the edge
> of my tongue and the English word, lost
> during the first moment
> of every question.
>
> Almost every day
> Mr. Landraf called Joey
> a "spaghetti bender."
> I knew that was bad.
> I tried to hide
> by folding my hands neatly
> on my desk and
> being a good girl.[3]

Dialect was what they had spoken in Italy, a clear and indelible
marker of their position in the Italian social universe. Their English
would long have a similar impact on them. Varying degrees of Italian
accent, of Broken English, and of lower-class urban patois accompany
the portraits of Italians in vaudeville (Jimmy Durante, Chico Marx), in
the movies (*The Godfather, Goodfellas*), and on television (*The Sopranos*). This is a set of American phenomena, so that the reader may

reasonably think it only sensible to treat any noticeably Italian American English as if it were what the phase implies: a form of American English. Italian American English uses the grammar and word list of the majority North American language, along with words and features clearly Italian, and it marks its speakers as belonging in the contact zone between speakers of standard American English and speakers of Italian dialects.

Dialectally, let us say, these forms of speech approximate forms of standard American and come to belong to the large spectrum of Broken Englishes (broken with Spanish, Yiddish, German, Greek, French, and many other languages) and of creoles that surround this national tongue.

Dialectically, on the other hand, Italian American English retains its orientation to Italian regardless how much it absorbs of the English language's stock of words and figures. To the extent that Italian American English exists, it retains a dialectic or protagonistic relationship to Italian. This relationship is as varied as such a relationship is likely to be when it survives through the medium of spoken language. As a way of sampling its range, we can consider some of its linguistic, national, commercial, and literary implications.

Linguistic

Written Italian American English develops a complex relationship with Italian at every social level. It can present local features, and the representation of Italian dialect is a favorite trope in Italian American writing from *Mount Allegro* (1942) to *Were You Always an Italian?* (2000).[4] Italian in Italian American English can also express the ambiguities of an interlingual situation. Such situations appear among Italians of every social stratum who come to the United States, not just among steerage immigrants. More important, Italian American English can reflect the transvaluation of Italian. Immigrants spoke an English broken with Italian dialect, a sign of social subordination. The American English of the Park Avenue Italian expatriate or of the third-generation Italian American who has been to college and has lived in Italy—as a student, a tourist, or a bourgeois expatriate—may use Italian, but it will be standard, or national, Italian. Such usage carries a dialectic implication: it is a mark of standing, and sometimes a trophy of victory, in the class wars.

Insofar as it is literature, and insofar as it is Italian, Italian American literature makes Italian language, geography, culture, and literature into abiding points of reference. These things do not simply mark cultural difference or signs of class subordination to the dominant Anglo-American culture of the United States. Rather, they are the foundational markings and global orientations that belong to the history of all that the word *Italian* has meant and continues to mean in the world market of cultures and commodities. For a U.S. citizen, assuming the identity Italian American means asserting salience to the powerful and persistent international myth of Italy as it expresses itself in many media.

Such salience had one sort of value at the end of the nineteenth century when the Great Migration was still going strong. This same salience has quite another value on the threshold of the twenty-first century when Italian America has become the home of a very large middle-class and upper-middle-class sector in the United States. Today, there are over fifteen million Italian Americans. They are no longer poor. For example, Italian Americans comprise 38 percent of the population of Westchester County in New York, per capita the wealthiest county in the nation. The magic of money has worked its powers on *italianità* as it does on so many signs of difference. Things that used to be stigmas can now be signs of distinction.

As Italian American writing in English progresses, its Italian claims return in forms that the immigrants would have recognized but could never have translated into terms acceptable to Americans of a century ago. Contemporary Americans and Italian Americans are working in an entirely different social environment.

The Italian difference in Italian American writing has an ideological value that both persists and varies with time. It sometimes takes the shape of a sacred object, valued very highly within the immigrant enclosure as a sign of Italy and in later years transformed into something of equivalent value in the American world outside. My immigrant grandmother cooked polenta on certain Sundays. She spread it out on a large board that covered the dining room table. Over it, she ladled ragù and placed a meatball in the middle. Her three children and their families sat around that table—twenty people with forks. Each person started eating. It was a race. The winner was whoever first reached that meatball. Quite a lot of polenta was on that board. The family manners were those of medieval mountaineers who had survived on cornmeal polenta through many a long winter when they had not much else to eat. Nowadays, elegant New York restaurants serve tiny slices of polenta as a delicate accompaniment to rabbit or truffles, all at prices that would make a peasant blanch. A change in class means a change in value.

Something similar has happened to many elements of *italianità*. They survive in both dialectal and dialectic relationships, but the values

and positions change sharply. The usual thing is that the Italian difference survives in two varieties. One kind becomes American, and this
American version becomes the dialect, or lower class, version; the other
returns to Italian, and this becomes the standard, or bourgeois, model.

Pizza is the most familiar example of this double transformation.
In its American English form, this Italian dish has become the sign of
what is persistently, even ruthlessly, inexpensive. Pizza is highway food,
fast food, midnight-delivery-to-the-dorm-room food. It resembles chow
mein in that it retains the class and race stigma that accompany mass
migration. It is archetypical food for people who do not have much
money to spend. But in its bourgeois Italian form, pizza has become a
delicacy in the United States. Restaurants advertise brick ovens with
wood fires, usually in Italian, *forno a legna*, as if one were dining in
Tuscany instead of Fairfield County, Connecticut. They serve individual
pizzas with expensive garnishes. This is not storefront by-the-slice Ellis
Island food. This is gourmet presentation; it features artichokes, caviar,
portobello mushrooms, and mozzarella imported from Sorrento.

The most tormented form of this double transformation is the Italian participation in international commerce. In its American English
form, Italian business has become the Underworld. Violent, crude, mur-
derous, and ungrammatical, the American version of the Italian Mafia
retains and revives every element of stigma that comes along with the
mass migration. This Mafia is as American as Hollywood.

But in its new bourgeois form, Italian American business has
returned to its place in the Italian world trade networks, as old as the
crusades and as opulent as Venice. Italians now come to New York not
to organize garbage trucks and cocaine dealers, but to represent major
manufacturers, traders, and banks. They have offices along Park
Avenue. They win lucrative contracts to build bridges and pipelines all
over the world. Magazines such as *Italia* and *Italy Italy* present glitter-
ing images of their prosperity and of their commodity splendors. They
import the most exquisite silks and worsteds, just as their forbears did
in medieval Brussels and Renaissance London. And their Italian American patrons are not John Gotti and Tony Soprano—or at least not
exclusively such persons. From Greenwich, Connecticut to Palo Alto,
California, Italian American professionals have the financial and educational capital to appreciate the finer—that is, the more socially dominant—meanings of the word *Italian*. Italian American business
managers preside over corporations that manufacture automobiles and
computing machines. These graduates of Stanford and Harvard do not
resemble the candy store bookies and Brooklyn torpedoes who populate

American Mafia films. As Italian Americans move toward the notion
that *Italian* means something central and authoritative, their impatience
with the immigrant stigma grows. Some spend huge amounts of energy
protesting the Mafia mythology. Others simply buy themselves villas in
Tuscany.

This process of transvaluation has an important place in the
growth of Italian American writing in English, and it underlies the argument of this book at every turn. From the start, I contend, Italian American writers in English have been aware that Italian precedes English
among the modern languages. Such an awareness is part of the ideological heritage of the Italian colonies. First-class liberal educations have
helped Italian American writers understand the weight of evidence that
accompanies such awareness. Meditating their own position as outsiders in this English-speaking culture, such writers have sought to recu-
perate the Roman authority of the Latin language that stands behind
Italian, French, Portuguese, Romanian, and Spanish. Through these
modern languages, Latin has had a mighty influence over the growth of
literary culture, as well as during the days when the ruling classes of the
British and American empires read Cicero and Virgil in school.

National

Italian American writing arises in the oscillating space that subsists
between two formidable national/imperial programs. In this arena, one
hears a steady noise of struggle for precedence. The United States—with
its victorious armed forces, its overwhelming economic engine, its political stability, its bottomless fund of natural resources—is a leading
power that makes its presence felt everywhere in Italy, thus giving it a
double presence in that part of the United States that connects itself in
any way with Italy. Nonetheless, Italy has its antique prerogatives.
Those Italian Americans who choose to thematize Italy in their thinking
and writing soon enough begin to compile claims of precedence that
have roots deep in the Italian national imaginary. In America, as everywhere in the international world, the Italian Renaissance can plausibly
be said to have strongly influenced contemporary life in many areas,
among them art, music, architecture, navigation, political philosophy,
theater, mathematics, geography, bookkeeping, and banking. Nowhere
is this influence more profoundly consequential than in the very project
of a national language. Italian literary and political history perpetually
returns to this project. It has followed Italians into the diaspora.

How did my mother come to know her own language as a dialect? She grew up in the United States, but the language map of Italy had been an article of faith among all Italians, including emigrants, ever since Italy became a nation in 1861. The magic of a national language was a basic element in the nation-building process. Massimo d'Azeglio is said to have framed this enterprise in a famous remark, "*L'Italia si è fatta, ma gli italiani non si fanno*" ("Italy has been made, but Italians are not being made").[5] Italian became a national language as a way of completing the making of Italy, consolidating the achievements of the Risorgimento by making not only a country but also people who belonged to it, rather than to one of its parts. Making Italians became a central purpose in educational policy. That purpose drew authority from antiquity and aimed at a glorious future as well. Since Unification, national Italian has presented itself as self-consciously incorporating the bodies of its ancestor tongues for many generations.

Until that time, Italian, which Dante first proposed in the fourteenth century, had became such a perennial theme for debate that it acquired an epithet: *la questione della lingua*, the language problem. The language was reformulated several times by Italian intellectuals during the Renaissance.[6] Centuries later, during the Risorgimento (1815–1870), Italian was still a literary project, rather than an actual spoken language. Alessandro Manzoni wrote a novel, *I promessi sposi*, which became a primary text for the makers of Italy and of Italians. When Manzoni was writing it, he was using a literary Italian full of Milanese regionalisms, but he came to accept the old idea that Tuscan ought to be the basis for the national dialect of Italy. In those days of no national dictionaries and no decent highways, after publishing the first edition of his novel in 1827 he took his entire family on the long and difficult overland journey from Milan to Florence so that he might revise his text at the geographical font of what would later become national Italian. In 1842 Manzoni published the definitive edition of the novel in the new literary Tuscan he had developed for it and for the future of Italian literature and speech. In 1868, for a commission appointed by the new Minister of Public Instruction, Manzoni set forth his linguistic program for the new nation in the treatise "*Dell'unità della lingua e dei mezzi di diffonderla*" ("On Linguistic Unity and on the Means of Promoting It"): the program covered everything from diction to pronunciation.[7] Insofar as Italian schools have enjoyed a national curriculum, this language and its ambitions have stood at its center.

Most immigrant newspapers used the national language.[8] By the time my mother came to America in 1919, at age three, Little Italys everywhere had effectively erected national Italian as a tribal totem. People could read it in the numerous Italian journals or understand when they heard it on the radio, although few immigrants actually spoke it. Their belief in its power was, and remains, unquestioned. People still apologize for speaking a dialect. Thus, to call English a dialect of Italian means referring to the political ambitions of United Italy, which from the start have been entwined in the powers and pretensions of its national tongue. Because Italians began to enter global diaspora in a large way only after the Risorgimento, when the full-scale promotion of the national language had begun, their socialization had taken place under the influence of this nationalist cult. Wherever they went, the belief in a national Italian inevitably came along with them. Most Italian Americans abandoned Italian in the early 1940s, after Mussolini's Italy had declared itself an enemy of the United States, but, strange to say, their respect for the national language persisted. To this day, many Italian Americans are reluctant to speak Italian because they know perfectly well that, like my mother, they "speak dialect." The prestige of the standard language shames them still.

Power was an object from the start in this story. Dante's claim to have invented a New Latin was an early Renaissance notion in that it underlined the attempt, something that would soon become universal in Italy and afterward in Europe, to recover the authority and imperial force of the Roman language. Italian was the first New Latin, but it was neither the last, nor the most successful. Italian immigrants, with their uncertain purchase of national Italian, soon found themselves facing the more powerful agenda of another New Latin, this time under the Anglophone aegis of the United States.

When two languages are in contact, the differences can be brutal. In crudest terms: the more politically powerful language can treat the less powerful as an unacceptable dialect. In 1887 the U.S. Commissioner for Indian Affairs, for example, wrote in his annual report:

> Schools should be established which children should be required to attend; their barbarous dialects should be blotted out and the English language substituted . . . the object of greatest solicitude should be to break down the prejudices of tribe among the Indians; to blot out the boundary lines which divide. them into distinct nations, and fuse them into

one homogeneous mass. Uniformity of language will do this.
Nothing else will. . . . It is also believed that teaching an
Indian youth in his own barbarous dialect is a positive detri-
ment to him. The first step to be taken towards civilization,
towards teaching the Indians the mischief and folly of continuing in their barbarous practices is to teach them the English language. . . .[9]

Italian immigrants to the United States found that the Americans
treated their Italian languages not very differently from the way they
treated the "barbarous dialects" of the Indians. And, back in Italy, the
promulgators of national Italian had treated with a similar contempt
the dialects of the rural poor.

Linguistic dominion is a very old story in Italy. Not all dialects
have the glorious military and financial histories of Venetian and
Tuscan. Citizens of today's Republic of Italy are descended from the
very first colonies that the all-conquering Latin tribes established in the
other regions of Italy, from Benevento to Milan. Samnites, Oscans,
Umbrians, Etruscans, Brutii, and Siculi entered the orbit of Rome, each
people having its own god to lay on the altar of Jove, its own tongue to
silence before the sword of Mars.[10]

In the United States, linguistic domination had three special
aspects. One was the ideological program of Manifest Destiny, which
kept Anglocentric linguistic ambitions at the forefront. A second aspect,
corollary to the first, was the general contempt the more powerful and
established native citizens had for foreigners of all sorts, particularly
those as poor and as numerous as the Italians. The third was the particular relationship that Anglo-Saxon culture had had with Italy and Italian for centuries.

English has long seen itself as a New Latin. The very notion of
Latin is intimately connected with linguistic dominion. As New Latin
became the basis for Italian, so French, Spanish, English—and all the
New Vernaculars that came to codify and standardize themselves as
ideals of speech during and after the Renaissance—belong to the category Dante established: all of them are New Latins. English culture,
after the Reformation, had to deal with contradictory motives. On the
one hand, it aspired to global authority. On the other hand, it drew
much of its own authority from its supposed filiation to the language of
the Roman Empire.

School English, which plays such a dramatic role in the formation
of Italian American language consciousness, presents itself expressly as

a New Latin, an imperial tongue with eight parts of speech. Indeed, schoolmasters in the eighteenth century portrayed the King's English as in every possible way conformable with Caesar's Latin.[11] The Renaissance motive of identification with Roman prestige and Latin universality is an area where English has been a dialect of Italian since Lorenzo Valla brought Renaissance humanism to England in 1420. As with the Renaissance Ciceronian prose of Lorenzo Valla and of his enemy Poggio Bracciolini, European New Vernaculars have imitated Dante in using Latin as the standard (in the double sense that it was both the ensign and the measure) of their enterprise and of their ambition. Humanist schooling from the fourteenth century onward practiced as a silent motto, governing much of its normative discourse, the saying of Petrarca, "For what else is history, all of it, but praise of Rome?"[12] To this day, some grammarians present the history of Italy's dialects as the history of their deviation from Latin.[13]

Standard English has a rank in the chart of comparative literary prestige. It stands ambitiously among the New Latins, alongside other European national languages, each with its library of dictionaries and grammars and rules of style designed to establish and enforce it hegemony.[14]

Nationalist and imperialist cults attend to origins and precedence; these have given to Italian and to the Latin that stands behind it an authoritative character that the bourgeois Italian American rarely hesitates to assert, placing American English culture into a perpetual dialectic relationship with Italian. *The Proud Italians: The Great Civilizers; What Italy Has Given to the World; Italians First!*—such titles proliferate.[15] Italians who migrate to the English-speaking world may first establish themselves economically, but soon afterward many of them turn to the notion of cultural seniority that is hidden in the project of a New Latin built upon an Old Latin, which belongs to Italy's myth of its national tongue. We think of dialectal relationships as existing in space—centers and peripheries. But dialectic relationships require time, past and present. In this medium Italy continues to claim precedence.

Commercial

The Italian American occupies a position that draws its vocabulary of self-construction from a world commodity culture in which the positions *Italian* and *American* derive much of their meaning from their mutual commerce. This was true in one sense during the Great Migration, and it is true in quite a different sense now.

When Italians were arriving by the thousands in the United States, they experienced their passage as an ordeal that changed them. No longer human souls, they became animal cargo, shipped in steerage alongside goats and cattle, medically examined on departure and again on entry, as if they were breeding stock or beasts of burden. During that same period, the transport of Americans to Italy was a luxury trade, and its passengers were treated as consumers rather than as objects of consumption. This difference of class agency persisted in the United States. Cabin-class Americans were conspicuously capable economic subjects who employed and deployed steerage-class Italians as objects of consumption. This trade functioned with the brutal insensibility that had begun in steerage; so-called free laboring immigrants had to negotiate the harshest laws of the market, their ability to function always dependent on certificates of acceptability as issued by the immigration doctors and the downtown police.

As in all such transactions, class differences only masked the fact that subject and object transformed one another. The Italians, as they learned to survive the Darwinian pieties of the New York labor market, began to become Americans and to acquire their own consumer fantasies. The Americans, as they decorated their palaces with ornamental plaster and polychrome mosaics, marked themselves with the eternal insignia of their ferocious dominance. They made themselves Italian in the most diabolical sense of the word. In their excesses, they aped the same Renaissance popes that their Protestant preachers had taught them to despise. The U.S. capitol building at a quick glance might be Saint Peter's. Architectural decorations that signify Italian artisan labor often also signify a fortune built on brutal exploitation. American millionaires such as Morgan, Carnegie, Frick, and Hearst built themselves vast Roman villas, in effect arrogating to themselves the spiritual force of the European immigrants whom they were reducing to the status of brutes in their mines and mills.

Now that Italian Americans have acquired position in the American commercial hierarchy, although they have for the most part lost the ability to speak any dialect of Italian, they have been able to surround themselves with fetishes of *italianità*. Madonna Ciccone in her video *Like a Virgin* wears a wedding dress while being poled through Venetian canals dreaming of being touched "for the very first time." This is the fantasy of the woman as possession who has become a woman in possession, what Madonna elsewhere calls by the ambiguous term *material girl*. Becoming a consuming subject, this Italian American woman transforms such emblems of her oppression as the Madonna and even virginity itself into the commercial tokens of the wedding dress, the Venetian tour, and the hired gondolier. With a similar extravagance of gesture, the bourgeois Italian American now can deploy her difference in that large segment of American shopping where Italian signatures guarantee high commodity distinction: Miuccia Prada, Giorgio Armani, Donatella Versace, and Ermenegildo Zegna.

An even deeper sense of physical validation rests on the use of Italian luxury comestibles in the United States. Many Italian Americans ritually celebrate their Italian distinction through regular consumption of water bottled in Piemonte, olives packed in Puglia, fresh gnocchi flown in daily from Abruzzi. Imported pastas, cheeses, wines, liquors, and cakes line the shelves of the "Italian store" to be found wherever Italian Americans congregate. Whether in North Beach—the old Little Italy of San Francisco—or in a suburban mall, the Italian store offers a long list of edible and potable fetish commodities marked *Made in Italy,* and these objects constitute the nouns and verbs of an Italian language that asserts itself substantially and regularly without ever needing to explain itself at all. Its precedence rises from stigma to distinction through its visible position in the hierarchy of conspicuous costliness and wasteful expense.

Literary

Literary relationships between American English and national Italian do not only subsist in the immigrant contact zone, where dialect words provide direct access to the immigrant mind and to the vaudeville comedy of ethnic subordination. Literary relationships between American English and national Italian also substand all of contemporary writing in English, whether in the United States or elsewhere.

English is one of the New Vernaculars whose literature grew in the world invented by Dante's New Latin. Dante's experiments with language and poetry initiated a series of startling innovations later in the fourteenth century when his admirers Francesco Petrarca and Giovanni Boccaccio followed him in showing Europe yet more new ways to use ordinary language to fulfill the purposes of literature.[16] These writers established long-lasting vogues for their innovations—their use of prose, their ingenious *canzoni* and *sonnetti.* In English, the flowering of the humanities in the schools, courts, and universities meant that there would continue to renew itself a steady audience for the determined linguistic innovations of the Italian Renaissance. Indeed, imitation of Italians became a major theme in the growth of the canonical school of

English literature: Chaucer, Wyatt, Surrey, Spenser, Shakespeare, Jonson, Milton, Fielding, Sterne, Keats, Byron, Shelley, Browning, Eliot—all major British writers with Italian stylistic agendas.[17]

Italian American writing may never forget its humble origins in immigrant poverty. But these origins grow more mythical with time, and the contemporary reality of Italian American life brings its writers closer to the literary traditions not only of English male poets, but also of Elizabeth Barrett Browning, Margaret Fuller Ossoli, Iris Origo, Shirley Hazzard, and indeed all the other bourgeois writers of both genders who have pursued the art of English composition using Italy as a source of material, as a place to work, or both. The Italian American who has acquired the economic means and social powers to pursue a literary career will quickly come on this international literary empire, which numbers among its citizens most leading British writers of the past two centuries and many Americans as well. This large English-speaking Italy belongs to the future of Italian America as a past it will inhabit after its own manner.

What will that manner be? How will Italian America plant its ambiguous flag on the contested territory of Italian prestige? That project will always require meditation because such gestures of appropriation have served racist purposes more than once.[18] This is not surprising. No past can be entirely usable, no heritage can rest exempt from the attentions of the critical mind. The Italian past must admit to poverty and loss quite as much as it can ever boast of trophies and masterpieces. Italy has many histories of its own as well: in some of these it is a golden dream made real; in others it is a delusional utopia, a lie bankers and politicians tell. In all these conflicted histories, the recurrent dialectic between what is American and what is Italian presents its own special difficulties. To confront such difficulties belongs to the proper work of literary history.

CHAPTER 2

De vulgari eloquentia
Ordinary Eloquence in Italian America

Dante's explanation of his language project has a bland self-confidence that is still striking. Finding that no one before him had "treated systematically the doctrines of eloquence in the vernacular" and seeing "that such eloquence [was] needed by almost everyone," Dante set out to "enhance the speech of vernacular speakers."[1] It was a difficult, even a bewildering, task. And it bears resemblance to the task that faces the Italian writer in the United States. Because this writer's language, like Dante's, is a confusing array of dialects and "grammars" (in Dante's sense of a secondary, acquired language). If, like Dante, the Italian writer in the United States wishes to employ the vernacular, the "speech . . . which we learn without any rules [from] our nurse" (p. 3), then this writer must do as Dante did: seek deliberately to devise a rhetoric that can employ the vernacular as the tool of a self-conscious literary art. If the project succeeds, this writer's language will rise above the idiosyncratic usage of the family or the hometown of the writer without becoming merely "grammar."

Every writer, of course, must to some degree face the same problem when setting out. Language is so various that the art of written expression demands of each practitioner a fresh solution, a new rule for the making of choices. The writer whose ancestral tongue differs radically from the language of his book has especially acute difficulties. Each writer whose work we examine now has a personal resolution of these difficulties and achieves a distinct degree of success in the endeavor. But all of these writers also share a common situation, and, not surprisingly, they have dealt with it in striking similar ways.

39

If Dante was able to hunt down his panther by imagining wider and wider categories of speech until he arrived at the "illustrious, cardinal, courtly, and curial vernacular of Latium . . . which belongs to all the Latin cities against which all the Latin municipal vernaculars are measured, weighed, and compared"(p.12), we may ask whether the English-speaking U.S. Italian may not do some similar thing. If this writer attempts to locate a common eloquence in the Italian spoken all over the United States, the effort may meet some success. Some, at least, claim that an American Italian *koiné* exists,[2] and this language may possess its own *vulgari eloquentia*. When the writer seeks a vernacular eloquence that will employ the English spoken and written by Italians in the United States, however, this is a great task in some ways more complex even than that which confronted Dante. The U.S. Italian seeks an English that will somehow comprehend and welcome the language of many forebears in Italy. English has enough of Latin in it to make such a rapprochement conceivable. The notion of reading English for the Latin it contains, however, is not an easy one for most people.

Then we have the hard fact that the language of this writer's forebears is neither the "illustrious, cardinal, courtly, and curial vernacular" of Dante, nor is it any descendant of that vernacular. It is, rather, much more likely to be the distant and fugitive heir of one of those many dialects that Dante merely waves away with a single gesture as irrelevant to the purposes of his vernacular eloquence. Can the humble speech of the immigrant, damned and derided in Italy, join itself to the demotic American English that the immigrant's children acquire? And can it, having done so, rise by easy stages—or by any stages at all—to the eloquence of the vernacular that one reads in the pages of Nathaniel Hawthorne or Henry James or William Faulkner or Willa Cather or James Baldwin? Can the U.S. Italian find a category of speech wide enough to accommodate such purposes? The examples of Baldwin, Cather, and Faulkner suggest that the Italian can succeed in fashioning a distinctly Italian form of American English. All of these writers enter the order of classic American English prose from a position that is distinctly marginal. Cather was a westerner, Faulkner a southerner, and Baldwin a black in times when the established styles belonged to white men from places between Boston and Princeton, period. Southern white men had fallen out of the central tradition after the Civil War (although before it they had sponsored stylists such as Thomas Jefferson and James Madison). Female and black writers had not achieved distinction appropriate to the quality of their work. Edgar Allan Poe, although he became a great god for Baudelaire and Mallarmé, in the United States never escaped his origins as an Irish poet from Catholic Baltimore. Poe never made it in Unitarian Boston. Even now, as far south as Yale University in New Haven, Connecticut, they poke fun at him, showing how alive is the tradition of in-group lampooning started by Ralph Waldo Emerson and John Greenleaf Whittier, faithfully sustained down to almost our own time by such as the late F. O. Matthiessen and our contemporary Harold Bloom. But if an Italian American writer were to equal the achievement of, say, James Baldwin, who constructed his own eloquence out of the ordinary speech of African Americans, where would the materials for such a triumph be found?

Some possibilities of effective interweaving between English and Italian come readily to mind but so far have failed to serve the purpose. Of all such the apparently easiest is merely to record the immigrant's broken English. But this language, filled as it is with signs of his oppression and shame, has generally not attracted the Italian writer in the United States. Indeed, its best-known virtuoso has been a member of the dominant language group, T. A. Daly, who was able to find broken English colorful and pathetic without needing, as an Italian would have needed, to portray in it any color or pathos of his own.[3] Recently, Fred Gardaphe has resurrected this dialect in his short fiction with enough success to suggest wider experiments to come.[4]

Frank Lentricchia tells a remarkable story of how the men of an Italian neighborhood in Utica, New York, managed to deal with a turn of events they found hard to accept: the great Joe DiMaggio was being replaced by the non-Italian Mickey Mantle!

> The Mick was not (apparently) Italian. He was just twenty and many of the twelve-year-old Little Leaguers on Utica's east side identified with him. *Worship* is a better word. An eight-year difference in age. What was that? They would be teammates in eight years. The Mick and me! And had not so many of the players' fathers transformed him into one of us? Mantle? Who were Mickey's parents trying to kid? We knew. *Mandolino* he was called on the Italian east side. *Mickey Mandolino*, this blond bruiser from Oklahoma was actually the secret son of the great DiMaggio. He had to be, to play ball that well, to replace DiMaggio, who was the father. How do you replace the father?[5]

Although this is an excellent application of the powers of Italians using Italian bluntly to bend English to their will, it remains fair to say that, thus far, the construction of a large-scale Broken English (English broken with Italian, that is) has not been attempted.[6]

At the other end of the scale, it has often seemed attractive simply to Latinize English eloquence, making it yet more "illustrious, cardinal, courtly, and curial" than it was already. This policy dangerously inflates a Germanic dialect that already for centuries has been devising eloquence with rich mixtures of Latin, French, and Italian. It has tempted largely the young, the pedantic, and the incurably grandiose. But they have not met success. Latinity has transfigured and elevated English writing throughout the history of British literature. But U.S. Italians have not needed to do, or at least they have not yet done, for their English what Tasso did for Milton's or Virgil did for Tennyson's. Indeed, to attempt this might in effect mean for the U.S. Italian to kiss the toe of the King's English, laying down as tribute any remnant of an ancestral dialect, treating it as a severed tongue, an embarrassing token of late arrival and immemorial social marginality—although indeed other politics are possible. The U.S. Italian must find an English eloquence that does not follow an English model. Even a Latinizing of how we read English writers such as Tennyson and Milton must await the development of an English prose with a new mixture of Italian in it.

This eloquence must be able to change English in a way that will look Italian, that will in some way be Italian, no less indelibly so than the writer's own name. It requires this property, even this identity, because of a purpose it shares with Dante's vernacular eloquence: it aims to suit the dignity of a nation that does not fully exist. This at least is the Risorgimento version of the story: Dante's policy hoped to bring Italy into being by constructing a tongue fitted for the deliberations of its putative princes and judges.

The Italian American writer—even before becoming a U.S. Italian, with U.S. citizenship and the British literary tradition to worry about—writes for a nation whose absence makes itself felt. Italian America has often seemed even more remote from the immigrant Italian than a unified Italy was from Dante, often has appeared a mythical place compounded of other myths—false memories of Italy and passionate dreams of America. According to Italian nationalist belief, Dante's Italian needed to be illustrious and cardinal and courtly and curial because it would thereby give sovereign attributes to a people that might then be induced to claim its sovereignty. The U.S. Italian's Italian American eloquence has aims that are slightly more diffuse. It does not imagine itself able to call a nation to sovereignty. Rather, it wishes to awaken Italian America to a sense of self, and then to console, to encourage, and to locate for this mythical nation a secure place that no one can confuse with its lost homeland or its fabulous landfall.

In both cases, one must remember the linguistic rule that what is called a language belongs to a community of users. Its inventors must devise it in a way that will make it possible for others to use it. This language, then, must, like Dante's, possess qualities that answer to the needs and habits of its inheritors. It must be liturgical to call up the power of lost Italy. It must be patriarchal to emphasize a continuity that often seems to have been broken. It must be heroic to reflect the nature of the immigrant Italian enterprise. It must, finally, be diplomatic to negotiate the terms on which Italian America can exist within the United States—exist, that is, neither as a mere political convenience, nor as the object of some altruism, but as almost a religion—something between a cult and a culture, something between a state of mind and a system of referents rich enough to generate works of art in a language that, howsoever American English or immigrant Italian any of its parts may be, remains irreducibly mingled.

Liturgical, patriarchal, heroic, diplomatic: these four terms, like Dante's *illustrious, cardinal, courtly, curial*, are not so much attributes of *langue* (the system of language) as they are of *parole* (specific acts of speech). They apply, that is, less to how the language is made and more to what it means to accomplish when someone uses it. The order of terms follows rising stages of negotiation. And the whole sequence from liturgical to diplomatic is necessary. Only in its diplomatic abilities does this language begin to fulfill the possibilities of Italian American expression. For the sake of clarity, I begin with the simplest term and work toward the most complex term; the explanations and exemplifications will be cumulative so that when we see how this vernacular is diplomatic, we will also see how it is liturgical, patriarchal, and heroic.

Liturgical

By *liturgical* I mean that the writer of Italian America fills his English with Italian that serves, before all else, the ritual purpose of invoking and celebrating the power of a mythical Italy. By *mythical* I mean that this Italy has exchanged physical for psychological presence. *Mythical* also means "real." Although the actual place be absent, the mythical Italy grows large enough to fill every available minim of perceived space and time, passing beyond the confines of nostalgia or even neurosis into a universal presence that writers of Italian America cultivate even if unconsciously or timidly. Writers who face the question directly invoke this mythical Italy by using Italian as a magical tongue that has power to bless, to afflict, and even to create a world.

In Lou D'Angelo's *What the Ancients Said*, for example, the narrator opens the novel with the sentence, "My brother Vinnie and I were brought up on Sicilian proverbs, most of them enigmatic."[7] Then he devotes a whole chapter to outlining how, within the confines of his immigrant family in East Harlem, these proverbs created a world filled with puzzles, fear, and doubt. Among this collection of gnomic sayings, he tells us, the most typical was,"King Solomon, for all his sapience, died without assistance" (p. 9). "I gave a good deal of thought to that one," he says, leaving us to contemplate the puzzlement of a young American boy who must learn to negotiate his surroundings in terms of such antique distillations. We only begin, however, to estimate their full power when he tells us how his grandfather finally explained the proverb to him:

> The meaning is that King Solomon was a very wise man of whom many people, including, and especially, his sister, were jealous. And for all his majestic learning, he died without help, with a spoon stuck in his ass. The ancients said, "Things there are, but we are not obliged to believe them."
>
> My grandfather had ended his explanation with the most quoted Sicilian proverb of all. What the ancients probably had in mind was authenticating Sicilian beliefs in witchcraft, ghosts, and evil omens, while noting their lack of ecclesiastical approbation. In our corner of the New World, this pronouncement served as an all-purpose comment on everything from small pleasures to major catastrophes. My grandmother, particularly, repeated it several times a day. (p. 11)

In subsequent chapters, D'Angelo writes in a similar fashion about the use of names—both the given name and the cruel nickname, *la 'ngiuria*.[8] He uses maledictions to create a state of terror, even of insanity. And he attributes deep madness both to his (or to his narrator's) own mother and to the presence of Italy in America. The mother tongue is the tongue of a lunatic mother in this novel, one that threatens to swallow into the darkness of her terrors even her own children.

D'Angelo rarely cites any of his proverbs or nicknames except in English. This seems part of a general policy in his works, a policy of keeping Italian at a distance, usually through irony, sometimes through outright burlesque. The fear of the mother that runs through *What the Ancients Said* and his subsequent *A Circle of Friends* provides a plausible motive for this distancing. The distance is not comfortable, however, and the satyr's mask that D'Angelo likes to wear is not always appropriate as a mouthpiece for the difficult things he wishes to say.

Some writers employ Italian to invoke a more benign power. In Pietro di Donato's *Christ in Concrete*, the characters speak an English that either suggests Italian word order or seems to translate Italian locutions literally. With the peculiar idioms that result, di Donato portrays the emotional and spiritual stature of this novel's immigrant protagonists. When Luigi is lying in the hospital after an amputation, he says to his sister, "Ah, the sheets are clean but God only knows how many Christians have decayed on this mattress, for the lice have grown big and bold in my hair and walk down my face. They do keep me awake, sister"(p. 123). Italian presses through the surface of this English. "Christians" is a standard synecdoche for "human beings" in Italian, not English. "They do keep me awake, sister" is an artificial locution meant to sound like a literal rendering of Italian and not like American English idiom at all. At moments of great agony—and many are found in this novel, which is built around ritually repeated crucifixions, life unfolding as recurring sacrifices that follow one another like priests to the altar of daily mass—this artificial manner will most likely disappear, and the characters will call out, as Luigi does during the amputation, in the sacred language: "Jesu-Giuseppe-Marieeeeee . . ." (p. 123).

One might multiply examples freely here. It would, indeed, be difficult to find an Italian American novel[9] that completely refrains from using Italian in this liturgical sense, although few do so as systematically as *Christ in Concrete*. Tag lines in Italian—these are commonplaces in immigrant Italian writing of many kinds. It will, for the moment, suffice to say why this liturgical use parallels Dante's sense of the illustrious quality of his vernacular, which, he says, means that this eloquence is "exalted both in instruction and power, and itself exalts its followers with honor and glory" (p. 29). I replace "illustrious" with "liturgical" because in Italian America, Italian may not bring "honor and glory" but seems always at least to carry "instruction and power"—"power" because it calls up Italy, always a strong presence, if sometimes an equivocal one; "instruction" because Italian is the medium, often enough, that brings the traditional wisdom of the old country into the discourse of the New World.

Of course, more needs to be done than merely invoking the old gods and gospels. But to rest content with such invocations has proved tempting and even inevitable for many U.S. Italian writers. In truth, the liturgical use of Italian in English is the most unmediated, and therefore the most powerful, way to join the two languages. Consequently, it is the easiest way, and the most dangerous, the readiest to the hand of the sentimentalist, the demagogue, the fraud. Literature must use liturgy but it must add, it must examine, it must dismantle, it must surround liturgy, with other powers, and the Italian American vernacular eloquence does this.

Patriarchal

By *patriarchal* we mean that the writer of Italian America fills the English of the text with signs of the patriarchal structure of the Italian family. Whether, indeed, the patriarchate or the matriarchate dominates in the Italian family is a question I do not pretend to decide because I am discussing the households not of the world but of the novel, where the patriarchal nomenclature of Italy has assumed in the English-speaking world what may, admittedly, be a disproportionate significance.[10] Names are the only Italian words that find their way into some Italian American novels. They appear if nowhere else on the title page where an Italian American's insistence on keeping unaltered the inconvenient patronym establishes a clear line to Italy.[11] In many novels, too, the importance of patronyms shows itself from the outset, where a novelist is more likely to define the social world in terms of them. Here, as a particularly apt example, is the first sentence of Garibaldi La Polla's *The Grand Gennaro*:

> The singularly narrow house, three stories high, in which the destinies of the Accuci, the Dauri, and the Monterano families became hopelessly entangled, still throws its late afternoon shadow in the East River.[12]

Names, important as they are, only begin to suggest the place that the language of patriarchy fills, particularly in fiction concerning Italian American men. To find a way of identifying American son with Italian father is one of the main purposes that Italian serves in these works. Robert Canzoneri's *A Highly Ramified Tree* invites us to follow the narrator, who is an Italian American professor of English, and his father, who is a Sicilian immigrant turned Southern Baptist preacher, as they return to the father's hometown of Palazzo Adriani. We follow the narrator, too, into his own childhood in the American South, where his father has married an American woman. But when they are in Sicily, we suddenly enter with the narrator a boyhood in Sicily that he has never had:

> "Roberto, Vene cca!" It is my grandmother, calling from the other room. She sits all day in the chair, dark and short; her little arms can reach out and grab me no matter how far around her I try to pass, pull me to her to be examined, scolded, hugged. "Come kiss your nanna good morning. It is a beautiful day, a very special day. . . ." Her voice chokes. She begins to cry. "Oh," she is wailing. "Oh, San Giuseppe be praised. . . ."
>
> "Mamma, mamma," my mother says. "He does not understand."
>
> "Sò papà," my grandmother cries. "He will get to see his father at last. He will not remember him."[13]

Two elements are crucial here. First, the opening phrase, "Roberto! Vene cca!" This is a ritual motif that recurs several times in the novel, invoking the Italian hidden within the American man. Second, the grandmother's speech about the boy's father. For in this fantasy, Canzoneri has imagined a boyhood in Sicily during the 1930s, an alternative boyhood, one in which his father has been imprisoned for three years by Mussolini; when this imagined father returns to this imagined village, he immediately plans to leave for the United States and so writes to his prosperous relatives there (who include, by the way, Tony Canzoneri, not imaginary, but in fact at that time lightweight boxing champion of the world, and in fact one of the author's relatives); they send a check to pay for passage to America, but at the last moment the narrator's father gives in to the pleadings of his wife and son and decides to remain in Italy. The fantasy fulfills in a complex way the narrator's desire to be one with his father. Complex because it moves in two directions: while the narrator and his father are joined in Sicily, still they are separated by Mussolini's prison, and so the fantasy makes the break between them seem inevitable, almost a kind of original sin. We see its importance when the narrator shows the father's desire to escape to America as a temptation to break the male chain of generation, a temptation that in the fantasy the father rejects.

Desire to mend the broken link runs through the language of Canzoneri's novel from beginning to end. In the first chapter, he arrives in Sicily, and the opening of the first paragraph recounts how his cousin greets him, "In black Sicilian suits and caps they sit in the sun like a flock of blackbirds far across the plaza. One is drawn stiffly from his chair as I approach. 'Roberto?'" (p. 3). With one word, the cousin calls up an entire inner body of feelings, and the narrator says, "He is my cousin, old enough to be my father; the look of him, the smell and feel of him I know from my father, my dead and dying uncles, myself" (p. 3). Thus, from the start, the narrator moves among a tribe of Sicilian men to which he does and does not belong. His need to resolve the contradictions of his own nature produces some striking results. Toward the end of the novel he is traveling through Italy and seeing little of it because his mind is on a younger woman back in the United States for whom he is planning to leave his wife. He feels the American in him tearing away from both his father the Sicilian patriarch and his father the American preacher. At this juncture, he writes a short story that becomes a chapter in his narrative: its hero is an Italian American just like himself who tries to join himself to Italy by having the whole cycle of paintings from the vault of the Sistine Chapel tattooed to his bald head and by then arranging to have himself murdered and to have his body hung in the catacombs. Alas, he cannot find an assassin willing to take part.

His plot fails for other reasons, too. At root the narrator wants not to be one with Italy, but to be united with his father. This means he must accept not only his own "crimes" against the old order, but also his father's transgressions as well: it is the father who has left Italy and brought the family to America. In the final scene, the son with his new wife, as well as with his father and his American mother, visit Vicksburg on a sightseeing pilgrimage. He concludes his narrative by reporting what his father says:

> When I get back to the driver's seat, my father turns to me; the senility seems fully taken into consideration, the flow of blood to the brain. Out of nothing, yesterday, he has said to me with this same clear look, I may be old but I'm still here. This time he says, "We going home now?" (p. 189)

The father's imperfect English, American speech despite its Sicilian echoes, suggests how highly ramified the Canzoneri tree has become at this juncture; and it points, at the same time, to a home that is neither fully America nor fully Italy but, whatever it is, stands where son and father are joined.

I am using "patriarchal" where Dante uses "cardinal," by which he means that his vernacular will be the pivot of a hinge, whose movement will affect all other vernaculars. I observe that the patriarchal impulse has a pivotal importance in the rhetoric of much Italian American fiction written by men. Many of the works where the tradition tries to define itself take the form of connectives. As Canzoneri's novel does, they aim to restore the continuity of the male line. Luigi Forgione's *The River Between*, an early example,[14] deals with the struggle for mutual acceptance between a father and son. Joseph Arleo's *The Grand Street Collector*,[15] though nominally "about" the murder of Carlo Tresca, follows the search of an American son for his Italian father. Rocco Fumento's *Tree of Dark Reflection*[16] has a narrator who struggles mightily with his immigrant father and can resolve his conflicts only after he learns in Italy the secrets of the old man's character. Even in Mario Puzo's *The Fortunate Pilgrim*,[17] a novel devoted to the portrait of a very powerful New York Italian matriarch, the strength of the heroine Lucia Santa develops only after her two husbands have failed to establish their own line of continuity; furthermore, her only male-bonded son, Larry Angeluzzi, displays the sterling masculinity that enables him to acquire a "godfather" and with that aid to arrive at a point where he can free his mother and her children from the bondage of New York City's West Side and then lead them into the Canaan of Long Island. We might also consider the importance of this theme in the plot of *Christ in Concrete*, where Paul's need to replace his father gives the book much of its shape—or in *The Godfather*, where Don Vito Corleone and his sons show us a wide range of the forms that father-son relationships can assume.[18] But the patriarchal themes of Italian American fiction are presupposed by our subsequent categories; and it will be appropriate, accordingly, to move on to these.

Heroic

I put "heroic" where Dante uses "courtly," which he finds appropriate because "if . . . Italians had a royal court, this vernacular would be spoken in the palace" (p. 30). The courtliness, in Dante's sense of the word, of his eloquent vernacular is a sign both of Italy's greatness and of her agony. One feels reading *De vulgari eloquentia* that it is almost the very lack of a court—that is, of a unified and potent Italy—that requires so elevated a tongue: the language must stand for all that is missing. For similar reasons, Italian American writers frequently use a language that is heroic: their words give stature and dignity to those whom no nation exists to ennoble. Novelists in this tradition wish to create alternative versions of a world frequently discussed in the dialects of the immigration officer, the social worker, the landlord, and the politician. Garibaldi La Polla, by profession an elementary school principal, was thoroughly familiar with the language of the oppressor. In this passage from the first chapter of his novel *The Grand Gennaro*, he specifically aims to revise the vocabulary of social science:

> The depression that really had its beginnings in 1890 but delayed the full force of its fury until 1893, had registered in Europe before it had become fully admitted into the United States. A stream of immigration began to pour into New York City. Especially from the southern portion of Italy great masses of people, for all the world like an ancient migration, braved the terrors of slow, weather-beaten steamers, and, once landed in New York, pooled into scattered communities throughout Manhattan. (pp. 3–4)

The simile "for all the world like an ancient migration" makes a gesture in the direction of historical dignity. Nonetheless, it amounts to little more than a grace note in a paragraph otherwise composed largely in the modes of settlement house economics and of newspaper sociology. The novel as a whole is a similarly incomplete attempt to show how these immigrants recreate, surrounded though they are by U.S. power and English-speaking bureaucrats, the intricate glories of an irrecoverable Italy.

A similar program—carried out this time, however, with professional thoroughness—underlies Mario Puzo's *The Godfather*. Here, liturgical and patriarchal elements combine in a sustained effort to reinvent the notion of *mafia*, to make it mean not "criminal world," but "refuge" and "heroic world." Puzo uses names with blunt allegorical intent. The first character to appear is the undertaker Amerigo Bonasera, the man who has tried to be "American." Denied justice by the New York courts, Amerigo Bonasera has now emphatically bid America goodnight and decided he must go on his knees to Don Corleone. *Lionheart*, the great Don, lives up to his name. To his world of relatives and allies, he is nothing less than the medieval honorific implies—leader, man of respect, dispenser of justice, arranger of high matters, Lord Godfather Lionheart. Puzo keeps all this afloat not only by labeling everyone carefully, but also by keeping persistently present an Italian diction that, literally translated into English and made part of the discourse, becomes in effect a heroic language. Don Corleone, we are told, refers to Santino as his "first-born, masculine son" (p. 31). *Figlio maschio* is idiomatic in Italian, but the gender epithet stands out in English as redundant and emphatic: it becomes a key expression in the novel, which elevates maleness to a level of heroic mystery. This heroic maleness enters, as it were, literally, during the wedding scene in chapter 1 with its description of Santino Corleone's massive sexual organ. After Sonny has made love to the maid of honor, the singers Johnny Fontane and Nino Valenti sing what Puzo calls "an obscene Sicilian love song" with a "sly, double-meaning tag line that finished each stanza" (p. 32). In the film this song is *"La luna mezzu o mari,"* and it is among the two or three most popular songs of the Italian migration, a bawdy dialogue wherein a daughter repeatedly asks her mother for a husband, and the mother asks what sort of husband she wants, pointing out that a baker husband will always be giving her his loaf, a fisherman his fish, a policeman his pistol, a fireman his hose.[19] All this phallic celebration echoes in the ordinary language of the characters, who call important people either big shots or *pezzonovanti* (*pezzi di novanta*, .90 caliber pieces, large six-shooters).

Puzo best succeeds at making this maleness seem the force of a heroic enterprise in those parts of the novel where the Don plays a major role, and most notably in his speech to the assembled dons, which begins, "What manner of men are we then, if we do not have our reason?" (p. 290). Puzo tells us that Don Corleone is speaking Sicilian here, and the English is stilted in a way that hints at literal translation (but is not because *avere ragione* does not mean "to have reason" but "to have right," "to be right") and moves with a marked stateliness. Later in the same speech, the Don offers this well-known defense of his world:

> "As for our deeds, we are not responsible to the .90 calibers, the *pezzonovanti*s who take it upon themselves to decide what we shall do with our lives, who declare wars they wish us to fight in to protect what they own. Who is to say we should obey the laws they make for their own interest and to our hurt? And who are they then to meddle when we look after our own interests? *Sonna cosa nostra,*" Don Corleone said, "these are our own affairs. We will manage our world for ourselves because it is our world, *cosa nostra*. And we have to stick together to guard against outside meddlers.

> Otherwise they will put the ring in our nose as they have put
> the ring in the nose of all the millions of Neapolitans and
> other Italians in this country." (p. 291)

This bravura performance takes the newspaper term *cosa nostra* and
turns its meaning inside out. Rather than sinister, Puzo implies these
men are admirable: not outlaws but heroes, crusaders, guerrillas, proud
and lionhearted men. The idea is not new. To make heroic the
excluded—the outlawed no less than the humble and the dispossessed—
is a standard operation in folklore, a maneuver that can sustain varieties
of revolutionary art. Little wonder, then, that it should find a place in
Italian American fiction at the end of the 1960s when the expression
"our thing" gave it a ready salience for an emerging community of self-
consciously Italian American readers.[20]

Puzo's very rhetorical success has troubled many readers who,
considering the complexity of U.S. Italian reality, find the heroic mode
misleadingly simple and, in Puzo's skillful work, dangerously seductive.
It is useful in this connection to consider a more modest text, Joseph
Arleo's *The Grand Street Collector*,[21] which concerns itself very directly
with the temptations of heroic language in an imaginary Italian America. The novel's title refers to Don Natale Sbagliato, a numbers collector
in New York whom Fascist agents flatter into murdering Guido Sempi-
one—a thinly disguised figure of Carlo Tresca (1879–1943), the notorious immigrant Italian anarchist editor of *Il martello* ("the hammer"),
active disruptor of Fascist meetings in New York, and high on Mussolini's list of people to destroy.[22] These are the words Don Natale finds
filling his reverie just before he engages himself to commit the crime:

> "The American right hand of Mussolini." A sudden surge of
> joy flooded through him. "That of all those in this country
> he knows so well, I, I am the one he reaches for. That the
> brotherhood of suffering is undeniable. That the Eternal
> Father makes me worthy. . . ." (pp. 29–30)

Arleo leaves us no doubt that this is the rhetoric of delusion. Don
Natale is thoroughly *Sbagliato*[23] in his reading both of Mussolini and of
his own role, and he comes to an elaborately terrible ending.

Puzo's novel, however, does not close its eyes to the moral paradoxes of its vision. It simply rests its case on the "ring through the
nose." The heroism is desperate because it has a desperate motive. In
Arleo's narrative the loss of heroic illusions acquires a tragic heroism. A

more straightforward heroism than that, and a less doubtful one than Don Corleone's, belongs to the humble bricklayers who are the protagonists of di Donato's *Christ in Concrete*. Here, the presence of Italian words and ways adds an almost entirely noble, even pompous, dimension to the narrative. In di Donato's text, Italian expression reveals itself not only magical, generative, and heroic, but also strategically ingenious. But let us reserve discussion of this text until we have added the last of our tetrad of epithets to the analysis.

Diplomatic

Dante calls his vernacular "curial" "Because curiality is nothing other than a balanced rule for things which must be done," and "we have come to call all of our actions which are well-balanced, curial"—and, as he says, his language has "been balanced in the very highest Italian court" (p. 30). The notion of a language sifted by many judicious speakers and writers with similar purposes in mind is a useful one to us here. I am employing a term that suggests something of balance as well, but *diplomatic* particularly suits the language of fiction concerning Italian America because it points to the mutual presence there of an Italian which is, as we have seen, liturgical and patriarchal and heroic, alongside an English that is—what? I shall propose here that the English component of Italian American language tends to reciprocate the gestures of the Italian component; that in the language of Italian American fiction, we find a play of reciprocal Italian and American gestures; that this interplay formalizes each of the two components out of the need each has to reply to the other, so that the character of this language is diplomatic.

When we speak of diplomatic language, we approach a dramatic situation from inside a very attentive policy of linguistic choice and a very instrumental notion of linguistic power. Diplomacy uses words to avoid the use of blunter weapons. Its closeness to action endows diplomatic language with something that resembles physical strength and mobility. The reciprocity of diplomatic discourse is no mere matter of binary alternation but more closely resembles the gestural interchange of a dance, where distinct roles for the partners remain visible while every action of each somehow reflects or predicts the movements of the other. There is enough of reciprocal constraint to suggest battle and enough of mutual self-constraint to avoid it. To call a literary language diplomatic, then, is perhaps to add an unwelcome complication to the act of reading: for a reader must not only follow the ordinary intricacies of language and structure, but that same reader must also attend to a drama that is purely linguistic, the encounter of two languages in the prose of the narrative. Unwelcome as this complication may seem, the material repays the effort it takes to follow it. As a strategy of reading, the discovery of diplomatic play in language offers necessary light for the scrutiny of Italian American fiction and may well provide similar illumination elsewhere in minority literatures that use majority languages. I shall use as a specimen passage here a few paragraphs from the opening chapter of *Christ in Concrete*; the narrator here describes bricklayers at work:

> The Lean pushed his barrow on, his face cruelly furrowed with time and struggle. Sirupy sweat seeped from beneath his cap down his bony nose and turned icy at its end. He muttered to himself. "Saints up, down, sideways and inside out! How many more stones must I carry before I'm overstuffed with the light of day! I don't understand . . . blood of the Virgin, I don't understand!"
>
> Mike "the Barrel-mouth" pretended he was talking to himself and yelled out in his best English . . . he was always speaking English while the rest carried on in their native Italian. "I don't know myself, but somebodys whose gotta bigga buncha keeds and he alla times talka from somebodys else!"
>
> Geremio knew it was meant for him and he laughed. "On the tomb of Saint Pimple-legs, this little boy my wife is giving me next week shall be the last! Eight hungry little Christians to feed is enough for any man." (p. 12)[24]

We might begin here without the aid of any of the analytic language we have been using. Reading simply for style, we can discriminate three clearly marked registers. First, there is the careful idiomatic English, sometimes marked by a degree of self-proclaiming artiness, that the narrator employs: "Sirupy sweat seeped from beneath his cap, down his bony nose and turned icy at its end." Second, there is the English equivalent of the Italian that the characters are actually speaking, and di Donato persistently emphasizes this doubleness by using locutions that appear literally to translate Italian expressions: "Blood of the Virgin" is scarcely something Americans say, while *"sangue della Vergine"* has a plausible ring. The third register is the broken English of "Mike 'the Barrel-mouth,'" which di Donato places here, on the second page of his novel, to indicate that the other characters are speaking not a pidgin or a creole but rather an Italian that di Donato is portraying in English. So much is clear.

But, having established these categories, we find that we must immediately begin to dismantle them. The narrator's English in particular evades easy classification because, although it generally has a highly self-conscious texture and shows a lively sensitivity to American idiom, it uses as well the English Italian of the characters when the need arises. The narrator, for example, habitually and plausibly calls his characters by the *agnomina* that *contadini* devise for one another: Nick is "the Lean" and Mike is "the Barrel-mouth." But di Donato can strategically refrain from using any such sobriquet. Geremio, the Christ who falls into the concrete, remains *Geremio* in the narrator's discourse, without any nickname, as indeed he does in the dialogue itself, where he even rises at times to the dignity of *Master Geremio*. Here we might pause and see how this language is diplomatic in the sense we are using. Both the Italian and the English in the narrator's prose are transformed by one another's presence. The nicknames of the characters, sure signs in Italian that these men are peasants, acquire in English a thematic emphasis so that these *braccianti* (physical laborers) become masks for spiritual states (and more subtle in their allegorical presence than Puzo's Corleone or Arleo's Sbagliato, whose names are precisely not diplomatic, not rewritten by any double direction of their messages). Thus, in *Christ in Concrete* a familiar rustic habit of speech in Italian assumes in literal translation a fresh eloquence that, in its turn, exerts a pressure on the idiomatic English of the narrator, moving it upward in tone, so that it treats even minor details with poetic precision in a language that has enough compression and visual attentiveness to suggest Dante as exemplar: again, "Sirupy sweat seeped from beneath his cap down his bony nose and turned icy at its end."

Nor is the narrator's English the only language here that evades easy categories. When "the Lean" says, "Saints up, down, sideways and inside out," the noun and the first two adverbs echo an Italian sequence, but *sideways* and *inside out* are American English music.[25] The joining of the two pairs of adverbs gives the whole expression the resonance of an epic formula or comprehensive spell, a dignity of estate that neither of the conjoined elements, each drawn as it is from the demotic idiom of its native tongue, could ever alone possess. Some of the other "translated" locutions seem to be at the very least mistranslated: *sangue della Madonna* is a more likely exclamation than *sangue della Vergine*. "On the tomb of Saint Pimple-legs," although it begins recognizably, ends in such a way that we can suppose that the Italian

original must be a very local idiom indeed or else that di Donato has
invented it for the occasion. The latter supposition seems to me the correct one because di Donato writes this novel in language that he pieces
together as he goes, an inspired bricolage that constantly draws on the
dance in his mind between the peasant eloquence of his childhood and
the bookish discourse he acquired in a youth that he spent (he boasts
elsewhere) as "probably the only apprentice-bricklayer in the United
States who [came] to the job site with the Divine Comedy, the Golden
Bough and Lamprière's classical dictionary under his arm."[26] We can, I
think, without troubling to annotate its every gesture, see the elaborate
dance of Italian and English in such a passage as the following, where
Geremio's wife grieves for him after his death:

> O Jesu in Heaven, and husband near, whither . . . and how?
> Pieced from the living are we now both. Bread—bread of Job
> and job of Bread has crushed your feet from the ground and
> taken your eyes from the sun, but nowhere are we sepa-
> rate—never—never in this breathing life shall I be away from
> you. Day and night will I kiss your wounds, with my flesh
> shall I keep the rain from you, these tears shall comfort you
> in heat, and with the cold shall I breathe upon you my
> warmth . . . husband great. (p. 49)

Here is the language of neither Italy nor America. This tongue —liturgical, patriarchal, heroic, diplomatic—belongs to a people whose expression arises in two countries, employing the mythical dignity of a mythical
Italy as a consolation for, as an incantation over, a real Italian America.

Jerre Mangione writes that his mother enforced a rule that her
children speak only Italian at home:

> Outside the house she expected us to speak English, and
> often took pride in the fact that we spoke English so well
> that none of our relatives could understand. . . .
>
> We gradually acquired the notion that we were Italian
> at home and American (whatever that was) elsewhere.
> Instinctively, we all sensed the necessity of adapting our-
> selves to two different worlds. We began to notice that there
> were marked differences between those worlds, differences
> that made Americans and my relatives each think of the
> other as foreigners.[27]

The double consciousness, entirely identified with language, that Mangione describes here, characterizes the situation of the novelist of Italian America. If this writer writes, as is generally the case, without di Donato's degree of poetic inventiveness, still the work means confronting the confusions of the situation. It means beginning to understand the civic and political codes that make one a U.S. citizen. The writer must play the diplomat. The writer must translate, explain, meditate. Mangione often takes on the role of interpreter, carefully explaining (pp. 54–55) the difficulties that arise from an Italian Americanism such as *baccauso*.[28] D'Angelo offers catalogues of proverbs and nicknames as a necessary initiation for a reader who would understand the insides of an Italian American household. For, finally, it is the diplomatic imperative that conditions every aspect of the language of Italian American fiction. To mediate between two languages is to maintain the existence of both.

The accommodation, it may be, is a fragile one. Some observers believe that coming generations will see the *Italian* in *Italian American* recede into a dim ancestry.[29] More likely, diplomatic counterplay will merely employ new terms to make the most of new arrangements in a relationship that has roots running back to the dawn of American history on the one side, and to the dawn of Europe on the other. Relationships so deeply rooted in the languages and cultures of the large world will transform and will survive.

The situation of the Italian American is changing as Italian America comes more sharply into focus. No longer an immigrant or the child of an immigrant, this dislocated Italian fares forth now as a pilgrim. The immigrant grandfather has become a brown photograph of an old man at a table where one can see ravioli, vino, and taralli. The photograph curls in the dresser drawer, but the grandchild is flying to Rome for the summer. Waiting for this traveler somewhere south or east of there, innumerable cousins will have prepared a vast ritual meal. This traveler will sit among them, rosy with the embarrassment of the anthropologist, not quite capable of using or understanding the dialect. Still, there will be blood between them, and one touch on the arm will claim the affinity. One such touch will open a passage for the Italian American to return. At the other end of the passage will rise the long, steep panorama of the immigrant grandfather's lost patrimony. Vittorini, Verga, Manzoni, Petrarca, Boccaccio, and Dante will make their musics heard. In that sound, the Italian American will hear a new complexity. Like many another returning citizen of the United States—like

Washington Irving in Westminster, Gertrude Stein in the Luxembourg Gardens, and Henry James in Rye—this traveler will find in the ancient sounds echoes that the natives never hear, and will discover then, it may be, as Irving, Stein, and James before this, another music of paradox, policy, and hesitation. For this traveler will have passed between two worlds and, belonging to both, belong then to a third, a world whose initiates are those whose ears have been opened and can hear in every word, like the shadow of a doubt, the echoes it will have in a foreign place. Such writers must always recognize themselves as diplomats, in the oldest material sense because they are doubles, folded double, turning at every corner to hear the ghosts of voices from the place in which they no longer find themselves.

CHAPTER 3

Il caso della casa

Stories of Houses in Italian America

Il caso della casa—"The Case of the House"—suggests a murder mystery, a crime, something formidable and stunning. "Stories of Houses in Italian America" is more relaxed, less formal: perhaps you will read about the seven-bedroom brick colonial that my cousin once owned in Westchester County, New york. The doubled and redoubled titles mean to suggest two self-conflicted and mutually conflicting attitudes that come into play as one turns the conversation to the question of Italian territory in the United States.

On the one hand, when Italian Americans speak of houses, they often tell a history of passion. I might tell about the house my grandmother almost bought after fifteen years of saving but did not because my grandfather got into a terrible bloody fight and the lawyer and the judge took all the money. On the other hand, this passion for houses is not merely a passion for passion's sake. Instead, it is a passion for stability. Italians have been pursuing and building houses—*case* in the medieval sense where *house* means *family* and *family* means *house*—for more than a century in Italian America, and doing so with stunning dedication.

Indeed, the Italian American passion for real estate requires some attention: and precisely because it is passion, one's examination of it might well aim to be a little cool, a little distant. So I will offer no stories of my own but will instead sketch a theory that will allow us to examine some stories that other writers have told, where the intensity of the enterprise reveals itself most openly.

The theory is simple. Contrary to the testimony of familiar maps, there is such a place as Italian America. It is not a contiguous territory,

59

although Italian communities certainly still exist; rather, it is a series of locations. Italian America is most frequently, most easily, to be found in Italian houses in America. In these places, the house is in one of several possible senses the old country itself. This chapter will isolate and exemplify four ways that this can be so. The house may be a shrine, a villa, a palazzo, or an embassy.[1] And any house may be all four of these at the same time, for these nouns must clear name purposes, and a house can serve many purposes at once.

Shrine

Lares and *penates*—the Roman names for household gods—are what make an American house Italian American, and here we may choose from innumerable examples. For anything that bears the mark of Italy can become a household god in Italian America. This extends from obvious artifacts such as the statue of Santa Rosalia or the panorama of the Golfo di Napoli to the subtle but all-enveloping atmosphere of cookery. Indeed, Mario Puzo goes so far as to identify house with family and family with food:

> I had every desire to go wrong but I never had a chance. The Italian family structure was too formidable.
>
> I never came home to an empty house; there was always the smell of supper cooking. . . . Many years later as [a] guest of a millionaire's club, I realized that our poor family on home relief ate better than some of the richest people in America.
>
> My mother would never dream of using anything but the finest imported olive oil, the best Italian cheeses.[2]

And so on. Puzo, like many other Italian American storytellers, employs as a standard trope the catalogue of the items of *la cucina casalinga*. And always, as here, the stress falls on the power, usually presented as a form of magic, that floats in the aromas of provolone and ragù.

What is that power? Certainly in the passage cited it has some of the features of guilt, and one thinks quickly enough of Freud's comparison of religion with obsessional neurosis. Reading Puzo, one often encounters the son who returns home precisely because he wishes to go wrong: his returns, that is, assure him that his "faithlessness" to the family has been avoided, while the home that he returns to is saturated in the glamour of taboos violated. By seeming to give himself up to the strictures of the "family structure," the son can in fact luxuriate in an unbridled orgy of self-indulgent fantasy. It is not merely that the family table is a thieves' banquet, although Puzo paints his mother as a kind of self-righteous Fagin who takes her poverty for an excuse never to inquire too far into the provenance of those fine imported oils and cheeses. Not only is private property violated here, but also the very propriety of privates: about *The Fortunate Pilgrim*, Puzo has written, "To my astonishment my mother took over the book and instead of revenge I got another comeuppance [Puzo's word]. But it is, I think, my best book" (p. 27). The touching collaboration of mother and son he describes there expresses the same fugitive fantasy of Oedipus victorious that informs the career of Michael in *The Godfather*. Michael who supplants the father that obligingly dies at the appropriate moment, Michael who murders all rivals with the panache of a race car driver slipping on his French gloves—Michael reaches apotheosis in the conclusion of the novel where, assuming the role of godfather, he poses before his friends even as he fills the reveries of his mother and his bride as they kneel every morning in church.

These fantasies, delightful as they are, bear a heavy price. Elsewhere in Puzo's work, the price appears to be nothing short of complete emptiness, a damnation deliberately chosen (see his early art-novel *The Dark Arena*[3]) and resounding with all the flatulence of a well-paid bad faith (see the interminable desert of his best seller *Fools Die*).[4] But Puzo, one hastens to add, has merely painted a picture, as it were, showing the inside of a shrine that generally receives more veneration than accurate portrayal. Those who give it genuine attention can scarcely ignore the crimes it commemorates. The guilty immigrant—the man who left father and the woman who abandoned mother in Italy, as well as the man who frees himself from the laws of life and property and the woman who frees herself from the laws of marriage in America—is the consecrator of this sanctuary.[5] The immigrant wrestling with his or her guilt is the mortar not only of the shrine, but also of the more complex purposes that may grow up around it.

Villa

Aeneas—from this angle, the prototype of the successful immigrant—owed his prosperity to *pietas*, veneration for ancestors so profound that he left Troy actually carrying his father on his back. Here is an exorcism of guilt that really works. For the immigrant who has abandoned father and mother, the symbolic path of Aeneas lies open, and many have taken this road, choosing to build in America a home that can advertise itself with whatever repression of absurdity, as patriarchal—*una villa padronale*. Stories of the *famiglia* which builds itself a house and then becomes a *casa* abound in Italian America. This is the narrative in mortar and stones as we encounter it glaring bleakly in the sunshine of Bensonhurst, New York, or South Philadelphia, its ambitions firmly asserting themselves even against the obvious contradictions of their surroundings.[6] When written, this narrative shows up most prominently in the promotional literature of the California wineries and on the back pages of menus in prosperous suburban *ristoranti*. The 1980s prime-time soap opera *Falcon Crest* (which for years appeared weekly on Friday nights right after *Dallas*, and which much resembled *Dallas* in ideology and plot structure) moved this vein of immigrant romance forward and upward into the Social Register. Novelists, however, are rarely content with the pleasure of writing the family patronym over the door (or even on the title page), and the pure type of this tale, the feudal romance of capitalism, almost never appears in fiction. When this romance does show its face, in such works as *Olives on the Apple Tree*[7] or *The Coming of Fabrizze*,[8] it wears, more likely than not, the frank colors of fantasy.

In the tradition of writing that concerns Italian America, the enterprise of the patriarch cannot escape its own inadequacies, cannot overcome the break in its line of generation, and it founders in failure and desecration, which are the very things that it aims to repress. A typical failed patriarch in this line is the father of Henry Molise, the narrator of John Fante's *The Brotherhood of the Grape*. Henry tells us:

> My old man had never wanted children. He had wanted apprentice bricklayers and stonemasons. He got a writer, a bank teller, a married daughter, and a railroad brakeman. In a sense, he tried to shape his sons into stonemasons the way he shaped stone, by whacking it. He failed, of course, for the more he hammered at us, the further he drove us from any love of the craft. When we were kids a great dream possessed Nick Molise, a glimpse of the glorious future lit up in his brain: MOLISE AND SONS, STONEMASONS.
>
> We sons had his brown eyes, his thick hands, his fire-plug stature, and he assumed we were naturally blessed with the same devotion to stone, the same dedication to long hours of backbreaking toil. He envisioned a modest begin-

ning in San Elmo, then the expansion of operations to Sacramento, Stockton, and San Francisco.[9]

Henry Molise, the narrator, tells us from the outset that this paternal empire did not materialize. The novel recounts one final attempt on the part of the old man to join his son Henry, a Hollywood screenwriter, in building something. Although his life's failure is already perfected when the novel opens, the father makes this parting gesture that Fante presents in the mode of tragic farce. The son humors the old man, whose problems include diabetes, heart trouble, and alcohol, complicated by raging satyriasis. Aged father and grown son, together this one last time, erect a collaborative monument. This, as it happens, is nothing more grand than a stone smokehouse. They build it using alabaster quartz—a mineral, Fante points out, that is ordinarily reserved for tombstones. Even this modest grandiosity is doomed. The old man, once a great builder, is now so drunk when he works that the building, almost the minute he finishes it, actually dissolves in the rain. One by one, the father's sins and weaknesses undo him, and when he dies, the only way his son can find to carry on for him is to make love to a nurse that the father has lusted after while dying in the hospital. The nurse is closer to his father's age than to his own.

Nick Molise, in a manner of speaking, dies into the house he fails to establish. The manner of speaking becomes a literal destiny in the story of Geremio in *Christ in Concrete*. After twenty years of striving, the immigrant Geremio finally succeeds one Holy Thursday in making the down payment on a house. The next day, Good Friday, he literally becomes the house that he too, at the last moment, has failed to establish:

> "Air!, Air!" screamed his lungs as he was completely sealed. Savagely he bit into the wooden form pressed upon his mouth. An eighth of an inch of its surface splintered off. Oh, if he could only hold out long enough to bite even the smallest hole through to air. . . . He had bitten halfway through when his teeth snapped off to the gums in the uneven conflict. (pp. 20–21)

Such are the ironies that fate has prepared for the immigrant Italian patriarchy that would plant itself in the New World with the same rocklike immobility it believes itself to have possessed in the Old World.

Di Donato's bricklayer father, like Henry Molise, fails in the ancestral role and reveals himself finally to be no more than an errant son—irresponsible, phallic, guilty, and doomed—who leaves to his own son an empty role to fill, a dishonored satyr's grave that the son seeks forever to bless with some further desecration. Henry Molise's interlude with the aged nurse only recalls rather mildly the hero of di Donato's *This Woman*, who marries a widow and then insists on making love to her on her husband's grave.

Palazzo

To many an enlightened immigrant, then, it has seemed that it would not suffice for *family* to become *house* and for it to erect the paternal totem in the form of a rooftree. This construction would bear the marks of self-enclosure, even of self-damnation. *House* must also become *community*. The logic, it may be, is the psychologic of the communion supper: in consuming a corpse, one must spread the guilt. Instead of consecrating oneself alone to the magic relic of abandoned Italy—the murdered parent—and instead even of merely planting the corpse to grow a new paternal tree, one must call together assemblies of fellow criminals and share the guilty meal. Each guest at the table offers the ritual, "*Domine non sum dignus ut intres sub tectum meum*" ("Lord I am not worthy that Thou shouldst enter under my roof"), and then can feel clear in conscience, can start eating with a will. Such is the solution, for example, adopted in *Christ in Concrete* after Geremio's death. Instead of moving into the *villa padronale* on whose altar the father has been immolated, the family thrives in a tenement (indeed, the central section of the book is called "Tenement") and lives the life of the *palazzo comunale*, where most events in life are shared, where the great building itself becomes a kind of *paese*. The subsequent life of the dead Geremio's family is rich with the features belonging to this manner of existence: the housewives send each other gifts of cooked food, the children mate on the stoop, great ritual meals occasionally take place, and the families gather in their dozens to share food after a wedding or a funeral.

This mode of living no doubt assuages some uncomfortable feelings and provides many of the advantages of community. But the idyll depends on material failure. Another version of *palazzo* in Italian America works quite differently. This one depends on material success. It occurs when a family owns the *palazzo* it occupies, renting apartments to others who inevitably assume positions of hierarchical subordination:

often a *palazzo ducale* wears the humble brick cloak of a three-family house in Bensonhurst or Astoria, New York. We easily imagine how it pleases the once-lowly *contadino* who has become its proprietor and has found in its hallways the answer to Leporello's prayer, "*Voglio far il gentiluomo,*"[10] ("I want to play the gentleman"). Leporello of course, changes his mind after he gets a close look at the fate of Don Giovanni. But the Italian American *servo padrone*, the servant who becomes the master, at least in fiction, generally gets to try the role out for himself. He also gets to pay the price.

The best example is Gennaro Accuci, hero of Garibaldi La Polla's *The Grand Gennaro*. The year is 1893. Gennaro, an illiterate Calabrese, has "without so much as a by-your-leave to the priest or mayor, to both of whom he owed money . . . slipped out of his mountain village and taken ship at Reggio for New York" (p.5). His unpaid debt to the *galantuomini* in Italy is the emblem of his career. He quickly gets rich in New York by stealing the business—literally stealing a thriving concern—that belongs to a boyhood friend who, remembering old days in Calabria, helps Gennaro and then promptly becomes Gennaro's victim. Once Gennaro is rich, he buys a pretentious three-story brownstone that bears, carved into its façade, the operatic name *Parterre*. Himself occupying the *piano nobile*, Gennaro installs two down-at-the-heels aristocratic *famiglie* in the upper floors. This constitutes a neat rearrangement of the social pyramid to be seen inside any opera house in Italy, where the nobility occupy the boxes in the parterre, and a Gennaro Accuci, if he is there at all, must make what he can of the spectacle on stage from a seat somewhere near the roof. Gennaro, truly realizing Leporello's fantasy, occupies not only the parterre of this opera house, but also its stage as well. He is forever marching past its imposing stoop at the head of some parade; he is, naturally, *un prominente* in the spectacular life of East Harlem. He lives out, too, a sentimental history that might have made even Metastasio hesitate and think, "Do I dare?" Gennaro becomes the romantic rival of his firstborn son, then rivals the father of one of his aristocratic families—in both cases seeking the love of the other aristocratic family's daughter. This girl, Carmela Dauri, a paragon of virtues and perfections such as one generally meets only in operas or in soap advertisements, at first loves Gennaro but at the end betrays him. The betrayal scene takes place—where else?—in the hallway of the Parterre: Gennaro accidentally, and unnoticed, sees his beloved Carmela embrace his own second son.

The Grand Gennaro has its weaknesses, but it has it elements of greatness as well, and, oddly perhaps, this florid melodramatic plot is one of its strongest features. For the plot accurately reflects the intricate doom of the *servo padrone,* whose whole life in America becomes a burnt offering on some ghostly *Ara Pacis:* he has broken the taboo of the great nobles of Reggio and Rome, and he must pay for his crimes. Gennaro, with the inborn sense of theater that such a hero needs, after witnessing Carmela's betrayal, walks straight out of his Parterre and into a revenge trap that he knows has been set by that same old companion whose business we saw him steal at the opening of the story.

This novel offers us the satisfaction not only that it records Gennaro's comeuppance, but also that he must pay for his crimes—his crimes against mother-father Italy as well as against his friends—just as his aristocratic victims must pay for their transgressions, and for Italy's transgressions, against Gennaro. This further twist remains in the guilt that the Italian American sacred space commemorates, enshrines, transplants, and glorifies: the sins of mother Italy herself, those sins that inspired the hatred, the abandonment, and the murder that haunt the immigrants, still burden their victims. These sins of the old country, in fact, make necessary the emergence of a fourth type of Italian American *casa.*

Embassy

Nothing will serve, finally, but that the breach be healed, that the hatreds give up their furies before the gentle forces of understanding and mutual absolution, the familial communion of love. For the sin, or at least the guilt, on both sides is great. To allude to its magnitude is only to begin to suggest the limitless extravagance of lies, of monumental misconstructions and ignorant betrayals that appear before the American Italian on that day when, moved by some irresistible anguish, this person first turns back and looks toward home. There she rises, Italy the terrible, Italy the insatiable greedy granddaughter of Tiberius Caesar, the whip of King Bomba, the leer of his priest. To forgive all this—even to look it squarely in the eye—will take whatever effort the immigrant's descendant can muster, all his understanding, all his woe.

I first encountered this Italian American in the pages of Jerre Mangione's *Reunion in Sicily,*[11] and I met him again in the elaborate turnings of Robert Canzoneri's *A Highly Ramified Tree.* But no account so clearly displays the issue as it expresses itself in houses as does Helen Barolini's *Umbertina,*[12] a novel that could indeed have furnished examples for every part of this chapter. *Umbertina* is a book about planting, about finding a house and a center that will hold. It has three central characters—Umbertina, the successful immigrant; Margherita, her granddaughter, who leaves her parents' comfortable life in country-club Italian America and chooses instead to live in both cisatlantic and transatlantic literary worlds as the wife of the Venetian poet Alberto Morosini; and finally, their daughter Tina, raised in both countries, marries into the Jowers family, an old Cape Cod clan, while maintaining for herself a great degree of independence. Each of these women inhabits several houses, and all of them come to similar conclusions: guilt and fear, like nostalgia, keep roots from sinking. Every house that lasts does so because it values itself where and as it stands.

Every such house is an *embassy*; that is, it refers freely to its own history; it achieves its stability by accepting its own impermanence, its own provisionality. Here is Tina, daughter of the restless Italian American Margherita and of the old Venetian Morosini, as she settles into her room in her new husband's family home:

> At the foot of the bed stood an old sea-chest used by a Jowers sea-captain on some trip to the ends of the earth. There were hooked and braided rugs on the floor and a child's Chippendale chair by the fireplace. . . . Everything was right. It was the equivalent of the fine Italian hand among the old families of the Veneto. Both were seafaring families; both had accumulated wealth and possessions and pride; but her father's family had been on the decline since the first World War and their possessions decimated, the style become faintly seedy. The Jowers family, however, were still enjoying their New World vigor.
>
> And yet, Tina thought, as she went to bed in that room, isn't it strange to realize that both places are doomed to vanish? First Venice will disappear beneath the waters of the lagoon; and long after, but still inevitably, the Cape will erode and go back to its beginning at the ocean floor. (pp. 421–22)

Only a reading of the novel itself can make clear how dear a purchase is this wisdom of the young bride. I cannot justify it here, but it may not be entirely frivolous to point out that Tina's is the direction in which many U.S. Italians will need, eventually to travel.

For *la casa italo-americana* must do more than offer shelf space to old Caruso records or a place in the garden to wrap the fig tree in winter; it must do even more than impress the all-seeing cousins; it must turn its face outward, as the embassy does, and must surely keep its inward gaze, recalling the strenuous doubling of the mind that makes immigrant Italians into Italian Americans. And in the mutual recognitions of such doubled and redoubled selves, certain crimes and fears of crimes will be, if never quite forgotten, nonetheless remarkably transformed.

CHAPTER 4

Immigrant Ambitions and American Literature

> The United States themselves are essentially the greatest poem. . . . Here is not merely a nation but a seeming nation of nations. . . . The American poets are to enclose old and new for America is the race of races.[1]

Walt Whitman's expansionist definition of the United States as the "greatest poem" and "a nation of nations" and "the race of races" has the air of radical democracy that is also radically imperialist.[2] In the nineteenth century, American literature as an object of desire became as grandiose as everything else to which the national label could be affixed: the army, the navy, the dollar. As an institution, this literature has long confronted immigrants with the same complacent hugeness as the steps of the Capitol or the concourse in Grand Central Station. American literature is not only transcontinental but it is omnivorous. It will eat your nationality and digest your race. This is its normal mode of operation. Many of its most frequently cited texts are monuments to its gigantic appetites: *The Pioneers, Moby-Dick,* and especially "Song of Myself": "I am large . . . I contain multitudes" (p. 55).

United States culture reached the exasperated apogee of its imperialist phase at the turn of the twentieth century with the triumph of Admiral Dewey in Manila Bay (1898) and the consequent destruction of the Spanish Empire. America's Great White Fleet (1907–1909) took dominion on the Spanish Main. During this moment of imperial glory, when the very seas became American, Europeans in unprecedented numbers were crossing the Atlantic to work in the United States. Those who came from Italy more often than not had the firm intention of

69

returning, but many remained. Those who settled in the United States
needed to confront, and to deal with, the staggering disequilibrium
between this political Leviathan and themselves.

They might, as many did, simply retreat into associations and
communities of an intensely local character, comprising people who pri-
marily had come from their own hometowns or regions in Italy. This
meant refraining from most kinds of civic life, and it certainly meant
refraining from Anglophone American literature.

Another option, more promising to anyone needing to confront
the national agenda of the United States, was first to find some way of
acquiring an Italian national identity, something most immigrants had
conspicuously lacked when leaving their native land. Italy had no Whitman of its own, but it too was "a nation of nations" and "a race of
races." After the close of the Risorgimento in 1870, successive govern-
ments in Rome worked to find ways of achieving a sense of national
unity and purpose.

War and empire, to some Italian leaders, seemed the best roads to
follow. Prime Minister Francesco Crispi believed in these methods, and
he designed Italy's invasion of Africa in 1894 with this kind of nation-
building purpose in mind.[3] Italy's miserable defeat that year in the battle
of Adua failed in this aim and indeed intensified the felt need for signs
and institutions that would embody an expanding Italian nation. At the
same time, every year thousands of Italian poor were climbing into
ships and leaving Italy forever, or at least for a very long time. When
they left, they were far more likely to think of themselves as carrying,
along with their Italian passports, an identity belonging to some sovereignty older, and for them much more real, than the new nation. They
were Neapolitans or Sicilians. They were Romans or Abruzzesi. They
were often illiterates with no knowledge whatever of the imperial Italian catechism: "My mother never heard of Michelangelo; the great
deeds of the Caesars had not yet reached her ears. She never heard the
great music of her native land. She could not sign her name."[4] Many of
the immigrants were no better prepared than Mario Puzo's mother to
think of themselves as Italians in any instrumental sense. Italy did not,
however, despair of them altogether.

Rather it conducted a tireless program of propaganda designed to
construct Italian identity at a scale adequate to the formation of a truly
national population. This program had an export mode. Italy's metropolitan literary institutions justified the migration and assigned the
migrant population a place, howsoever subservient, within the Italian
national agenda.[5] The newspapers of *la colonia*—the Italian-speaking

quarters, that is—in any American city were filled with appeals to patriotic feeling of one sort or another. Military glory and imperial ambitions were favorite themes. Another was misery: Italy is a volcanic country, rich in natural disasters, and funds were often being solicited to relieve the distress of Italians who had suffered earthquake, flood, or famine. Italian poets and essayists had plenty to offer on the subjects of king, flag, and fatherland, and much of this work was regularly disseminated in the daily, weekly, and monthly press. In Rome, work went forward almost entirely throughout the period of the Great Migration (1880–1924), on national edifices of staggering scale: the Ministry of Justice on the banks of the Tiber (1889–1924) and, above all, the monument to Victor Emanuel II, Italy's first king, a vast edifice known as the *Vittoriano* (1880–1911), which was meant to project the idea that the new national capitol in Rome was the equivalent of the imperial capitol on whose ruins it rose.

These were energetic and striking projects. For someone approaching the imposing institution of American literature, however, they offered little help. Indeed, in their concentration on the massive and the military, they missed the point altogether. Their ideals, even when they could be imagined to correspond to some social or historical reality, did not amount to an effective ideological armamentarium for anyone confronting the radical democracy of American literature, where a continental expanse could imagine itself as the body of a single man. In American literary history, ideological warfare takes place not only on the field of battle nor yet on the field of government buildings, but on the field of self-construction.

This has powerful implications for the task that faces anyone wishing to enter the order of American literary prestige. William Boelhower has written definitively on the importance of the autobiographical genre in immigrant literature. Boelhower cautions that immigrant autobiography does not automatically gain acceptance as a literary achievement. One who studies American culture, Boelhower writes, "must not forget that immigrant autobiography is preeminently a model fighting for status in American literary history."[6] The struggle is a long one. This is certainly the case where Italian immigrants are concerned because Italian literary history does not place any special value on the machinery of self-construction. Italian culture is not likely to appreciate either the challenge or the necessities that face the immigrant autobiographer, who must find means to present a self that is either in itself imperial or else at least directly in contest with the imperial self that speaks in the voices of American literary history.[7]

One of the first Italian immigrants to achieve American literary standing was Pascal D'Angelo, who came to the United States an illiterate peasant, taught himself to read and write, began to compose poetry, and after intense rounds of solicitation managed to catch the attention of Carl Van Doren, editor of *The Nation*, who published his verses in that journal in 1922. D'Angelo came to be known as the "pick-and-shovel poet." In 1924 he published his autobiography, *Son of Italy*,[8] which outlines the process by which immigrant ambition carried D'Angelo into the pages of a journal whose very name certified it as a national literary institution. He needed to find himself, and to establish his name, as a son of Italy before he could claim a place in the literature of the United States.

Son of Italy opens with an introduction by Van Doren telling how he discovered the young writer. Much of D'Angelo's narrative follows familiar patterns. In his Abruzzese boyhood, the autobiographer is an unreconstructed rustic who might have stepped out of a pastoral elegy of Virgil or Theocritus. Gardaphe reads D'Angelo's narrative as originating in this moment, signaling the passage from the *vero narratio* of oral tradition into the mythic mode of prose narrative (pp. 24, 37–47). Emigration interrupts this bucolic idyll and flings him into a world of dark sadness, brutal exploitation, and catastrophic disappointment. In the United States, he travels with a group of *compaisani* that includes his father. Although these immigrants earn money working on the roads and rails around the United States, the company stores and other conditions of their existence make getting ahead practically impossible for them. Eventually, Pascal D'Angelo's father gives up and returns home to Italy.

Although D'Angelo himself has always intended, like so many immigrants, to complete the circuit, he finds himself obscurely but firmly rooted in the United States. His hard life there now grows even harder. Eventually he begins to learn to read from some Mexican immigrants. Soon he is writing puns and jokes that he is forever trying out on his coworkers. Then he has a moment of transformation:

> During the summer of 1919, I began to hear much about "Aïda," but I did not know exactly what it was. Federico up on Hudson Heights had been to see it; but he was unable to tell me much about it except that there was a fine parade in it.
>
> About the same time I happened to glance over an Italian newspaper and saw an advertisement that this opera was to be represented in the open air at Sheepshead Bay race

track. I decided to go and hear it. I went there by asking my
way right and left, for I knew nothing about the intricacies
of Brooklyn.

And there in the middle of the confusion that attended
the performance, I succeeded in worming my way to a seat
right next to the orchestra, where my ears were eloquently
feasted.

And all at once I felt myself being driven toward a
goal. For there was revealed to me beauty, which I had been
instinctively following, in spite of my grotesque jokes and
farces. The quality of beauty that is in "Aïda" I have found
only in the best of Shelley and perhaps Keats. There were
parts of such overwhelming loveliness that they tore my soul
apart. At times, afterwards, when on the job amid the confusion of running engines, car screams, and all kinds of bad
noises, I heard those supreme melodies around me. I felt the
impulse to rush home to our box car and compose another
Aïda, even though I did not know one note from another.
(pp. 149–50)

This unexpected vision of beauty eventually leads him to write poetry in
English, particularly in the style of Shelley and Whitman.

D'Angelo's pursuit of what seems an impossible career follows a
pattern that Boelhower recognizes as an instance of the classic American narrative of the self-made person. D'Angelo's autobiography concludes at the point where Van Doren's introduction to it begins, in the
editorial offices of *The Nation*, where D'Angelo takes on his public role
of pick-and-shovel poet or exemplary immigrant writer. His private self-
image is still startlingly grandiose for someone who has assumed so sub-
sidiary a niche in the pantheon. But D'Angelo understands the strategic
algebra that is in play here. He uses Shelley as a model because he figures himself as Prometheus, a good European counter for Whitman or
for what Boelhower calls the "sovereign democratic self."[9] Prior to this
moment, D'Angelo's writing has lived on the border between two languages, comprising mostly puns and other explorations of linguistic
uncertainty. Now he has found a model for something much grander.
What has happened to him as he listened to those "supreme melodies"?

What constitutes a "supreme" melody in *Aida*? This question in
fact has a precise answer. In the opening scene, the high priest Ramphis
announces that the Ethiopians are once again planning to invade Egypt.

Radames, the Egyptian general, asks if the priest has consulted the goddess Isis:

> Ramphis: *Ella ha nomato dell'Egizie falangi il condottier supremo.* [She has named the army's supreme commander.]
> Radames: *Oh lui felice!* [Oh happy man!][10]

D'Angelo has picked up "supreme" from the very *introit* of Ghislanzoni's libretto, where the careerist outcry of Radames, enlivened by the stirring music Verdi has written for it, plunges the audience into the center of the action almost as soon as the curtain rises. D'Angelo's choice of the epithet "supreme" tells us that, in effect, the immigrant watching this opera witnesses the creation of an ideal Italian male and in that moment comes on the scene of his own nationalization. No longer simply an Abruzzese peasant, he has seen himself on the stage of Italian national myth. He too can be the voice of a "nation of nations."

Aida is an opera that celebrates nationalization. Written at the end of the Risorgimento, its place in the history of Italian opera is not unlike that of Whitman's "Song of Myself" in American literature. That is, it is a myth of nation-building that includes the subsuming of other nations, other places, other races. Radames, the Egyptian fighting against the Ethiopians, is in the position of the victorious national leader, who enacts the triumph of the Savoyard King over the King of Naples. Turin against Naples is parallel to Egypt against Ethiopia, a North/South dyad that has continued to inspire political and economic conflict in Italy,[11] to say nothing of racial strife, where fair-skinned Northerners call Southerners *Africans* and *Turks* and treat them as racial subalterns. Aida, in this story, is the daughter of the South, dark and enslaved and yet hopelessly in love with the Northern general. The priests fill the function of the Masonic lodges that had an important role in making the Risorgimento; their anticlerical mummery here transforms them into clerics who are as nationalist and merciless as they are pious and pompous. When Pascal D'Angelo unconsciously casts himself in the role of the "*condottier supremo,*" he assumes the position of Italian national hero with all the self-contradictions therein implied.

Some of these contradictions would belong to any Italian, even in Italy. Radames, like Aida herself, is caught in a bind of conflicting loyalties, faithful both to the King of Egypt and to his beloved who is the daughter of his king's enemy. Such divided loyalties are constitutional for Italian national identity. No one can make the passage from a regional to a national identity in Italy without acquiring something of this same divided loyalty. This is especially true for Italian literature as Carlo Dionisotti has definitively argued.[12]

But certain aspects of this opera gave it a special importance for Italians living in other countries. For one thing, it was written for performance outside Italy, an aspect of its genesis that bears some thought. The Khedive Ismail Pasha, who commissioned the work, was aiming to reformulate Egypt as a European nation with a capital on the model of Paris or Milan. Written for the opening of the Suez Canal and of the opera house in the new European quarter of Cairo, this opera uses an Egyptian context and vocabulary but its "Egyptian identity was part of the city's European façade."[13]

This staging of Europe in another place has given the opera an extraordinary *fortleben* in the Italian diaspora, where it serves as a way for emigrants to experience the forces of nationalization that have driven them from Italy with the same hand that has reached out and drawn them into the nation's global trade network. D'Angelo is not the only Italian American writer to register a profound response, even an identification, with an Italian opera. In *The Right Thing to Do*, Josephine Hendin uses opera to situate the heroine's "gendered position in the family." Flavia Alaya constructs her entire memoir around operas.[14] Diane Di Prima writes that opera was forbidden to her grandfather because he was too fond of it for his own good: "he had a bad heart—and so moved was he by the vicissitudes and sorrows of Verdi's heroes and heroines that the doctor felt it to be a danger."[15]

D'Angelo's narrative allows us to locate his response to *Aida* within the historical logic that gives it shape. This opera, written by Italy's most successful nationalist composer, in effect marks the conclusion of the Risorgimento by recapitulating the contradictions that went into the making of Italy and that were going to continue to torment the new nation. The Italian immigrant's entry into this drama ensures that Italian America will remain a part of that same conflicted economy. This conflict gives D'Angelo's title a degree of nationalist force that is striking in a book so consumed with American Anglophone literary ambitions. *Son of Italy* can serve as a sample of such ambitions as they have been worked out during the years since its publication. Italian America from this moment can measure its Italianness by the depth of its conflict with Italy. And to the degree that it experiences that division, it will find itself free to seek the terms of its entry into American literature, where it can continue to be Italian simply because it has a quarrel with Italy.

D'Angelo has entered the arena where Italian national identity reveals its fullest ambitions and with them its own inner contradictions. In composing *Aida*, Verdi displayed an artistic will whose form would have been familiar to Richard Wagner or Walt Whitman. Without ever visiting Cairo, he wished to control every aspect of the production there (Said, pp. 122–23). He was ready to swallow, digest, and incorporate the modal melodies and hieroglyphic postures that anthropology had taught Europe to associate with ancient Egypt. But he was not ready to abandon his own ambitions as the definitive composer of national Italy. He wrote for this opera two scenes of "supremacy," each of them supplied with a rousing anthem that he himself compared with the *Marseillaise,* that archetype of all national marches.[16] This nationalism has proved to be in its way as successful as Whitman's. For Italians *Aida* has always been among the most resonant of operas. Its Italian fame had an especial pertinence in summer 1919 when D'Angelo saw it because it was at the very end of that summer, on September 20, that Gabriele D'Annunzio, another Abruzzese poet, led the national/imperialist raid on Fiume. And not only Italians were susceptible to imperialist fevers in those days: during the American period when D'Angelo saw the opera at the Sheepshead Bay race track, *Aida* was the "all-time Metropolitan [Opera] favorite," having 142 performances between 1900 and 1921.[17] Clearly, American audiences responded to the imperial anthropology and Wagnerian brass choirs that made this work so effective a machine for reproducing the making of Italy and Italians.

After his moment of transforming recognition at the opera, D'Angelo feels himself qualified to enter the nation made of other nations. In the public library in Edgewater, New Jersey, he has a profoundly democratic experience of exactly the kind that America's national bard likes to advertise:

> Going there, I was kindly received in spite of my broken English and the ragged appearance of my working clothes. And it was there that, while browsing among books, I finally wandered upon "Prometheus Unbound." In a flash I recognized an appealing kinship between the climaxes of "Aïda" and the luminous flights of that divine poetry. (p. 157)

The poet is ready to take on Shelley, the universe, and even God:

Omnis Sum

On the Calvary of thought I knelt, in torment of silence.
The stars were like sparks struck from the busy forge of
    vengeful night.
The sky was like a woman in fury
Dishevelling her tresses of darkness over me.
It seemed as if the whole universe were accusing me
Of the anguish of the Deity. (p. 119)

Gardaphe calls this poem "Whitmanesque" (p. 43). Somewhere between Whitman and Prometheus, the Abruzzese shepherd acquires the universal ambition that makes him first Italian, then American, and then a witness to the "torment of silence."

Italian immigrant ambitions have always had to negotiate the terms of national disparity between the place they left, whether or not they saw it as a nation, and the place where they arrived.[18] When that place was the United States, immigrant writers soon realized that they were confronted with a powerful and hungry national/imperial agenda that was able to use literary forms, even lyric poetry, as engines to propel its progress. Often, in such circumstances, they found themselves, as D'Angelo did, far more closely in touch with the culture of Italian nationalism than they ever would have been had they remained in Italy. That culture had its special appeal for immigrants who needed it as a counterbalance or a psychological template that would allow them to stand on level ground with the powerful sovereignty of radical democracy in the United States. There subsisted, slightly below the threshold of national ideology, a powerful economic machinery that repaid Italy for this ideological benefit by promoting a brisk export trade in food and drink and other value-added exports, which found captive markets in the Italian *colonie*.[19]

But this substructure did not, could not, address the political conflicts that were bound to arise in a century of warring empires. When Italy and the United States went to war in 1941, neither the marches of Verdi nor the authentic appeal of *grana padano* was enough to make possible the kind of allegorical embrace of titans that D'Angelo could so readily imagine. Harmonies became far more difficult to achieve. At that point, it became evident that the one Italian heritage that could still serve an immigrant ambition was the deep, even constitutional, force in Italy of divided loyalties.

To call oneself an Italian meant, and still means, to have loyalties divided against themselves. *"Mille Italie, una patria"* ("A Thousand

Italies, One Fatherland") was the title of a recent exhibit at the Museo del Risorgimento in the *Vittoriano*.[20] No Italian person answers to only one Italy. This complex fate has transferred itself into American literature with the writings of ambitious Italian immigrants. Think of Pietro di Donato, an Italian American worker who was also an American Communist. He resolved his many conflicts of loyalties during World War II by becoming a conscientious objector. Think of Mario Puzo, who fought in that war and who constructed, in *The Godfather*, a myth of divided loyalties that has found a central place in American ideology.[21] Not only does Michael Corleone fight for the Americans (over the Pacific, Puzo is quick to specify), but also his father refuses to accept this as a show of heroism, insisting that Michael "performs those miracles for strangers" (p. 16). *Stranieri*, in the Italian that underlies all of Don Corleone's speech, means "foreigners." For his own part, Don Vito Corleone erects a separate *paese*, a sort of Italy-within, and thus reconstructs the kind of divided loyalty that has been, from the start, constitutional for Italians in Italy. As Chris Messenger has shown in detail, *The Godfather* has proved to be attractive to American readers and writers alike. Supporting this attraction is Puzo's construction of a national identity that is both more and less than national, equally local and imperial.

On June 2, 2002, the *Vittoriano*, which had for decades remained mostly closed to visitors, was opened to the public. One can now climb its many flights of blinding white marble steps and look out at the city of Rome from heights that are only equaled on the dome of Saint Peter's or the peak of the Gianicolo. The other great monuments of Rome are made of travertine marble, which is brownish in color. The *Vittoriano* stands out as the unmistakable sign of a vast white national/imperial self in process of construction. The equestrian statue of Victor Emanuel II rides at a commanding height over a pedestal decorated with statues of women who represent the great Italian capitals that preceded the construction of the nation: Venice, Florence, Rome, Naples, Milan, Palermo, and so on. These stand for subjected sovereignties that managed to sustain a sense of their individual histories even under the rule of the kings of Piedmont. Italian national literature has now begun to pay attention to works not written in the national language but rather in the local and regional languages, still called *dialects*, of cities and regions comprising the actuality of Italy's history, its territory, and its divided self-awareness.[22] Such a sense of doubleness and self-division has been constitutional in Italian national identity in various ways ever since unification. Italian immigrant ambitions were certainly not immune to this structural feature, which replicates itself in the very conditions of the diaspora, where people are separated from Italy and often enough from its language too but are still solicited to buy Italian things, to eat Italian food, and to visit Italian places as sites of pilgrimage. As American readers reconsider the American Renaissance and its monumental appetites for other nations and races, this model of internal self-division comes to seem more humane, more accurate, and more democratic than Whitman's "sovereign democratic self."

Imperial postures inevitably rest not only on the silence of the suppressed, but also on the insincerity, whether conscious or not, of the imperialists themselves. Joseph Kerman once famously remarked on the "curious falsity about *Aida*."[23] As American literature brings the curious falsity of its own ambitious declarations more clearly into focus, the massive insincerity of the gangster-hero who is at the same time a loving *paterfamilias* has an astonishing resonance for American audiences.[24] Tony Soprano is the American Everyman of the present moment, not because Americans despise Italians as much as because Americans have learned not to trust themselves and have turned, as so often in the past, to the Italians for models of their own interiors. Italian Americans, like other Italians, have long experience of insincerity as one of the necessary elements of civilized life. Whitman's "barbaric yawp" over the roofs of the world is only convincing to someone who has yet to learn that one cannot correct a false note by playing it louder, or that there are sounds to which the only possible replies are patience and silence.

CHAPTER 5

The Text in the Dust

Writing Italy across America

Immigrants to America have always confronted, before anything else, the blankness of the place. America has generally struck the settler's eye as empty and illegible. At the outset America had no map, no connection of its swamps and pampas with any articulated purpose a European could recognize. No kingdoms enfeoffed to the Vicar of Christ. No boundaries, indeed, of any sort recognizable to the European eye.

Columbus's discoveries eluded the mapmaker. Columbus himself, subtle and ambitious geographer that he was, never quite succeeded in impressing on the world a single impression of where he had found himself in relationship to Europe or to China.[1] *Something* was needed. The supplier of this something was Amerigo Vespucci (1452–1512). Vespucci's bold assertion that Columbus had not found Asia at all but an unexpected continent, a New World in its extent, took a commonplace of conversation and turned it into an incredibly successful piece of mythmaking. His focus on this idea afterward earned for Vespucci a startling immortality. Martin Waldseemüller, a German cartographer who was preparing a chart to register the newly discovered lands, having read the *Mundus Novus* of Americus Vesputius (as the cover of his book called him, in Latin), made Americus namesake of a space otherwise blank to European recognition, which later mapmakers came to use to name no fewer than three distinct major landmasses: North America, Central America, South America. Vespucci's idea of a *Mundus Novus* or New World was the kind of real estate allegory that, ever since its first entrance into the general conversation, has exercised mass appeal among Europeans. The pamphlet *Mundus Novus*, translated into Latin from the Italian of the letters Vespucci wrote to his colleagues

81

in Florence, was published exactly fifty years after the invention of printing. No book before it had so powerfully demonstrated how printing can
change the world: within a few weeks, *Mundus Novus* was reprinted
"over an area spanning Venice, Paris, and Antwerp."[2] It became the first
best-selling book of the sixteenth century, and its impact glistens in the
literature of that Golden Age, from Thomas More's *Utopia* to the *Essaies*
of Michel de Montaigne to Shakespeare's *The Tempest*. But, despite the
intellectual and practical successes of the mapmaker's innovation, the
shapeless world that the grand Italian initiators encountered has never
submitted entirely to the European frame of mind. It has continued to
puzzle new arrivals and to exercise their powers of cartographic imagination. Luigi Barzini Jr. tells how even New York City, approached from
the Italy in the 1920s, seemed unbearably new and, with its reticulated
grid of numbered streets and avenues, imposingly blank. Only after visiting the rest of the country and reapproaching New York City from the
American West would the traveler perceive this metropolis as a place
with a long history, after all, and a complex of storied lives in its pas-
sageways and corners.[3] Most of the North American continent, of
course, offers much less to the European eye.

Writing across America

Writing the American map is a necessary drama in the eyes of Europeans who come to the New World, a basic task that often imposes
challenges of grave consequence and deep feeling. Lucia Perillo's "The
Oldest Map with the Name America" conjures with the incompletion:

> In Martin Waldseemuller's woodblock, circa 1507,
> the New World is not all there.
> We are a coastline
> without substance, a thin strip
> like a movie set of a frontier town.
> So the land is wrong and it is empty,
> but for one small black bird facing west,
> the whole continent outlined with a hard black edge
> too strictly geometric, every convolution squared.
> In the margin, in a beret, Amerigo Vespucci
> pulls apart the sharp legs of his compass—
> though it should be noted that instead of a circle
> in the Oldest Map with the Name America
> the world approximates that shape we call a heart.[4]

American immigrant literature is rich with examples of hearts seeking their images on this map or design for appropriation.

And not only Italian hearts. Consider the Norwegians in the Midwest. The Great Plains stretch level endlessly toward and beyond the horizon in the wide Dakota lands. The Norwegians in their covered wagons, as one encounters them in Ole Rolväag's classic *Giants in the Earth*, appear to be wanderers lost on a great empty sheet of paper, a map on which their God has forgotten to write.[5] This Norwegian American novel (although written in Norwegian, it was for decades a steady United States schoolroom classic in English translation) tells a story of how a story can work. It shows European immigrants using a narrative to make a map. The immigrants need to textualize the prairie, to inscribe on it a story of their own past, their own enterprise, their own future—and not just any story, but one they can actually believe. Although the hero Per Hansa does his best to accomplish this inscription, making furrows; cutting boundaries; building houses, roads, and walls on the virgin page of the land, his wife, Beret, remains unconvinced. She slowly but irresistibly becomes oppressed with the unwrittenness of the place, where she finds no names, no past or future marked down, in characters she can read. Her husband has taken hold of his land by violating Indian graves. Beret lives inside the sacrilege. The turning point in her destiny comes with the arrival of a Norwegian minister in their settlement. Baptizing children, solemnizing marriages, and, especially, delivering a sermon in which he compares the migrants to the Israelites in the Promised Land, the minister cures Beret's *anomie*. She, her husband, and their prairie have all now found a place in the divine narrative of salvation. After this, everything that the immigrants do has a meaning. It is part of a story they know very well indeed. Like the Israelites in Canaan, the Norwegians have entered the Land of their Covenant. Beret's cure, as it turns out, is her husband's doom; the very text that gives meaning to the enterprise also imposes on Per Hansa the task of imitating Christ, giving up his own life in the vain attempt to save that of his friend. Of course, unlike Christ, Per Hansa pays for crimes he actually has himself committed. So his story, guilt and all, both resembles and is folded into the larger story of how Christ redeems all guilt. Per Hansa's sacrifice completes the Covenant parallels. It brings the New Covenant of Jesus, another sacrifice of the same kind, into the story so that he may fulfill, as the Christian narratives always teach that Christ fulfills, the promises of God to Abraham in the Old Covenant. Per Hansa's love for his friend redeems his hatred for his enemy.

Rolväag finds great narrative authority when he employs the
theme of the Promised Land as a way of writing into the prairie some
convincing allegorical line. It institutes a process in which the immigrants' debts are paid and their crimes are absolved by the purposes of
their large and inscrutable Deity, who forgives all their sins, especially
the ones committed in His interest. The Promised Land, among tropes
of guarantee, has been the most consistently successful for European
Protestants who wished to engrave on the continent the divine characters that could secure the shape of their own destiny. From John
Winthrop to Cotton Mather, the visionary Puritans who settled New
England established in remarkable detail the set of parallels that made
of the Bible a pattern to certify and to bless their own collective purpose, all evidence and witnesses to the contrary notwithstanding.[6] God
had to them as to the Israelites made a Promise of this land; and the
Promise was a Covenant, a contract that offered benefits and extracted
corresponding duties from the People thus Chosen to dwell in this New
Eden. So deeply did the Puritans succeed, so well-embedded in the land
remained this contract, that we can easily read the works of their
descendants—such monumental meditations as *Leaves of Grass* and
Moby-Dick—as commentaries, not just on America, but also on America as Promised Land.[7]

Most immigrants to the United States until the mid-nineteenth
century were Protestants. For them the Bible retained its effective power
to map the American destiny. Among more recent immigrants, European Jews whose long diaspora represents an earlier volume in the same
saga of textualized exile have not found it inconsistent with their own
traditions to see, and to see deeply, how America might be a Promised
Land. The heroine of Anzia Yezierska's *Bread Givers* goes off tri-
umphantly to college, leaving behind her in the Lower East Side a father
whose devotion to God's Promise in the Torah comes to stand as an earlier version of her own belief in God's Promise in America.[8] The hero of
Henry Roth's *Call It Sleep* seeks the divine power that burned in the
bush for Moses and cleansed with a burning coal the lips of Isaiah. In a
denouement that makes improbability convincing, the hero finds this
power in the electric current of a trolley rail on Avenue C. Its channeled
lightning runs along the tenemented streets no less mysteriously potent
than the hand of Him that led His people there.[9] Yahweh indeed quite
plausibly in such a work appears to guide his people in America, as earlier in Babylon or Egypt, Spain or Poland.

Even the Hebraic-Protestant map, of course, does not live only in
books. One detects in its construction many signs of a more comprehen-

sive act of possession. Roth's trolley line is an earthworks, a line drawn across the land by the electric finger of God (a persistent image, this finger recurs in Cecil B. DeMille's *The Ten Commandments*, where it inscribes the tablets of the Law). Per Hansa's death is a living crucifixion. His transgression of Indian grave markers early in the story is felt as powerful magic by his wife, Beret, magic that only the healing word of God can counteract. *Leaves of Grass*, too, is not only a matter of writing words in a book, but it also engages in acts of eminent domain at every turn, marking the ground with the very body of the poet. "If you want me again, look for me under your bootsoles," Whitman writes at the end of his greatest poem "Song of Myself."[10]

Still, at the very least, one must remark that standard U.S. literary history would find the authority behind these ritual gestures in the familiar textuality of the Covenant. The Covenant arises in the rhetoric of the theocrat divines of the seventeenth century; and it subsists, returning as contracts, as guarantees, as commentaries, as anything written. This standard map of Anglo-America resembles the map of Israel, residing in a Covenant with God, beginning and ending in a book.

But Italian immigrants brought with them no such textually lucid relation to the God of Abraham. The Risorgimento used the Promised Land as a metaphor for Italy. It became an ideological compass point in that political struggle, something one read in the newspapers, part of the nationalist conversation in which their fates in the labor market were to be discussed in the newspapers. Immigrants could transfer it to their American enterprise. But it did not have a large place in the daily rituals of social reproduction that characterized Italian immigrant life. In the rituals of their daily lives, the Italian immigrants were not textualists, they were performers. They did not, like Protestants, have the habit of reading their destinies in the pages of Genesis. Their church stood firmly between them and the Bible, which priests and deacons read and chanted before them during ceremonies, mainly in Latin, a language they did not understand. Priests taught Catholics that the daily ritual Sacrifice of the Mass reenacted the central act of the Christian Revelation directly: a continually returning act of Incarnation. Italian Catholics participated in the drama of redemption with their very bodies.

Roman Catholicism's daily life depends on human performances: the priest is speaking words, marking circles in procession, squaring the altar stones, all the time that he is celebrating the Sacrifice of the Mass. Where Roman Catholicism has set its hand, one finds not merely a few books but a worldwide architectonic rebus. In Italy one knows this as the ubiquitous plan of the *comune*: piazza, church, *municipio* (city hall), houses, streets, and walls. Catholic Christendom repeated the scene everywhere it went, from Edinburgh to Buenos Aires. Fragments of it survived into the icy Calvinist topography of the New England village, even if in desperately simplified form. It was not a version easily recognizable to the Italian eye. All wood, no stone. Very few items of furniture. No pictures, which smack of magic. No plays, which teach immorality. No puppet shows, which show violence against authority. No graven images, which honor false gods. No statues, even of Jesus Himself, lest they become golden calves. No courtesans in sedan chairs to enliven the streets. No dancing dogs and high-heeled fiddlers clattering down the twisted stone staircase into the porch of the church as the cardinal's boyfriend throws up in the choir loft. None of that.

Introducing Latin ritual into a Protestant America suspicious of its ways of making meanings, an Anglo-America that had already for two centuries been reading itself written down in Hebrew and English by the sons of Harvard and Yale, has proved to be a complex task for Roman Catholics, Italians among them. Italians carried a history, a sense of how to produce themselves as a society, that required them to engage in this secular ritual task, frustrating and even impossible as it has often seemed to be.

Writing Italy across America

It might not have seemed so. Often, indeed, the enterprise of the Italian writer in the United States promises a much smoother passage than it can deliver. Those names, *Columbia* and *America*, have persistent implications: the primordial Italians wrote their names across what Europeans thought of as a virgin page.

Not so, of course. The place was not new, only new to them. But even as European settlers, however, these heroes of heritage, the so-called Discoverers, have remained more than a little out of reach for the Italian writer in the United States. They can be precursors, but they are often simply problems. Yes, they are in some sense Italian, and that ought to mean something. But just what it ought to mean is not so plain. The inscriptions, taken alone, do not speak unequivocally. First of all, Columbus, Vespucci, Verrazano, and Cabot expressed the purposes of others, who were definitely not Italians. The circles these others inscribed had originated in, and would always return to, not Italy but the Atlantic countries where Italian navigators found employment: Spain, Portugal, France, the Low Countries, Great Britain.

Then too were the issues of class. Amerigo Vespucci, whose forebears had lived inside the Medici family for two generations, belonged
entirely to the millionaire faction. He was more a Medici—that means,
among other things, more an international capitalist—than he was an
Italian.[11] *Italian*, after all, was still a theoretical word in the year 1500.
Except in the speculations of think-tank dreamers such as Machiavelli,
Italian remained a cultural expression; it did not have a clear and certain political referent. *Spanish*, however, had. The kings and bankers of
Spain had purloined the golden ring of Christendom. The famous Dis-
coverer Italians, meanwhile, had far less interest in the future of their
own imaginary nation than they had in the futures of their own families, friends, cities, and fortunes.

Families lay at the basis of all their achievements. Vespucci
acquired his experience of the world during fifteen years in and around
the High Renaissance capital of Florence, where he managed the estates
of Lorenzo di Pier Francesco de' Medici (first cousin to Lorenzo il Mag-
nifico).[12] Vespucci inherited from his father the frame of mind appropriate to the steward of a great estate. The Medici interest was his own.
Even Columbus, howsoever high his personal pretensions, was a servant
to the queen and king of Spain and a man whose family ambitions
leaned entirely on the Spanish Crown.

The whole order of international capital stands behind Columbus
and Vespucci. And yet the Italian immigrant wants to think of them as
fellow Italians. They have those names with vowels attached to the
ends, and the Americans (used to) admire them. Nothing to be done
about it. As long as immigrants remain Italians, they are reluctant to
divorce themselves altogether from other Italians, even their own class
enemies. The result is a stalemate. An unresolved contradiction in their
own Italianness in the United States leaves Italian writers to face the
American continent as bearers of a self-contradictory identity, in some
deep way incomplete, and in some way irresistibly drawn to postures of
dominance that they cannot really sustain.

The writers, thus incomplete, can only record the problems they
encounter when they set out to write on the American page. The narratives of Italian American historians richly explore the theme of cultural
self-contradiction.[13]

The United States of America likes to call itself *America*, an act of
massive appropriation somehow appropriate to the Roman gesture
implied in this succinct Latin version of its own name. That sounds
promising to an Italian, but this America greets the immigrant—he or
she that arrives here in 1880 or 1920 from the port of Naples—with a

seamless universal murmur of abuse. This America speaks in a jargon
for which the immigrant does not possess any codebook or Rosetta
stone. That is, not only does the English language seem harsh to the
immigrant's ears and impenetrable to the immigrant's mind, but also the
immigrant meets a vast Protestant context that regards this sort of
person as distinctly un/Clean and un/Chosen. And this lofty prejudice
does not receive any ready rebuttal from the codes of complacent feudal
Catholicism, which are the immigrant's only ecclesiastical armor. The
feudal Catholics of Southern Italy had no need for religious defenses of
the kind that were going to be required in the United States. The deep
complacencies of the antique Roman Catholic religion are what the
immigrant Italian knows. No defenses, and in the new environment
many vulnerabilities, come with those old Catholic codes. Indeed, all
unknowing, the immigrant has become their unarmed crusader.

The immigrant is a victim. Soldier in a religious war who has
innocently set out to be a settler in a friendly land, the immigrant has
even supposed himself or herself to have some title to be there, has even
claimed a cultural descendance from the Discoverers. Instead the
immigrant Italian has the fate of meeting, often as not, a profoundly
complicated hostility that he or she persists in reading as simple incomprehension. Gay Talese suggests that the pain of the migrants was so
great, their humiliation so bottomless, that most of them could never
bear to tell the story of their disappointments. Still many of them did
tell their stories.

Darkness and confusion form the pith of innumerable and lamentable pages of immigrant history.[14] The Sicilians lynched in New
Orleans could scarcely have appreciated in 1891 that the Americans
regarded them with something yet more terrible than hatred—with,
instead, disgust, which denies its object a dignity even hatred must
grant.[15] Woodrow Wilson did not so much argue as hold his nose
against the Italian presence in his America.[16] Unclean! Not like other
Americans, not born to the antisepsis of the covered wagon, which
leaves behind it as it goes that which it no longer needs, the Italians did
not have the help of biblical inspiration when they thought of themselves as seeking a Promised Land.

Italians thought they were settling another Italy. Their imagination
of home was powerful because it survived in innumerable rituals of settlement that belonged to the places they had come from. *Settlement* is
the operative word here: Italians came from a sedentary culture, where
the great aim in life was to make and keep livable, productive, beauti-

ful, charming, and secure one single place, one *paese*, one *comune*. To them Christian charity meant in practice often as not *civiltà*—that intricate ritual of habitation that, mingled with the old Franciscan sweetness and humility, has made it possible for families to live successfully together within the same town walls for centuries. The written scripture that records this view of life is the *Comedia*, the poem of the love of Florence; its great image, its transferable inscription, is the circle.

The circle in its highest manifestations becomes the symbol of God's universal love, just as on a level a little lower down it shows His mercy and, lower still, His justice; on a terrestrial plane, the circle calls to mind first and last the enclosing maternal comforts of the city wall. A central element of Italian American literary history is the enterprise of inscribing this circle. To write the circle matters to the Italian writer much as inscribing the Promised Land on the American continent matters to the Protestant or the Jewish writer. The circle writes Italy across, around, and through the American continent.

The history of this enterprise is littered with failures. Circles at this scale are hard to construct or, in the U.S. context, even to imagine. For one thing, U.S. cities have no walls. That simple fact underlies much of the poignancy in *The Grand Gennaro*, Garibaldi La Polla's 1935 novel about the Italian Harlem of the 1890s.[17] Its hero needs to inscribe such a circle but absolutely cannot do so. Gennaro, a poor immigrant, becomes the strutting leader of the compact, teeming, thriving community of Italian newcomers in East Harlem. With his *prominentismo* he conquers even the imported Neapolitan gentry—*gente per bene*—who find themselves stranded in his orbit. But although Gennaro leads, he cannot contain his little world. It is forever leaching away into the larger and more mysterious United States world that surrounds it: the heroine disappears for years into a Baptist home for girls, where she learns to be "clean" in Anglo-American fashion; her family moves to a farm in the shapeless hinterlands upstate; Gennaro's first son dies in the U.S. Army; another son goes to Columbia University, where, despite the Italian American name of the place, he grows so completely estranged from his father that he comes at last, unwittingly, to cause the old man's death. No number or extravagance of parades and churches can build around Gennaro's Italian Harlem the castellated fastness it would require if it were to keep his world from eroding so rapidly and uncontrollably as it does.

New York City has no walls, but at least it does possess some natural boundaries: the Harlem River on one side and the Hudson River on the other. These provide Gennaro with a species of open-air back-drop against which he can stage the doomed splendors of his processions and carnivals. He makes a feast for the dramatic sociologist because his city certainly has the sense of a theater. But what if the city lacks, as Los Angeles does, even in any visible sense a shape?

The Text in the Dust

Here the crisis of Italian America as the object of writing enacts itself in its purest form in the work of John Fante.

The city of Los Angeles, westernmost megalopolis in the continental United States, rises and subsides in the landscape with the random rhythm of dunes in the desert. One approaches and leaves across wide dry wastes. The city is famous for appearing to shamble and ramble haphazardly, growing up inside the fringes and creases of a tectonic chaos. It can seem so even now, but in the 1930s this was often all it seemed: at its best, it was no more than an irrigation project destined for success (see *Chinatown*), whereas at its most grimly familiar, it loomed as a seedy immensity writing itself a phantom history across the desert. Its 1930s, the great days of Hollywood, form a large chapter all their own in this history. The cheap oranges, cheap sunshine, and cracked plaster all made history in *The Big Sleep* and *Farewell, My Lovely*.[18] The peculiarly florid underclass of those times has found immortality in art and in film. A rough-and-tumble young fellow either is looking at a heap of discarded movie sets, such as Nathaniel West's *The Day of the Locust,* or else he is standing behind a bar serving a beer to Roger Rabbit.[19]

This same Hollywood of the 1930s also forms the background of John Fante's *Ask the Dust*, a novel that appeared in 1939.[20] The hero of this work is offered to us as the thinly disguised figure of young John Fante, whose *Wait until Spring, Bandini* had in 1938 won him some measure of fame.[21]

In *Ask the Dust*, the writing young man Arturo Bandini has arrived in Los Angeles, fresh out of a Jesuit college, anxious to escape his immigrant family in Denver, and vowing to establish himself before the world as a great writer.

His ambition founders on his contradictions. Morally, he is incoherent: he aims at the career of a romantic libertine, but he pursues it with armaments he acquired, as students do in Jesuit schools, by living the *Spiritual Exercises* of Saint Ignatius. In his relations with others he is self-deceptive: he wants to be at the same time a *conquistador* and the servant-lover of a Mayan princess. The consequent mismatch of ends and means, both personal and historical, is remarkably complete in this novel.

Like an uneasy seminarian, Arturo develops a Flaubertian fantasy life of untrammeled brilliance at the same time that he practices the prescribed monkish disciplines of poverty, chastity, and obedience. Poverty: Bandini lives in a fleabag hotel eating oranges that he buys for five cents a bag under the Palestinian sunshine of Los Angeles. When he manages to earn a little more cash than he needs for subsistence, he immediately squanders it or, immigrant fashion, mails it home to Mamma in a money letter. Chastity: Bandini falls in love with a Chicana named Camilla Lopez. Contact fails. According to the narrator, Camilla offers herself to him as a whore, but he wants a Madonna. The more hopeless the situation grows, the more desperately attached to her he becomes. Obedience: Bandini writes long letters to an encouraging editor in New York (offered as the thin mask of Mencken, who indeed first published Fante's fiction), to whom he pays the reverence a novice owes to a Father Superior.[22] The sincerest form of flatterer, the young man apes the elder in attitudes and prejudices. When Mencken loves him, Arturo is happy; when Mencken falls silent, the youth is sad.

Life in the fleabag grows worse and worse, but the editor grows more and more encouraging; through his agency, one of the young man's "letters," hundreds of pages of bared soul, is published as a novel. Meanwhile, the affair with Camilla begins difficult and then becomes impossible.

The action of the novel makes clear that the young man's love for this girl and his devotion to his literary career are in fact two aspects of the same enterprise. Arturo Bandini meets the waitress Camilla at the Columbia Buffet. Their encounter is that of the Italian with the indigenous daughter of the pre-Columbian place. Bandini wants to connect. Through Camilla, Bandini is vainly attempting to write the mark of Italy. He wants to make a circle with Camilla. His failure with Camilla is the failure of this circle.

He goes at his work methodically. First of all, we see him wanting to give the city a center. He does this by making a pilgrimage. The goal of a pilgrimage, by definition, is the center of a putative circle. Bandini's center is the church. In this place he is accustomed to find meaning. But the meaning of a writer as he conceives it and the meaning of the church as he conceives it fail to connect. Indeed, they mutually exclude one another. This is what happens when he gets to the church:

I pulled the huge door open and it gave a little cry like weeping. Above the altar sputtered the blood-red eternal light, illuminating in crimson shadow the quiet of almost two thousand years. It was like death, but I could remember screaming infants at baptism too. I knelt. This was habit, this kneeling. I sat down. Better to kneel, for the sharp bite at the knees was a distraction from the awful quiet. A prayer. Sure, one prayer, for sentimental reasons. Almighty God, I am sorry I am now an atheist, but have you read Nietzsche? Ah, such a book! Almighty God, I will play fair in this. I will make you a proposition. Make a great writer out of me, and I will return to the Church. And please, dear God, one more favor: make my mother happy. I don't care about the Old Man: he's got his wine and his health, but my mother worries so. Amen. (p. 22)

His own contradictions are going to undo him before he begins. "Make a Nietzsche out of me, and I will return to Church." "Oh, and make my mother happy." The novel is one long series of variations on this character's incoherent prayer life. When leaving the church building, for example, young Arturo ties himself in knots with a very Latin complication: after praying for Italian mother in Roman sanctuary, he steps outside and hires a Mexican prostitute. This encounter, too, fails him farcically. Its straightforward failure serves to rehearse the far more elaborate collapse of his relationship with Camilla, whom he meets shortly afterward. She is a waitress and, we discover, a woman with a taste for being mistreated. But Bandini persistently reads her as a *donna*, a courtly object of love and service. Camilla has no use for this approach, and soon enough she simply reduces him to a convenience, a way to get money for the drugs that increasingly dominate her life, a refuge for recovery when her other lover, Sammy, abandons her. Sammy hates women. Camilla, no less courtly and abased than Bandini himself, bends her knee to this superb attitude.

Bandini and Camilla never can agree on rules for their encounter. Which shall be slave and which shall bear the burden of mastery? Their confusion, we see repeatedly, reflects the themes of both *Ask the Dust* itself and of the novel-within-the-novel that Bandini is writing, which he calls *The Long Lost Hills*. Bandini shuttles between the church and the sandy wastes of those hills. From Nietzsche to Ignatius, Bandini is the famous hopeful skeptic. The more acidulous his doubts, the more he keeps returning to the Blessed Virgin Mother whom he beseeches to write the shape of meaning onto his quest. She does not oblige.

The close of the novel is instructive. Bandini's book has come out. Camilla, he learns, has followed woman-hating Sammy to a shack in the desert. Sammy does all he can to get rid of her. Bandini goes to "save" her, but when he arrives the girl is gone. He searches for her:

> I remembered road maps of the district. There were no roads, no towns, no human life between here and the other side of the desert, nothing but wasteland for almost a hundred miles. I got up and walked on. I was numb with cold, and yet the sweat poured from me. The graying east brightened, metamorphosed to pink, then red, and then a giant ball of fire rose out of the blackened hills. (p.164)

The aboriginal continent surfaces there: on the maps, no roads or towns or other marks of human life. But the solar journey at the close of that paragraph, a parody of what we find in *Paradiso*, suggests there may be the sign of meaning in all this yet. But no. He goes on:

> Across the desolation lay a supreme indifference, the casualness of night and another day, and yet the secret intimacy of those hills, their silent wonder, made death a thing of no great importance. You could die, but the desert would hide the secret of your death, it would remain after you, to cover your memory with ageless wind and heat and cold.
>
> It was no use. How could I search for her? Why should I search for her? What could I bring her but a return to the brutal wilderness that had broken her? I walked back in the dawn, sadly in the dawn. (p.164)

He fails to connect the circle of the sky. The repeated and saddened dawn is a sign of the Dantean sun, now filtered as neither justice nor mercy nor love but simply as indifference, "supreme indifference," and so emptied of meaning. And he continues:

> The hills had her now. Let these hills hide her! Let her go back to the loneliness of the intimate hills. Let her live with stones and sky, with the wind blowing her hair to the end. Let her go that way. (p.164)

And the way that his Beatrice disappears into the blankness of this uninscribable page, so also is the way of his book:

> Far out across the Mojave there arose the shimmer of heat. I
> made my way up the road to the Ford. In the seat was a
> copy of my book, my first book. I found a pencil, opened the
> book to the fly leaf, and wrote:
>   "To Camilla, with love,
>   Arturo"
> I carried the book a hundred yards into the desolation,
> toward the southeast. With all my might I threw it far out in
> the direction she had gone. Then I got into the car, started
> the engine, and drove back to Los Angeles. (pp. 164–65).

Los Angeles, that shapeless and futile encampment, has the last, ironic word: what angels has this *Comedia* found?

The failure of love, the absence of angels, the breaking of circles—these themes recur often in Italian American fiction. It would require considerable space to follow even a representative sample of the recurrences. Lou D'Angelo's *A Circle of Friends* and Pietro di Donato's *Three Circles of Light*, merely to cite two of the more obvious cases in point, both assert the great image.[23] But D'Angelo recalls a garland of pornographic Beatrices that the hero of his novel makes love to in a spiral of masturbation fantasies. His victory at the end has him actually sleeping with secretaries instead of dreaming about them, a paradise to recall more *La Ronde* than *Paradiso*. With di Donato, we will enter a different territory. But in this enterprise, as we have traced it thus far, the dust has been the victor. And the text, whose nouns are cathedrals and *castelli*, whose verbs are the great circular walls, and whose theme is the love of San Francesco, the text of Italy—in this narrative, the great Italian American novel—still hovers at the edge of the American blankness, waiting to be written. Fante's greatness is the denial of greatness. His critique of Italian American self-aggrandizement stands as a corrective to many less-balanced attempts at resisting the temptations of an illusory grandeur.

CHAPTER 6

The Semiology of Semen

Questioning the Father

In the year 1939, John Fante was publishing *Ask the Dust,* his novel about the impossibility of writing a Great Italian American Novel, and in the same year Pietro di Donato was publishing *Christ in Concrete,* which certainly looked like a contender.[1] *Christ in Concrete* made an impact on the national audience. Jerre Mangione reviewed the book in the *New Republic.* The Book of the Month Club chose it as an alternate selection. Di Donato had a book tour and a portfolio of photographs. On the book tour, he always afterward claimed, he had an affair with Edith Wilson, President Woodrow Wilson's widow, who was traveling to promote her own memoir. Not only di Donato was making progress in American society, but U.S. Italians were visibly moving toward the central currents of literary and cultural history. Fiorello La Guardia, mayor of New York City, was one of a large group of East Harlem *virtuosi* that included at various times the seven Piccirilli sculptors; the poet Arturo Giovannitti; the sculptor Onorio Ruotolo, who published *Leonardo* (the magazine of the group); the politician Vito Marcantonio; and the educator Leonard Covello, who was principal of Benjamin Franklin High School and author of *The Social Background of the Italo-American Schoolchild.*[2] It was not surprising, in that context, that sooner or later a work of immigrant narrative art would be able to capture that combination of popular appeal and artistic originality that characterizes what used to be called a Great American Novel. Two leading exemplars of this category were *Moby Dick* and *The Sound and the Fury.* One sort of Great American Novel, at least, fits this description: it has an epic scope but works from inside a very localized professional position, as in *Moby Dick,* where whaling becomes a language, or from within a marginalized social and geo-graphical location, as in *The Sound and the Fury*, where the Southern aristocracy develops its own distinctive rhetoric of defeat. Di Donato's novel explored the immigrant Italian world as a vision of the worker's destiny in the empire of industrial capitalism.

But World War II put an abrupt stop to all of that as far as Italian immigrants and their offspring were concerned. Italy became an enemy nation. Italians lived under suspicion in the United States. After the war, for an entire generation, Italian Americans directed great cultural energy into proving how American they were. Frank Sinatra, Frank Capra: American standards. The most successful Italian American nov-elist of the 1950s was the author of *Blackboard Jungle*, who called him-self Evan Hunter. John Ciardi, still in 1998 the most widely read of Italian American poets, heard that Robert Lowell had called him an "Italian American poet." Ciardi regarded the term as an insult. He wanted Lowell to call him an American poet, as Lowell would have called himself.[3] Not until after *The Godfather* (1969) did U.S. Italians begin to discuss publicly their *italianità*, did they begin to look for new ways to be Italian. Di Donato's career was interwoven with this history of finding and forgetting and finding again.

Forgetting

Di Donato comes back into the story at the point when forgetting began to be a visible problem for U.S. Italians. Although he published some works in the early 1960s, di Donato did not command a national audi-ence again until the 1970s, when the American Italian Historical Asso-ciation, founded 1967, had begun to establish an intellectual network among scholars working in U.S. academia. Against the background of the works of Rudolph Vecoli, Joseph Lopreato, Sal LaGumina, Frank Cavaioli, Richard Gambino, Jerome Krase, Luciano Iorizzo, Alexander DeConde, Frank Femmenella, Giovanni Sinicropi, Rose Basile Green, John Cammett, and many others, di Donato's career looked like a far-off lonely eminence, a lighthouse on a hill, isolated on the other side of a great historical divide, the one immigrant narrator of the 1930s who had understood what it meant to remember on purpose.

Trying to deal with all the forgetting was a major theme of U.S. Italian thought in the 1970s. The greatest single monument to that period is Jerre Mangione and Ben Morreale's *La Storia: Five Centuries of the Italian American Experience*.[4] Knowledgeable as its authors are, they do not find space in this history of Italian Americans to trace the development of their sense of ritual. Nonetheless, these authors themselves are engaging in a new ritual for Italian Americans, the grant-funded construction of a collective history as an act against collective forgetting.[5]

This was a period when new rituals of remembering began to appear everywhere in Italian American life. Once very serious and traditional in the tone and aims of their observances, Italian American elders created some startling innovations in the 1970s and 1980s. I offer two examples from my own experience.[6] The Italian American Club in Clearwater, Florida, for example, an organization comprised largely of senior U.S. citizens who had spoken Italian and lived in the northeastern United States when they were children, appeared on Columbus Day 1978 marching down the main street of that retirement colony in a mock funeral. Everyone wore black. The women draped themselves with veils and rosaries. They followed an empty pine box painted black, and they howled and fainted and tore their dresses, calling on the saints and pretending to bare their chests. Everyone agreed that this was among the most diverting celebrations the club had ever staged.[7] In the early 1980s, I attended a fund-raising dance at St. Margaret Mary Church in Astoria, Queens. The dance took the form of what Italian Americans call a football wedding. The organizers, husky middle-aged people with grown children, played the parts of bride, groom, bridesmaids, ushers, flower girls, ring bearers, priest, parents, and so on. The band played "Let Me Call You Sweetheart" and a long tarantella. The bride had a large silk bag for envelopes. Every detail recalled the weddings of thirty and forty years earlier, and each was hailed with general hilarity and delight.[8]

These funeral and wedding ceremonies had in common a striking and surprising quality of burlesque. What was leading these Italian Americans to travesty with such exuberance sacred rituals that their parents, and even they themselves, not many years earlier had practiced with a remarkable degree of intensity and solemnity?

Most evident in the travesties was the exaggeration. Becoming Americans, immigrant Italians and their children learned to look on their own rituals as excessive, laden with affect that other people's observances avoided. No one raised as I was, mostly among these immigrants and their descendants who lived nearby, can forget the shock of a first visit to a non-Italian wake: the absence of tears, the muted conversations, the undisturbed hairdos, and the pink dresses all seemed to us shockingly inadequate to the occasion. "These people," we said to one another, "do not know how to grieve properly." But soon enough we began wondering whether we ourselves were doing it wrong. Likewise with weddings. How dull the "American" weddings seemed with their expensive bland dinners and their absence of children, their spastic fox-trots and insipid toasts. Compared with our marathon bouts of drinking and dancing and eating and laughing, how pointless, how inappropriate they were! How useless were their presents! Their butter knives and tea services and Revere bowls were as so much wind next to a great white *peau de soie* satchel fat with cash. But then, soon enough, we were all staging formal wedding dinners with no children, and we even began buying sterling silver pickle forks and mint trays. We loved our ancient customs so much, it now seems, that we could not bear our repudiation of them in silence as we moved toward standard American manners; we had to cure our memories of how we once did things as if we were driving out devils, making elaborate public fun of them at the same time that we were recovering them.

The 1970s and 1980s were a collective adolescence of our history in the Italian United States, where even old folk still struggled through travesty and sarcasm to free themselves of their parents. We had no more talented or determined ancient teenager in that period than the late Pietro di Donato (1911–1992). Those who heard him at one of our ritual convocations of scholars will generally agree that on such occasions he was almost unfailingly the spirit of burlesque. His performance in Chicago in 1978 was for years afterward spoken of under raised eyebrows. In May 1982, invited to address the theme "The Italians of Brooklyn" at a conference at Brooklyn College, di Donato elected to read a story about attempting to lose his virginity in Prospect Park the same year he was about to be confirmed in a church in Bensonhurst. This charming tale, when it was first printed in the pages of *Oui*, must have seemed positively innocent in its evocation of a teenager's fantasy of what awaited him under a woman's clothes.[9] But as an offering for an academic conversation of the sort we were conducting at Brooklyn, di Donato's story sounded thoroughly scandalous. A working-class boy's appraisal of his sexual object uses the language of sexist oppression. That language, indeed, plays an important role in teaching the youth the practice of such oppression. Several women understandably stood up and walked out as di Donato was reading. His use of the demotic dialect of sexual aggression in his narrative was flawless: terms such as *gash, cunt, ass, fuck, blow, suck, prick*, and *cock* floated along in his sentences with the irreproachable plausibility of used condoms in a sewer pipe. And di Donato read these terms with gusto. As a septuagenarian he had retained the vivid sexual fury of the fourteen-year-old who has just decided there had better not be God. This fury, and the powerful longings that fueled it, always came across very plainly in di Donato's reading of such a story, and they never failed to shock those in the audience who had come to hear the man who had written *Christ in Concrete* so many years earlier,[10] the man who, as they supposed, must by now be a wise elder, a Solomon, a Pope John. When instead they encountered this randy old village atheist, they raised their hands in horror and in general grew terribly dignified, outraged, and foolish. This, of course, was very funny to di Donato and was, moreover, exactly what he claimed he wanted. Indeed, an unsympathetic reader might say that di Donato, throughout his career, played the professional adolescent.

But a fuller comprehension might lead us to decide that di Donato had rather acted the part that fate allotted him, that of the bewildered and abandoned son. It was a resonant role, and di Donato played it with all of the generous energy at his command. He did so in, I think, three ways: his first move was to create a language that maintained in the immigrant son's English as much as possible of the lost father's Italian; this was a poetic victory, but it did not go far to ease the son's pain at his loss. Thus, at the same time, there was a second move, the raising of an insistent question, the question of Jesus to his Father, "My God, my God, why hast thou forsaken me?" This question expresses a good deal of anger as well as the obvious frustration and pain we hear on its surface. Di Donato acted as if he had received an answer to this question, not from the heavens but from his own body, which spoke to him in the secret language of genes by which—according to the linguists of molecular biology—our forebears transmit themselves to us. Di Donato's effort to read his father's answer in his own body and behavior I call a *semiology*, an attempt to understand the sign language of semen. This becomes his third move: the way he practiced and taught a powerful art of remembering. But this is to leap ahead. I will take these three moves as they revealed themselves in the turns of di Donato's exemplary career.

The language of language recovery. We can begin with a scene that took place in 1935, before the novel was written.[11] Di Donato's friends from Communist summer camp were praising Clifford Odet's working-class melodrama, then a hit on Broadway, *Awake and Sing.*[12] This is how I remember him telling the story:

> "*Awake and Sing*! That's nothing," di Donato said. "Self-pity and whining. I can do better than that."
>
> "Can you?"
>
> "I already have!" He paused for effect. "It's called *Christ in Concrete*."
>
> "It was an idea I had had for a long time," di Donato remarked, many years later, when he was telling the story. "But I had not written a word of it."
>
> "So what did you do?" someone asked.
>
> "I had boasted to them. I had to show them a story. So I went home and wrote it. It had been in my head for years."

The story in his head was in Italian, and di Donato wrote it down in the place where Italian memory and American English met in his mind. It was the story of how his father died falling into a cement foundation on Good Friday, lying there in the hardening concrete, his dead body not able to be extracted until Sunday morning, Easter. Di Donato had been elaborating this obsessive interpretation of his father's death during the long years of his adolescence when, instead of going to school, he had needed to work every day with the men laying brick, first as a helper, then as a carrier, and finally as a bricklayer himself, so that his mother would be able to feed the eight children her unfortunate husband had left behind when he fell into the cement. Di Donato wrote the story of this definitive catastrophe in his own life with the accumulated energy of his frustrated youth. As a short story, "Christ in Concrete" made a hit with di Donato's friends, who had good connections. "Christ in Concrete" appeared in *Esquire* in 1937, and soon di Donato had a book contract. He was going to be the Italian Richard Wright, the Italian Henry Roth. In the novel, which he wrote immediately afterward, he presented the now-famous short story as the first chapter of a long narrative, all written in the new English Italian dialect of his invention. This language is the vehicle of the desire to remember.

Christ in Concrete employs a dialect never spoken by anyone except the American son of the lost Italian father. It is itself an act against forgetting. Take, for example, the following passage, describing the arrival home of the slaughtered parent's corpse:

> On the entrance door-jam was pinned a visiting sign of thin ribbons and white carnations. Hands clutched breasts, and mute respect cried, "Attend! By the love of God, attend! The man of the house has come home!" (p. 32)

This is the language of impossible desire, the son bringing with him into his lucid, literary, and even elegant English as much as he can carry of the coded symbols and gestures that belong to the poor, illiterate *paesani* of the preceding generation, so that the ribbons, the carnations, and the hands clutching breasts are transformed into a ritual dance that demonstrates how these immigrants are subtle and civilized even if they have not had much schooling. The careful poetic English of the prose generally just misses being ridiculous. What saves it is the intensity of emotion. Thus, when di Donato renders "*Attenti!*" as "Attend!" we do not smile, as we might in some other circumstances; instead, the cognate mistranslation gives to the English a tragic firmness that the verb— being the word for *pay attention*, and being the Italian word one would use in any ordinary situation—lacks in Italian. The effect is to make the moment strange, to give it some of the effect that the coffin coming in at the door makes on the young boy who is telling the story. The word dramatizes the moment. Its interlinguistic flicker resembles what Shakespeare obtained by sprinkling his Warwickshire proverbs with sesquipedalian coinages out of Latin, French, and Italian. But there is a notable difference: the Italian rises always to the surface of di Donato's English in this book because of the overwhelming motive it everywhere indicates—the son's desire to recover the lost Italian father and godfather whose deaths are the turning points in the story. I have called this desire of recovery impossible because that is precisely how di Donato presents it: recovery is impossible, he says, because death is final, the father is dead, the godfather is dead, and so, he decides, God too is dead. But however hopeless, the desire persists. And the persistence of impossible desire is the theme of di Donato's career, just as it is the force driving the language of *Christ in Concrete*.

The persistence of desire. The son's desire for the father is not only impossible; it is, as it persists, also criminal. When Jesus calls out to his father across the blackness, "My God, my God, why hast thou forsaken me?" we hear him in his most human moment, when he most resembles that most human of his great forebears, King David, whose Twenty-Second Psalm he is in fact quoting at this crisis.[13] The full measure of this divine humanity is that Christ's question, when we consider it, tells us that He feels the emotion that Christianity calls the unforgivable sin: despair. Orthodoxy might say that Christ's despair is shown as a sign of fleshly weakness, which is the absolute weakness of all mankind, and therefore, by complement, the full measure of Christ's divinity, which can suffer even this, the coldest torture of Hell. But

when di Donato asks the question, and in *Christ in Concrete* he does
so repeatedly, it is more the human weakness than the divine reply that
we are given to explore. Why have I abandoned you? I have forgotten
you. The father becomes identified with abandonment and oblivion.
Let us consider the scene of the loss of the father, the burial of Geremio
in the concrete:

> The rescue men cleaved grimly with pick and ax.
>   Geremio came to with a start . . . far from their efforts.
> His brain told him instantly what had happened and where
> he was. He shouted wildly. "Save me! I'm being buried
> alive!" He paused exhausted. His genitals convulsed. The
> cold steel rod upon which they were impaled froze his spine.

Notice that di Donato has begun this passage by castrating the father,
and remember, as we go along, that all of this is purely imaginary
because no witnesses saw this actually happen.

> He shouted louder and louder. "Save me! I am hurt badly! I
> can be saved I can—save me before it's too late!" But the
> cries went no further than his own ears. The icy wet concrete
> reached his chin. His heart appalled. "In a few seconds I will
> be entombed. If I can only breathe, they will reach me.
> Surely, they will!" His face was quickly covered, its flesh
> yielding to the solid sharp-cut stones. "Air! Air!" screamed
> his lungs as he was completely sealed. Savagely he bit into
> the wooden form pressed upon his mouth. An eighth of an
> inch of its surface splintered off. Oh, if he could only hold
> out long enough to bite even the smallest hole through to
> air! He must! there can be no other way! He is responsible
> for his family! He cannot leave them like this! He didn't
> want to die! This could not be the answer to life! He had
> bitten halfway through when his teeth snapped off the gums
> in the uneven conflict. The pressure of the concrete was
> such, and its effectiveness so thorough, that the wooden
> splinters, stumps of teeth, and blood never left the closing
> mouth. (pp. 20–21)

The fever pitch of this writing reminds me of a rule of composition that
di Donato once shared with me: "the scene is a spike that you drive
through the reader's head."[14] The reader's pain, however, should not

obviate a few pointed inquiries. What, for example, is the dominant theme of this passage? It begins with the father's castration, and it ends with the breaking off of his teeth, and in the next few paragraphs, it will turn to his suffocation. All these themes—castration, burial alive, splintering of teeth, loss of breath, and suffocation—come straight out of the Freudian back room of Edgar Allan Poe,[15] but here they are transformed by the very clear message we receive that the author is writing under thin fictional allegory about his own imaginings of his own father's death.

And it is hard to avoid the recognition that, as he writes, the author makes himself guilty of that death: driving the spike through not so much the reader's head as the imaginary father's. In the vividness of the writing is an emotion almost of glory, certainly of fury. The writer's pen grows in monstrous power precisely as he details the removal of the father's power to express himself. We have here the very primal scene of writing, the son stealing the power of words from the father. It *is a terrible scene,* in the old Italian sense of *terribile,* that it displays and makes us feel the absolute terror of terror. To read it is to see, actually to see, di Donato in the moment of becoming a great writer by assuming through the rage of the writing the guilt for his father's murder. Next to this scene, even *Macbeth* reads like polite literature.

Why did di Donato write this scene? The risks involved were enormous. And although the rewards were great, the price, as we shall see, was greater. The risks were enormous because to write this was to commit the most vivid possible sacrilege and to perpetuate in writing the primal crime. Why did he do it? Di Donato's entire subsequent career attempted to provide the answer, which was always that he felt an intolerable and irrepressible anger at his father for dying and abandoning him, as the father did, just as the boy was crossing the threshold of puberty. "My God, my God, why hast thou forsaken me?" Jesus, we might say, allows himself to be crucified as a measure of his willingness to suffer what many sons in their anger have wished on many fathers in their distance. Jesus's meekness, eternal and boundless, is the exact measure of the wrath his love must deny. It is this harsh equation in the heart of Christianity that di Donato in his career repeatedly demonstrated, availing himself of the consoling and consolidating relief that flows from written confession in the pages of commercial publication to register his anger against this silent father.

His later work demonstrates the anger under many forms. The novel *This Woman,*[16] published in 1943, as well as the later manuscript (late 1970s, early 1980s) entitled *The Venus Odyssey,*[17] details the story of an obsessive marriage. Paul, the hero of *Christ in Concrete*, has grown up and become a successful author. Rich and famous, he squanders his money and marries a beautiful widow. This marriage, from the first, is shadowed by his inability to stop thinking of the woman's dead husband, whose ghost he encounters in the most private moments and places, and whose body he finally exhumes and pommels into a foul amorphous jelly, just as, we might say, he has earlier done with his father's body in the pages of *Christ in Concrete*. Di Donato wrote under no illusions about the source of this obsession: *The Venus Odyssey*, in particular, is filled with detailed comparisons between Paul's dead father and Helen's dead husband. In both novels, di Donato paints Paul as a man paying the price of Oedipus, experiencing a love that is a form of eternal punishment. Di Donato is always aware that one way out of this dilemma is the way that Jesus took: to sacrifice himself on the altar of the violated father. He tries sometimes to follow that path. The two hagiographies he wrote, *Immigrant Saint*[18] and *The Pentitent*[19] suggest by their titles the preoccupations that moved him to undertake them. They are uninspired and willful work. Di Donato's imitation of Christ needed to follow a less orthodox path.

In *Three Circles of Light*[20] he abandoned the simple Christianity he had been attempting and tried instead to justify his fury, outlining the treacheries, double identities, and fornications of his father, almost painting the father's death as a just punishment for the life he had led. If this had been the case, then the son's murder of him in the pages of *Christ in Concrete* would have been excusable as well. But *The Venus Odyssey*, a later work, suggests that neither the prayers of *The Pentitent* nor the excuses of *Three Circles of Light* were very effective. Di Donato could neither play the saint, nor could he play the defense lawyer at the throne of judgment.

In short, di Donato marked out a path for facing the deepest fear blocking memory: the fear of what one will remember. The guilt, terror, threat of extinction, powerful uncertainties that give life to every effort to erase the past to avoid recognizing what is going on in the present.

The fool for Christ. His third move, the way he practiced and taught a powerful art of remembering: di Donato's art of remembering returned to a modest but steady vogue in the last two decades of his life. U.S. Italians had begun to want a way of finding something important that had been forgotten. What di Donato offered them was not only an engagement with language and with desire but also with the history of forgetting. He had himself lived as something forgotten. His life enacted the immigrant Italian engagement with lost memory.

During World War War II, di Donato, who had been a Communist in the prewar years, became a conscientious objector. Strenuous politics typified Italians during the first sixty years of the Great Migration. The names of Generoso Pope, Carlo Tresca, Arturo Giovannitti, and many other immigrant Italian writers in New York were associated with the extremist politics of those decades: the calls to strike, to protest, to revolution; the appeals to resistance, to secrecy, to war. World War II changed the political temperature among U.S. Italians. In the cold light of the first day after the ignominious death of Benito Mussolini, Il Duce, the Leader who had arrogated to himself the whole intensity of Italian self-regard, everything Italian suddenly seemed terrifyingly reckless. In the quiet of its victorious streets, the great United States of America seemed to expect of all citizens that they henceforward act as if they had been good soldiers. World War II had discredited Fascism. The peace discredited Communism. After World War II, U.S. Italians wanted to forget their history of violent political expression because both the Fascist Right and the Communist Left had become positions for pariahs. During the 1950s and 1960s, as U.S. Italians set about forgetting their Italian languages and customs in favor of Anglo-American language and customs, they also industriously went about forgetting their own past.

When this process had reached a crisis in the cultural revolution of the late 1960s, di Donato was still there where other U.S. Italians had left him thirty years earlier: still Italian, still radical, still able to say with a straight face that his father had been a god.

Of course he too had changed. The act of being what he was during the years when he was not supposed to be what he was had hardened di Donato into the mode of antic criminal, comic sinner, fool for the Christ he had known *di persona*, the worker Christ who had fallen into the concrete. This flamboyant sinner was the unpleasant comedian on the stage at Brooklyn College, the vulgar tough workingman whose every gesture amounted to an act of social resistance. My mother had a cousin, Bill Mastrodicasa, whom di Donato resembled in several points. Bill was Abruzzese, and he too had worked in construction, he too had the weathered aspect of men who spend their working lives outdoors, and he too was proud of his class identity. Bill died of lung cancer in the act of lighting a cigarette. By his own request, he was buried with a pack of Lucky Strikes tucked into his rolled-up shirt sleeve. When my family staged its first sit-down wedding in June 1955, with American food, Bill insisted on being served a plate of spaghetti and meatballs. I still have the Kodachrome of Bill holding up the dish of spaghetti as a sign that, among all the strivers in this room, he alone had insisted on continuing to eat like a workingman. Di Donato did most of his insisting in that same class-conscious mode. Ralph Fasanella (1911–1997), the painter of immigrant Italian life, never would wear a tie, never gave up the union (he made his living as an organizer), and never gave up saying *fuck* and all those other words that reminded one in every sentence that this was a worker, not a boss.

The outrageous is what still retains a flavor. Di Donato remained a free-thinking Italian bricklayer to the end of his days, never pausing to try to make himself more decorous, more restrained. In retrospect, this witness resembled a Christian sign of contradiction, a witness to another and superior way of seeing the world. Saint Paul says of Christians, "we are made a spectacle unto the world, and to angels, and to men. We are fools for Christ's sake" (1 Corinthians 4: 9–10). *Fool for Christ* in the context of di Donato's career is a precise term: it means that di Donato elected to work out his salvation—or, as we might prefer to say now, the meaning of his career—by confessing his sins publicly and in the antic mode, endlessly.[21] In *The Venus Odyssey*, di Donato demonstrated how this policy had made him an absurdly literal reader of the semiology of semen, the genetic language by which fathers transmit themselves to sons, making sons resemble them in surprisingly elaborate, unpredictable, and inescapable ways. All sons read this language, but few carry the enterprise as far as di Donato in *The Venus Odyssey*, where he writes, for example, "[Paul] wrote about [his father's mistress], and in the fiction laid her the way his father did."[22] Di Donato's penance was to immure himself inside his imaginary father's imaginary body as if it were itself a concrete coffin. Like his father, he felt obliged to play the great lover; like his father, he felt condemned to court eternal scandal.

All of these gestures became allegories for reading U.S. Italian history from exactly the point in time, the late 1970s, where di Donato had returned to the public stage and was enjoying a steady national vogue among students of what was becoming the U.S. Italian canon of Italian American literature.[23] To many students and readers di Donato's blunt insistence on the reality of class positions, despite the years of political and economic warfare that had misdirected his career and deprived him of an audience, by the late 1970s had come to seem a noble and important witness, a guarantee of values di Donato had continued to employ in his reasoning. He had always possessed a good command of artisan aesthetics and of trade-union political theory. He had long been a technically accomplished modernist: in *Christ in Concrete* he had used the innovations not only of Joyce, but also of the Italian Futurists who had designed a prose specifically to represent mechanical speed and force. Now he emerged as a philosopher in the village-intellectual style. Like Fante's Arturo Bandini, di Donato always read his Nietzsche. In later years, it encouraged him to see his own career as an example of how to overcome the curse of smallness and fear that seemed to have descended over most other U.S. Italians after World War II.

Christ in Concrete read against this context becomes an ambiguous title for a novel. Ostensibly it defines the heroism of the martyred plebeian immigrant bricklayer father. But by the end of the novel, the bricklayer son Paul seems as stuck in the mortar as Geremio was before him. Di Donato found himself in the same place where he had seen his father. He never really escaped. After *Christ in Concrete*, di Donato's subsequent career only intensified his sense of immersion and of social death. This, as much as the great language of his great novel, is di Donato's most notable achievement: that in his career he dramatized the contradictory emotions, the love and hate, nearness and absence, faith and despair, which had moved him from the moment when as a boy he had lost his father in a cloud of love and fury. All this he enacted as a form of public history: he had overcome his father; he had become his father.

An old story and always difficult to tell correctly, di Donato's version had particular salience to a whole generation of immigrants' children who had overcome their fathers by leaving them behind, forgetting their language and their music, and then had emerged, after the Cultural Revolution of 1968, finding themselves to be Italians all over again.

What did this mean? Settling on an explanation of the force in this return of impossible desire was difficult. All solutions to the riddle seemed provisional and more than slightly ridiculous. Di Donato's performance struck a grateful chord among Italians in the United States who found themselves amazed and even relieved to hear their own strangled sense of displacement and inappropriateness speaking so sharply as it spoke every time that Peter stepped up to the podium.[24] They had seen their immigrant progenitors disappear into a growing foreignness, a growing incomprehensibility, a distance they could not measure, could barely bring themselves to recognize. When di Donato questioned the father, "Why hast thou forsaken me?" he echoed not only King David and King Jesus, but also every immigrant's son who comes home from college. He sits down again to the wine and the hard bread and looks up to the head of the table. There he sees the red face and the strange manners of a man from a world where the boy may now visit but can never live again. Di Donato asked the question for all such sons. And when he made them move restlessly about in their seats at the scholarly convocation, as he dreamt aloud of the divine vagina and the innumerable hells of desire and need, he simply confessed for them all. In this he played the priest—confessing that he, like other sons, found written in his fingers the semiology of semen, the secret language of the genes the sons have stolen before they could inherit them, the stolen goods, which like the ghost of the murdered God, possess them forever.

Guilt and confession were the leading themes of di Donato's burlesque. They have a place in many Italian American rituals. In this Italian Americans do not differ from other sons and daughters. But Italians, of whatever provenance, develop their own individual and local styles of masquerade and of florid liturgical inventiveness: what they employ, for example, when they atone to their parents with a mock funeral in the streets of a retirement village or a mock wedding in a Catholic-school gymnasium, or the mock suffering that di Donato's Paul displays in *This Woman*, when he ascends his wife's bed as it were a scaffold, or the mock scandalousness of di Donato himself who used to tell his terrible stories, stories of guilt and horror worthy of Poe or the Ancient Mariner, delivering them with a boyish relish for the gory details that put one in mind, not of the haunted hero di Donato played onstage, but rather of the Abruzzese peasant child his father must have been, scaring his sister with stories about the slaughtered pig and the mating bull. He was his Father, but he was his Father as a boy.

The Son, in the circle of return, becomes the Father, and yet he is always the Son. He never grows up. God, it appears, is dead, and yet one never can think of anything else. And di Donato was that fool who is at least faintly wise, who questions his father obnoxiously, embarrassingly, and then stays, as some do not, to decipher the answers he receives, to read the secrets in the seed. His books are canonical scriptures of Italian America. For what he was—a Catholic, a hero, a fool, a lost child, a man traveling in circles of light—is what the Italian fathers have written in the hands of their American sons. In every case, di Donato was the outraged and outrageous son who became the outraged and outrageous father: in the semiology of semen, men struggle to win the right to speak.

The Morals of Remembering

The act of speaking and the act of remembering appear together in the career of a canonical writer. Di Donato as a young writer recalled, and as a senior citizen embodied, the world he had seen as a boy. His elaboration of that vision became the meaning of his entire career, from start to finish. The old man embodied the ideal of a man whose actions the young man had recorded. Di Donato represented in 1939 the best that the Italian migration had produced until that moment. He began his career as a man whose thoughts he represented in all his work—in the books he published and, later, in the public acts of self-representation he performed on stages and in seminar rooms. He saw the art of remembering as a practice: "The magic of writing is the catharsis of being able to look back."[25] He saw his witness to memory as a moral act:

> "I look to the present, too," he says, pointing to a neighbor fiddling with a speed boat in the driveway next door. Di Donato shakes his head and the color drains from his face as he takes a long drink from his glass of wine. "He is the present. All through the Vietnam War, he pretended it didn't exist. And now (in 1985) millions like him have no regrets, no memory. *They have no conscience.*" (p. 58)

Di Donato's appeal to conscience in *Christ in Concrete* spoke to U.S. readers in 1939. His language experiment had a direct moral meaning. He put Italian into the English language because he was representing Italians bargaining for their lives in the English language. He recorded the harsh terms of the bargain. It called for their blood and sorrow. It did not call for their language. That might remain to them, in some form, but only as a result of their own initiative. When di Donato used the English language to render a portrait of Italian speech, thought, ambitions, and humiliations, he was marking the lives and sufferings of millions of persons.

Di Donato's art of effective witness requires performance because it enacts a relationship between the representative remembering and the memory he represents. Making this relationship real, giving it the force of a social fact, is the key to constructing a literary history. Di Donato stands in direct salience to the U.S. Italian community as it passes across the post-World War II silence because he offers it a language, not just as a way of choosing words, but as a way of occupying a position in the history of Italians in the world.

The real use of *Christ in Concrete* becomes clear when we compare it with *Ask the Dust*. Both novels inscribe circles. Fante's fails in a way that many readers find paradoxically successful. It is an act of honest rage. Di Donato's circle, as we will see in the next chapter, succeeds. It succeeds because it begins where one begins in inscribing a circle, by establishing a center. The center that *Christ in Concrete* establishes is the entombment and sanctification of Geremio in the concrete. This is an act reminiscent of the first Cyclops, the loneliest creatures in earliest Greek antiquity, long before Homer, who lived alone in caves, who built rings of stone around themselves, the Cyclops who a little later in remote antiquity were famous for building the circular walls of Mycenae.

Immigrant narrative begins something important in di Donato's exemplary career. He ritually enacts an originary solitude—not for some literary reason, but because this is what Italians, to their great surprise, experienced for the first time in many centuries when they came to the United States of America: what it is to be alone on the planet, not to know how to understand or make oneself understood. Di Donato begins the construction of Italian circles in the English language literature of the United States. Imagery of planting semen, of fucking on dead men's graves, of spilling semen uselessly, of inescapable aloneness all suggest major preoccupations in Italian American writing. They lie at the center of things that cannot speak. He defines their inarticulateness as a language problem. Speech must be English. Speech must be Italian. How is that to be managed? That question surrounds the solitude di Donato works to interrupt.

CHAPTER 7

Circles of the Cyclopes

Concentric History

To use immigrant isolation as a center to describe large circumferences in U.S. writing has required strategic thought and a willingness to struggle. Italians living in the English language experienced from the start absence, abandonment, and other effects of systematic isolation. Language encloses an immigrant people within walls made of secrets and passwords. It is not only a question of breaking the code that confronts the immigrants. It is a question, too, of imposing their own code for the transmission of their own messages. If they escape isolation only at the cost of obliterating their own signatures, then they proceed from isolation to erasure. To retain a sense of connection with the global Italian condition in the diaspora of the twentieth century, U.S. Italians seek ways to circulate in American English their clearly recognizable Italian signatures and considerations. And for this purpose they cannot use only the postures of Renaissance dukes or the beliefs of Risorgimento ideologues, although these will certainly enter the equation. Italians living and writing in English must always be ready to use a language they invent as they go along.

We should not be surprised, then, that explaining immigrant narrative might call for a few of its own secrets of language, for example, this book introduces a new word, coined for the occasion: *heteroglossolalia*, which means a "word that enters another language in the form of nonsense." Whether this word answers a pressing need may not be clear.

Any new word needs an excuse. Some literary people still have the notion that an essayist ought to avoid new coinages, either personal inventions or inventions of others. In its strongest form, this notion is a rule. The "literary artist," as Walter Pater most definitively expressed

111

the rule well over a century ago, "will feel the obligation of those affini-
ties, avoidances, those mere preferences, of language, which through the
associations of literary history have become a part of its nature, pre-
scribing the rejection of many a neology, many a license, many a gypsy
phrase, which might present itself as actually expressive."[1] Avoiding
such intrusions on one's diction, the literary artist learns to use a style
of intricate avoidance, replacing the strange word with a circumlocution
in plain English, rather than making up new words for new realities,
hoping this conveys a sense of grace and power in the sentences.

Whose grace and power one may wonder. Pater himself is not so
attached as one might expect to the old notion that an author is the
authorizing authority of his own usage. One might have expected Pater
to ask the usual question: Grace and power in a writer's words belong
to the writer, do they not?

Pater's rule, if we look back at it, is specific on this point. He
writes that "the associations of literary history" prescribe the rejection
"of many a neology, many a license, many a gypsy phrase which might
present itself as actually expressive." "The associations of literary history" is a phrase that one is probably meant to read as an allusion to
William Godwin's psychology, where associations work in the manner
of hypertext links: pleasure in the language of a given text depends on
what it calls to mind of other texts, texts well established by the traditional pleasures of one who reads the books prescribed by some canonical literary history. But when Pater uses words here such as *established*,
traditional, and *prescribed*, a new meaning forces its way into the question. "The Associations of Literary History"—if we capitalize the words
this way, as if the phrase referred to actual people organized in groups
rather than to some private rites of recollection—are no longer merely
mental phenomena. The Associations of Literary History (as groups of
people or even as mental phenomena that groups of people share) are
social facts: groups of people produce and reproduce them, real persons
in real buildings holding real positions in the world, recognizing very
clearly visible group interests and working in large systems of very real
social constraints. The Associations of Literary History exclude the
"gypsy phrase" because they exclude the gypsy.

The Gypsy Phrase

Italian American English employs precisely the "gypsy phrase," along
with its history, its prospects, and all that accompanies a migrating
people into a strange language. What becomes of the language of a

great mass of outsiders as they labor painfully, generation after generation, to work their way inside?[2] That question is my theme and in the
spirit of it, I have decided to allow myself this awkward eight-syllable
neology *heteroglossolalia*. This is not an act of bravery, however.
Rather, it is one of imitation. Most students of Italian American writing
respect the Associations of Literary History, but when I wrote this chapter I had been reading with admiration a critic who had allowed himself
to use to good effect some remarkable and even startling new terms.[3]
My entry may be odd but is, I think, precise.

I am using this word, *heteroglossolalia*, to mean "the production
of meaningless speech in another tongue." It has the advantage of being
at first sight an example of the very phenomenon it names, but that is
not why I am introducing it.[4] Rather, it specifies an interruption in systems of communication that occurs as a result of large-scale migration
into a nation with foreign language, customs, and political institutions.
Words or other signs that enter one language from another in the form
of nonsense—an expression such as *moo goo gai pan*, familiar to many
Americans who only rarely can define it [5]—are the clearest examples of
this phenomenon. Italian words such as *spaghetti* and *penne* generally
retain their derived meanings as names of kinds of pasta, but rarely
their prior meanings of *thin strings* and *quills*. Signs that change their
meaning radically in the new language so that they are understood in
mutually exclusive senses by the migrants and the natives also fit this
category. A wide sample of such signs occurs in Lou D'Angelo's book
How to Be Italian, where much of the gestural vocabulary of Italian
face-to-face communication is explained for American readers in various burlesque ways that would have little meaning, and give less pleasure, to native users of this dramatic language.[6]

Any community produces sense through endless transactions
about meanings. The first level of communication is a transaction, a
double process of cognition and recognition.[7] One party produces signs
and the other recognizes them. A common language is a necessary pre-
condition to successful communication. The common understanding of
a series of patterns is the medium of any such transaction. In a successful communication, the receiver knows certain patterns and recognizes,
even creates, them in observed phenomena and received messages.

Italian American writing deals with problems of mutual understanding beginning with the narrowest of circles, the ones enclosed by
nonsense-effects or heteroglossolalia. Around that circle of isolation, it
inscribes wider and wider circles. This process of continual reencir-
clement is a figure for how a community disseminates a communication,

how it reaches out to its surrounding communities. The circle is, literally, a figure of speech in that it draws a geometric shape to represent what speech actually accomplishes. Mediterranean mythology offers this figure as one that may either close off communication or open it up widely. In literary language, a centered communication is called a *periphrasis* or circumlocution. Such a circle may widen communication or else preclude it.

Looking to the prehistory of the immigrant Italians, we find both of these meanings standing at the cave of earliest Mediterranean island memory where circles enclose the one-eyed giants or Cyclopes. Two models of Cyclopes—one drawn from the *Odyssey* of the preliterate poet Homer (c. 800 B.C.) and one from the *Aeneid* of the imperial ideologue P. Vergilius Maro (70–19 B.C.), summarize the relationships between success and failure in making sense across a linguistic divide. Comparing these two models shows what it means to begin widening the circle.

The Homeric Cyclopes

Both the circle of the single eye that lacks perspective and the hole of the cave where each monster Cyclops lives have preliterate meanings. These circles correspond to the more ancient legend that paints the Cyclopes as wall-builders who erected the ring of stones around the Acropolis at Mycenae; each Homeric Cyclops is entirely cut off from the world outside the cave, entirely surrounded by his own enclosure. "They have no laws nor assemblies of the people," Odysseus reports, "but live in caves on the tops of high mountains; each is lord and master in his family, and they take no account of their neighbors."[8] In our terms, the only circle a Cyclops can recognize with his monocular vision is the family circle that he entirely dominates (in the case of Polyphemus, his cave family seems to be comprised entirely of sheep and goats). Thus he lives inside a speech community all his own: a ripe field for the confusions of heteroglossolalia. Odysseus the traveler is an old hand at exploiting this kind of situation. He is the same man who is famous for having coined the gift of a horse to confuse and to undo the Trojans inside their walls, where they were cut off from the complex understanding of travelers such as the Achaians. Polyphemus's isolation makes him a perfect victim for Odysseus's highly developed expertise at the play of diplomatic language, and the hero in fact tricks this Cyclops with a sophisticated pun worthy of a double agent or a stage Jesuit. When Polyphemus asks the hero his name, Odysseus responds,

"*Outis*," which means "No-man" in Greek but sounds close enough to a cognomen for "Odysseus" that it is not entirely a lie.[9] To Polyphemus, who speaks with very few people, only the literal meaning "no man" occurs, so that his curiosity is provoked in a very different direction from the hero's actual name, which indeed was so notorious as belonging to the inventor of the Trojan Horse that even Polyphemus might possibly have recognized it and might have grown accordingly suspicious. When Odysseus blinds him, Polyphemus cries out for help, and the other Cyclopes hear him and call out, asking, "Who is trying to kill you?" Polyphemus shouts, "Outis [No one] is trying to kill me." And so no one comes to help. Odysseus is able to carry off this heteroglosso-lalia exactly because the Cyclopes' communicative network is not secure outside his own narrow circle. That circle encloses, shuts off, and isolates. That circle makes all meanings literal—that is, it sticks to one meaning, which it takes as self-evident—making all other interpretations illicit. Avoiding mistakes and nonsense using so narrow a frame is difficult.

The Virgilian Cyclopes

Although they too are one-eyed, Virgil's Cyclopean monsters have undergone Romanizing, and they belong to a system of divine bureaucrats who trade favors like any network of cousins in modern Campania. They live together, not alone, in the Lipari islands north of Sicily where they work as forgers and smiths for the god Vulcan. When Venus desires armor for her son Aeneas, she seduces Vulcan to obtain it. Vulcan gives the order to his Cyclopes, and they produce a great round shield in which the entire history of Rome is portrayed in advance on a concentric pattern.[10] The circle works as a pattern for extension both inward and outward. Inward extension is suggested by the proleptic accuracy of the shield, and the Cyclops's single eye at the center of the composition becomes a sign of literal in/sight: at its center the shield foretells the critical battle of Actium, where Augustus would defeat Antony and Cleopatra a thousand years later. The shield can be prophetic because Virgil's Cyclopes, being one-eyed, can understand the recurrent truth implicit in any center, its exemption from the laws of time. Outward extension, building of empires, and the experience of time is suggested by the outer circle of the shield, which embraces a huge historical range. Because they work in a group, Virgil's Cyclopes negotiate continually the complexities of multiple visions, of parallax—of time. The story of how the Cyclopes made the shield of Aeneas, placing one circle around another, neatly suggests the reduplicating tactic that Virgil's patron Augustus Caesar had laid down for the Roman *imperium*: Rome would recreate its own temples, altars, and other focal institutions everywhere it went—many circles, but always one center.[11] *Focus*, or *hearth*, which in Homer excluded outsiders from each Cyclops's individual world or else simply ate them alive, in Virgil becomes a device for placing the group of Cyclopes into a continuously expanding circuit of communication that aims to embrace the entire world and can convey messages of every kind.

The figure of speech for this transformation is called *periphrasis*, which means literally "declaring in a circle." Periphrasis shows how one story grows around another. In its oldest use, periphrasis applies to the art of avoiding a subject: instead of calling a dangerous divinity by name, one uses a periphrasis: Lord of Thunder, Son of Chronos, the Holy One Blessed Be He. Making something sacred means surrounding it with circles—walls, processions, circumlocutions. Periphrasis in this performative sense belongs to the ritual of founding a city, when the priest/king/commander plows a furrow around the walls and then consecrates the walls by pouring blood into the furrow and calling on the gods to inhabit and protect the place. In literary usage, periphrasis may still attach to acts of city-making, or civilization. We make a thing sacred by enclosing it in a circle. We make the circle sacred by enclosing it within another circle. But having done as much, we have entered the province of history and of literature, where two times, two places, two stories can coexist around a single center. One goes around the other.

Circumlocution as circumambulation, walking around a city as the ancient Etruscan way of making it sacred, is still practiced in the streets of Italian neighborhoods when they dance the saint, carrying the effigy or the relic in a processional circuit to mark the territory of their assembly (*ecclesia*, Latin for "church," comes from the Greek word for *assembly* or "calling together"). They encircle their territory singing hymns and carrying the saint: this is periphrasis, or circumlocution, as a performance. All forms of commentary, from linguistic footnotes to allegorical interpretation, are forms of circumlocution or periphrasis, one story wrapping itself around another on the page, beginning with the sacred text at the center and working outward toward the margins of imaginable reality. In books of style, the practices of circumlocution and of periphrasis sometimes come with warnings attached: "Watch out for these figures of speech. They suggest big talk." An old synonym for *circumlocution* in English is "ambition," which begins its career as a word meaning "walking in an ambit (circular path)," and often refers to the act of canvassing for votes by going around the district or among the voters collected in a forum or piazza. By definition, *periphrasis* and *circumlocution* mean "avoiding the matter at hand." In company with ambition, these practices lend themselves to denial, hypocrisy, even fraud.

But these circular figures also imply the very deliberate making sacred of things, the very deliberate tracing of a story around a story around a story, not only to avoid a truth, but also to make something sacred and to require one's support of it, one's defense of it, one's awe of its presence. The Shield of Aeneas presents a vision of many cycles, showing how a text, in this case the text of a prophecy, becomes canonical, a stone cast into water and occupying the center of rippling circles of interpretation. This is how periphrasis constructs a community's entire history. The interaction of language with deliberate geometry (the figure of a circle) produces periphrasis. The geometrical abstract figure of the circle generates effective magic for the city-builder, helps the priest or king or commander to create order. "In Xanadu did Kubla Khan a stately pleasure dome decree": the circular figure becomes the magic instrument that produces an ordered human world. So says even so tight-lipped an authority, so parsimonious a stylist, as Fowler:

> The periphrastic style is hardly possible on any considerable scale without much use of abstract nouns such as *basis, case, character, connexion, dearth, description, duration, framework, lack, nature, reference, regard, respect.* The existence of abstract nouns is proof that abstract thought has occurred; abstract thought is a mark of civilized man; and so it has come about that periphrasis and civilization are by many held to be inseparable.[12]

As one would expect, of course, Fowler is hard on the ambitious language of those who use periphrasis to inflate the importance of what they are saying. But his elevation of "abstract thought" in effect recognizes the original motive of avoidance; abstraction removes one a distance from uttering the dangerous word. Periphrasis, the art one needs to guide the plow, is also the beginning of thought, the art one needs to order or to arm a social circle.

The Homeric Cyclopes and the Virgilian Cyclopes suggest with considerable force two distinct stages in the history of immigrant Italian writing where intense self-enclosure or fear of outsiders can impose a severe regime on immigrants, but then can sometimes give way to methods that cultivate a growing inclusiveness, beginning with the immigrant literality of an isolated person for whom words have a limited circulation, and moving toward the arts of interpretation as these are practiced by persons who learn to see across boundaries of language, physical boundaries, and boundaries of elapsed time. These persons use ambition in its double sense of circular speech and of desire for promotion.

At first, like Polyphemus, many immigrants live inside language barriers, so enclosed by nonsense-effects that making themselves understood outside their own families is formidably difficult, even impossible, for them. In a second stage, like Virgil's Cyclopes, they belong to a larger history, once they have learned to overcome their own isolation. The passage from one stage to another uses periphrasis, declaring in a circle.

Periphrastic analysis: Because the construction of circles, geometric and narrative, architectural and ritual, is a means that immigrant Italians use to establish effective models for widening their collective scope and articulating their collective self-reflection, having a method for at least beginning periphrastic analysis is beneficial. Three ways of performing a periphrasis are especially useful for understanding what happens when a circle widens its scope: commentary, pomp, and explanation.

- *Commentary.* One may imagine Commentary portrayed wearing a muslin robe and holding a quill over the inkwell. Commentary, often copious and wandering, can lead us to think of periphrasis as aimless and boring, but commentary is also how we center a narrow focus for a story that afterward, without its having lost anything of its particularities, will be found to have general application. Virgil's own text became the center of commentaries written around it. Commentary resembles hypertext in its ability to adduce parallels and metonymies. But unlike the nomadic hypertext universe, Commentary professes a position, postulates a center.
- *Pomp.* One may picture Pomp dressed as a cardinal on his way to the theater, preceded and followed through narrow Roman streets by a retinue that included bishops, monsignors, and liveried torchbearers. Pomp may cause one to think periphrasis overbearing and rich in self-congratulation (*pompous* is generally used in an even less complimentary sense than its cousin *ambitious*), but pomp also gives necessary solemnity to propi-

tiatory rites and to ceremonies of possession. Processions and
ritual dances are serious business in many forms of Italian culture, beginning with what we know of the city-founding Etruscans.[13] In Little Italys, processions extend the boundaries of
narrow family enclosure out to the proportions of a neighborhood or even (as in ancient Rome) of a city.

- *Explanation.* We imagine Explanation standing before a policeman or a judge. Something humble, even humiliating, attaches
to this form of periphrasis. Explanation applies to our sense
that periphrasis is a way to avoid admissions of weakness or
guilt, but Explanation is basic to any diplomatic negotiation of
boundaries, to any effective transformation of a communication from nonsense-effect to effective sense, and to any case of
not uttering the dangerous word. Periphrasis helps us to understand the social use of allegory in the construction of a literary
history.

The literal Homeric Cyclopes and the allegorical Virgilian
Cyclopes are two importantly recurring types in immigrant Italian narrative. I offer three examples of each type.

Immigrants as Homeric Cyclopes

The Martana family in Lou D'Angelo's *What the Ancients Said* lives
according to a set of proverbs that Polyphemus could have known: "All
neighbors are werewolves." "The neighbor is a serpent; if she doesn't
see you, she'll hear you" (*"Michelune lassa dittu: Cu fa bene e
maledittu."*)[14] A magic circumference of such protocols is drawn in the
first chapter of the book, "The Ancients." The family patriarch embodies the authority of the ancients when he offers these laws; the action of
the novel centers around the attempts, mostly failures, of his children
and grandchildren to cross the lines inscribed around them and to make
contact with the larger world outside. Because they expect in advance
that this world will teem with invisible werewolves and serpents, they
interpret it using a codebook that turns into nonsense every message
they receive. So that they have a very difficult time dealing with life outside the house is no surprise. D'Angelo's second novel, *A Circle of
Friends,* takes up a similar theme, portraying a young man so tied to his
mother and sister that the "circle" in the title refers to no real society,
but instead to a garland of women who populate his masturbation
fantasies.[15]

Periphrastic analysis:

- *Commentary*: D'Angelo's entire novel is a commentary on these imprisoning circles, a quasi-psychoanalytic attempt to cure painful memories by talking about them. His mode is that of the editor of an ancient text: Here are the fragments (what the ancients said). These are the circumstances of their discovery. This is what people say about them.
- *Pomp:* The characters become abstract principles of themselves, not just the parents or grandparents but "ancients" who speak through them, so that even the smallest transactions of daily life move to the rhythm of massive inherited forces that the characters continually invoke in their rituals of conversation. This makes for an interior family life intensely differing from life outside the walls of the apartment-cave.
- *Explanation:* Guilt and shame ripple across the surface of D'Angelo's prose on every page. He not only writes commentaries, that is, but also apologies, self-examinations, and records of self-humiliation and self-abuse.

Masturbation, indeed, is a Cyclopean theme, not restricted to D'Angelo's narratives. Masturbation certainly has an important place in the Cyclopean work of Vito Hannibal Acconci, an Italian American writer who in the late 1960s turned to conceptual or performance art as a practice. Acconci's most famous early performance work was titled "Seedbed." At the Sonnabend Gallery on West Broadway in New York City for several days in January 1972, Acconci hid under a false floor masturbating for six hours at a stretch, fantasizing into a microphone about gallery visitors walking above his head, who could not of course see him but could hear his fantasies about them piped through loudspeakers in real time.[16] This piece is harmonious in theme with yet more evidently Cyclopean works such as an album composed entirely of snapshots of Acconci's mother written over with the son's expressions of desire to see her continue living.[17] The piece most worthy of Polyphemus is the performance entitled "Claim," where the artist blindfolded himself and stood for three hours at the foot of a stairwell with an iron bar in his hands threatening to kill anyone who came near him. These works represent a sophisticated performance of Cyclopean isolation, showing by their very form how a wall or a floor or a blindfold takes the discourse of the artist—which is meaningful to himself in a way as absolutely direct as are one's masturbation fantasies or his

good wishes toward his mother or his desire to protect his territory—
and turns such discourse into a set of meanings almost nonsensical to
his desires, and even more anomalous to the audience, which is
expected to react to these avant-garde outrages with the surprise and
confusion traditionally associated with successful crossings of the
boundaries of common sense.[18]

Periphrastic analysis:

- *Commentary:* In these works Acconci often provides a running
report on his fantasies and feelings, either through the microphone, as in "Seedbed," or in journals and other handwritten
materials that show that Acconci's Jesuit teachers (at Regis
High School and the College of the Holy Cross) had helped him
to learn well the Renaissance use of periphrasis to achieve
amplitude.[19] In Acconci's use, amplitude grows from an obsessive and omnicomprehensive impulse to document every
uttered syllable, every scribbled graffito. This is Commentary as
an act of perpetual motion.
- *Pomp:* In his Cyclopean works Acconci turns rituals of daily
life into deliberate performances with frames around them. In
his case, the frames are enlarged. No longer rectangles on the
walls of galleries, Acconci's pieces use the galleries themselves
as frames. At one point he staged a show in an art gallery that
consisted of carrying all his personal possessions from his
apartment to the gallery, one by one, and installing them there
for public inspection.
- *Explanation:* In his early days as a performance artist, Acconci
would appear at the Artists' Space or in the large hall of some
art school. An interviewer would ask him a question about his
work, and Acconci would talk for two hours. Next question.
Everything requires explanation, and no explanation is ever
enough. The force and amplitude of the apology makes even
the tiniest infraction into an epic transgression.

My final example of Cyclopean isolation is Jerre Mangione's
Mount Allegro: A Memoir of Italian Life.[20] The narrator constantly
plays on the difficulties the immigrants have in recognizing a pattern of
communication in their new setting. The family circle of his relatives,
fortunately for them, is not confined to a single household, as it is in
D'Angelo's Martana family, but nonetheless Mangione's family in

Mount Allegro directs its gaze pretty thoroughly inward: "My relatives were constantly seeking each other out to celebrate the existence of one another," the narrator remarks[21] in a nostalgic aside considerably complicated by ironic distance. That distance, a chronic holding back, is in fact the most pronounced heteroglossolalic effect in the book. Heteroglossolalia isolates. It interrupts communication the way a neurotic disturbance interrupts an inner serenity. To speak inadvertent nonsense by employing a minority language in a majority speech community can lead to a condition of chronic hostile isolation. This is the Polyphemus posture that Vito Acconci strikes with an iron bar in his hands in "Claim." Mangione's narrative tone uses mutual incomprehensibility not only as its theme, but also as the guiding principle in its choice of diction. Mangione repeatedly seeks ways to demonstrate that he understands the languages of the *paesani* and of the Americans equally well. This obsessive insistence on a double competence gives a distinct flavor of self-contradiction to the irony in Mangione's voice: it flows from his attitude of American superiority to his own Italian self, an attitude that battles with his attitude of Italian superiority to his American self. Mangione bases these inconsistent superiorities, in either case, on his ability to foresee and to forestall the nonsense-effects that separate the Sicilians, who are his theme, from the Americans, who are his audience. The narrator mediates between these two discrete circles with the Homeric wit belonging to a veteran traveler who can accommodate comfortably conflicts that might inspire sadness in a more innocent mind or exhaustion in a less flexible spirit. His tone can accommodate, but not resolve, these conflicts.

Mangione straightforwardly explains his self-division: "My mother's insistence that we speak only Italian at home drew a sharp line between our existence there and our life in the world outside. We gradually acquired the notion that we were Italian at home and American (whatever that was) elsewhere" (p. 52). In practice, this endowed him with a very rich inventory of duplicities, twinned versions of the same phenomena, versions that tended less to contradict than mutually to exclude one another by their tendency to engage in pitched battle. His parents had notions concerning religion, politics, education, and, indeed, all extrafamilial life—notions that seemed irrelevant to the world as the boy encountered it in the streets and schools of Rochester, New York. The Italians had contempt for the American ways, a contempt that Americans warmly reciprocated. As these two circuits, familial and political, often confront one another in this narrative of Mangione's youth, there occur innumerable instances of heteroglossolalic communication, of translation as nonsense. Nonsense is what you cannot use or understand, although it sounds sensible enough and seems to require that you pay attention, as if it were all going to come into focus at any moment. Mangione exploits the nonsense-effect frequently for its value as comedy, sometimes to achieve pathos and other times to project the figure of a leisurely observer, as if he were Baudelaire or some other perambulating dandy watching the world go to hell with itself before his eyes and for his mild amusement. As in many scenes of translation, the nonsense runs in both directions, into the immigrant circle and out of it, at the same time. The Italian spoken by the immigrants includes terms such as *storo* for store, *barra* for bar, and *baccauso* for bathroom—a word that mystifies Sicilians, Mangione says, when he uses it in Italy, "a nation without backhouses" (p. 55). But even more frequently, Americans in this memoir are mystified by the immigrants' attempts to make themselves understood in English. These attempts include the idiosyncratic, such as the father's decision to use *she* as the only pronoun in English and to use the present tense as the only tense; these attempts at communication also include the semiologically startling and symptomatic, as when Mr. Michelangelo, a Sicilian who can speak no English, wishes to express his disapproval of his neighbor, a Canadian woman who understands no Sicilian. The woman dislikes the narrator and his friends, boys who play ball in the street before her house. She confiscates any balls that land in her yard. Mr. Michelangelo shouts at her in Sicilian, a frightening performance that only increases her intransigence. She whips a boy who chases a ball into her yard. Mr. Michelangelo tells the police she should be taken away and electrocuted, but the police do not understand Sicilian any more than the nameless woman does. Mr. Michelangelo does not feel that he has made his message clear. So, unsatisfied with his stymied communication, Mr. Michelangelo gets the boys to help him erect a huge brick wall between his house and hers. "In two weeks' time, the brick wall was up and painted, a strong white monument to the old man's dislike for the old woman" (p. 47), the narrator says, to which one may add that it was a strong white monument standing in the place of a common verbal medium that might have allowed, at worst, for satisfying invective, and, at best, for successful negotiation with the Canadian lady. And she might indeed, had there been a shared language, have had a more precise identity than Mr. Michelangelo can ever find for her. He calls her simply *la strega*, the witch.

Mangione's memoir chronicles a great deal of this kind of short-circuited communication. Readers who are tempted to make of *Mount*

Allegro a utopian vision might want to pause over the long list of courtships that founder, jobs that are lost, lies that are told by child to parent and parent to child, along the borders of two languages in this work. And particularly should such readers reflect on Mangione's flat assertion in his 1981 epilogue to the 1942 book that "Mount Allegro no longer exists as a neighborhood."[22] Failing to create a wider circle around its own center, Mount Allegro survives only in Mangione's account, a work intricately alert to the messages received in both directions.

   Periphrastic analysis:

- *Commentary:* Mangione casts himself as the expert who understands everyone, the memoirist whose prose offers itself a medium of continued existence for all the people in it who, he thinks, would otherwise not matter much any more.
- *Pomp:* The story of Mr. Michelangelo shows the construction of a wall as a religious act, enclosure of a sacred space. It focuses attention upon the dangers associated with walls and boundaries.
- *Explanation:* Explanation is the major mode in *Mount Allegro*. Mangione explains the *paesani* to the American reader, just as he shows himself explaining, or trying to explain, America to the *paesani*. Explanation of conflicts replaces resolution, indeed gives reasons to abandon the possibility of resolution.

Immigrants as Virgilian Cyclopes

Attempts to make the family circle into the pattern of an widening concentricity are not uncommon in Italian American discourse. Mangione himself engages in such a process, beginning with the autobiographical narrative that binds together his account of Mount Allegro, and expanding its range considerably in the circular journeys described in *Reunion in Sicily*,[23] *A Passion for Sicilians: The World around Danilo Dolci*,[24] and *An Ethnic at Large: A Memoir of America in the Thirties and Forties*.[25] But other Italian American narrators provide us with more succinct examples. I discuss three of them.

   The first is paradoxical. The family of Demetrio Lyba, in Louis Forgione's 1928 novel, *The River Between*,[26] appears grimly Cyclopean in the Homeric sense. Isolation, paternal tyranny, incest, fear, half-blindness, primeval superstition, a life devoted to building with stones, and a phlegmatic stiffness that only can express itself in great outbursts on melodramatic occasions—these Cyclopean motifs enclose the unhappy existences of the characters in this novel. The paradox here is that Forgione, working in the mythological manner made fashionable in the 1920s by T. S. Eliot and James Joyce, presents all of this oppressive isolation precisely in terms not of the lonely Homeric, but of the socially integrated Virgilian Cyclopes. Forgione clearly saw the need for this second step. *The River Between* is a determined effort, more willed than imagined, at transcending Cyclopean isolation. Demetrio Lyba comes from the very island where Virgil's Cyclopes worked. The crisis of the action turns on a picture that, like the shield of Aeneas, has magical powers. The daughter-in-law whom Demetrio, unknown to himself, passionately desires, is presented as "a true daughter of Aphrodite"— that is, an avatar of the goddess Venus whose impulse is the efficient cause of the shield in *The Aeneid*. What is the point of this allegory? Following a poetic logic he never quite succeeds in dramatizing, Forgione attempts to elevate the suppressed mutual love between Rose and her father-in law Demetrio, making it into a place where he can imagine a new interpersonal connectedness, a new personal freedom. At the novel's end, Demetrio is completely blind, a homeless beggar. Rose, for her part, has long since fled the family home, terrified by her husband's unconscious ferocity and troubled by her father-in-law's unconscious desire. She has tried to live a glamorous life as the mistress of an American jazz composer who seems to live in George Gershwin's apartment on Riverside Drive. The codes of that social world are too bourgeois for Rose's comfort. She cannot manage to belong there. Eventually, she loses her frail grasp of middle-class life and becomes a prostitute. Blind Demetrio does not know her at all when she finds him wandering destitute on the Lower East Side; Rose takes him in to what we are left to suppose is a kind of unconscious mother-and-child reunion, Venus and Aeneas, Demeter and Demetrio, living in a preconscious libidinal utopia beyond the reach of confusion, sight, or even language itself.

Periphrastic analysis:

- *Commentary:* In its purest form, commentary grows around a text like a frame that grows another frame that grows another frame. Forgione's use of classical mythology has a directness reminiscent of autodidactic painters such as Henri Rousseau

and Ralph Fasanella. *The River Between* represents, very early
in the tradition of Italian American writing in English, a determined intent to place the Italian American story within a frame
of classical stories, a Shield-of-Aeneas way of enlarging its
range with rippling rings of comment and of interrelationship
among ages and among measures of greatness. In such a context of reference to past, present, and future, all three can be
seen at once. Thus, the spiritual gesture of beginning something
will give great eventual importance to even the smallest things
it uses (names, stories, slabs of marble), and that importance
will grow as the circumference of ripples increases with the passage of time and the repetition of the gestures of origination.

- *Pomp:* Focusing on any single aspect of pomp in this novel,
where the characters move about under a weight of heavy feelings so huge that it slows them down, is difficult. They address
each other with a deliberation and circumstance more appropriate to characters in a serious opera than to ordinary people
living ordinary lives. *Opera seria,* both in recordings and on the
radio, gave to immigrant Italians a steady domestic spectacle,
which they used to model their styles of communication. Immigrant Italians often named their daughters after operatic
heroines: Eleonora, Gilda, Elvira, Rosina. The dramatized
musicality of Italian speech in nineteenth-century Italy thus
supported, among twentieth-century immigrant Italians, a habit
of hearing themselves as *dive* and *divi* (goddesses and gods) as
well as an easy relationship to the ancient stories (classical
myths) and pagan dramas that give these operas their plots.
Thanks to this new diffusion of the opera, with its intense psychological portraiture and its powerful techniques for the
expression of feeling, Pomp became normal not only to the
public life of Little Italy, but also to its daily life at home.

- *Explanation:* Forgione's book belongs to that large category of
periphrastic explanations that manage to explain nothing,
intense confessions that never exactly specify which sin they are
disclosing. The opening situation of *The River Between* has the
harsh brilliance of a well-remembered painful scene, something
out of a bad dream. But the story as it unfolds loses itself in
stageiness and improbability—periphrasis of the kind that composition manuals (even that of Erasmus) generally warn writers
to avoid.

Forgione's book, as its blunt Freudian algebra suggests, has the charm of primitive painting. As is often the case in such work, the execution is not cosmopolitan in style or polish, but the design shows good artistic instincts and has been prophetic of more successful experiments to come in the works of later writers

In my second example, the Cyclopean immigrant family expands into a utopian pattern of itself. This is the first circle that the immigrant Italian narrator can outline clearly. This is his first escape from isolation. Enlarging the family circle into a utopian projection of itself is what Pietro di Donato manages in *Christ in Concrete*. Di Donato succeeds at this exercise, giving to his text the sacred authority of blood sacrifice that it has since acquired in Italian America. This novel has two simple movements. First, the blinding, castration, and death of the immigrant Cyclops, the ill-fated father Geremio, who falls into the absolute isolation and aphasia of concrete; the concrete swallows and kills him as the final indignity in the long process of humiliations and losses that, for Geremio as for so many other immigrants, constitutes the ritual of migration. Di Donato renders this death by concentrating all his focus on the solitude of a sudden, painful, untimely death, the total enclosure of the immigrant. Second, the transformation of this same Geremio into the type of Christ. Once this transformation is established, then Geremio's death—like Per Hansa's death at the close of *Giants in the Earth*—can serve as part of an all-inclusive Christian narrative that for the immigrants explains and justifies their lives in a satisfactory manner. Di Donato's Christian Communist theology proceeds according to a steady and familiar liturgical rhythm: on the afternoon of Good Friday, the worker-Christ dies alone, calling vainly on God in heaven, according to the pattern of Jesus. Not only does Geremio die at exactly the same hour that, in liturgical time, Christ is dying; but he is raised out of the concrete on Easter Sunday, when the risen Christ disappears from the tomb. According to the Catholic teaching concerning liturgical time, these events can in fact take place simultaneously. All events that repeat the Crucifixion are happening, actually taking place, in the same moment that the celebrant and the congregation are performing rites whose slightly changing patterns follow the lunar calendar recurrences of days devoted to the performance of the many aspects of the story.[27] Thus that the novel's *paesani* draw the mythological parallels is hardly a surprise. The event binds them together (*religio*, binding together) in the shared process of the Divine Family's Divine Life unfolding with the progress of the moon and sun through the sky. As the story unfolds, one sees that within the shared vision of this eternal present Geremio stands revealed as the transfigured Christ, the central figure, his poverty and his shattered body the universal signature of the Italian mass migration as we find it written on the stones of the United States by waves of immigrant Italian poor. In this capitol of capital, men are made of money, and Job (*the job*, mingled with an echo of the sorrowful human Job in the Hebrew Bible) is God. The pattern of the composition is strict ritual periphrasis: at the center stands the lonely Cyclops—in a Catholic church the isolated human would be the body of Christ on the cross, whereas in this case it is the corpse of Geremio. Around this central sacred body, this untouchable fact at the heart of things, Commentary, Pomp, and Explanation walk and talk in concentric circles of Periphrasis.

Their circular talk has a diplomatic power. It overcomes isolation. Geremio's resurrection as a Christ frees the *paesani* from the enclosure of the English language barrier that reduces them to babbling, to heteroglossolalia or unintentional nonsense, the enclosure of critical moments when they learn how totally unable they are to make themselves heard or understood in the face of the foreign power that dominates and restricts their lives with its money, its language, its traditionally strict anthropological categorization of subject peoples. In di Donato's text, the language of the immigrants marks itself as foreign, but it does not succumb when English speakers at the Workmen's Compensation office treat the immigrant Italians as if they were speaking nonsense. Instead, the text creates a new kind of sense, becoming a mode of communication that passes freely between languages. Instead of heteroglossolalia, the *paesani*, and the narrator along with them, can now speak "in tongues," a gift the New Testament calls *glossolalia*. In New Testament Greek, that word means that anyone who listens may understand them. *Glossolalia* means "the ability to transcend boundaries and to inscribe larger circles." It gives power and, with power, courage. According to the Acts of the Apostles, glossolalia enabled the followers of Jesus to transcend differences of languages in the throng assembled at Jerusalem for Sh'vuit. No longer afraid, the apostles shared their gospel with any and all; and, what was more miraculous, any and all understood them. Greeks, Egyptians, Syrians, Romans— everyone in the crowd who listened that day understood what the Apostles said. Catholic liturgy reenacts this day on Pentecost, the seventh Sunday, or fiftieth day, after Easter (Sh'vuit is the fiftieth day of Pesach). The gospel for Pentecost Sunday recalls how glossolalia had loosed the tongues of the Apostles and opened the hearts of their hearers.

Periphrastic analysis:

- *Commentary:* Di Donato composed the novel *Christ in Concrete* as an act of physical periphrasis, composing it around the short story "Christ in Concrete" he had written about his father's death. Thus the novel *Christ in Concrete* is a material circle of stories di Donato inscribed by hand around the story of his father's death. He would do something similar—and more plainly—twenty years later in the book *Three Circles of Light*. In *Christ in Concrete*'s concentric circles, the *paesani* are endowed with their own Gift of Tongues Confronted by the incomprehension, greed, and prejudice of lawyers, police, and compensation-board bureaucrats, the immigrants at first seem driven to a hopeless isolation.
- *Pomp:* But then, in the sort of dialectic move that takes the place of a plot in this novel, di Donato inscribes a circle around their isolation. He conducts a narrative procession: there occurs a wedding scene where the participating *paesani* suddenly realize—they enact and they at the same time see—all the possible promise of their improvised community. They expand for the occasion into utopian demigods, offering one another care and stroking and, especially, food and drink, in a self-consciously proletarian vision of a beggars' banquet; di Donato's prose moves around their entire predicament—symbolized and embodied as it is in the death of Geremio their particular Christ.
- *Explanation:* In the manner of a priest at noon proceeding to the altar for high mass in church, he goes at a measured pace, emphasizing the pastoral plaster cornucopia spilling out nuts and flowers, bosoms and dancing legs, without ever quite touching the ugly question of who paid how much for what or who got what in return. This is an act of explanation by avoidance: periphrasis in a pure form. And the explanation works. Only the eternally hungry grandchildren of hungry grandchildren could take this much delight in praising table abundance (and not want to talk about the money because it is so painful that it becomes irrelevant).

The language of the banquet scene (called "Wedding"), as of the whole novel, makes nonsense into high poetic sense, turning all the peculiar heteroglossolalia of the immigrant Italian into an idiosyncratic eloquence that has no exact parallel in the English language before this. Periphrasis, a speech declared around a circle, names the shape that represents this transformation from nonsense to sense. A ritual periphrasis performs a Figure of Speech in the most literal sense possible: speech making a visible figure or visual pattern. Di Donato's nonsense-as-high-sense is that kind of performative periphrasis at its root of utterance, English wrapping itself around Italian. This continuous act of simultaneous translation is di Donato's epic vernacular. It supports the dialectic image of the wedding feast. The powerful growth of the family circle in this scene, to the point where it includes not just relatives but friends and even neighbors who are not Italian, has a place in the history of Italian America resembling the position of the Mayflower Compact in U.S. Protestant discourse. The primal contract. The immigrant wedding represents the first achievement of a universal Roman—or, if you prefer, Roman Catholic—ritual contract for an American future among Italians.

The immigrant Italian family has in U.S. advertising folklore long since possessed as its distinguishing attributes the qualities of stability and generosity, as well as the habit of effective internal communications. These attributes have proven a rich vein for such prospectors as the marketing ideologue who invented Aunt Millie and the ambitious gambler who wrote *The Godfather*. Michael Cimino used an apotheosis immigrant Italian wedding scene as the prototype immigrant wedding in *The Deer Hunter* by translating it into a Russian wedding, rediscovering the Italian fondness for circular passages in ancient rituals of the Russian Orthodox church that plainly resemble the way these ceremonies were performed in Italy fifteen hundred years ago (Italian churches from that period, such as those in Torcello and in Ravenna, are circular in plan, maps of liturgical progresses during the second half of the first millennium, when differences between Greek and Latin churches had not yet become motives of war). But the most straightforwardly Augustan use of the family stereotype as a figure of concentric history has appeared in the discourse of a Catholic rhetorician with a Roman name, Mario Cuomo.

When Cuomo campaigned for governor New York State on the allegorical program that the government should work as a family does,[28] the candidate spoke in the visionary political tradition that he shares with Italian writers in every age—Virgil, Dante, and di Donato, no less than many humbler talents. Cuomo's focal image can see the nation around the dining room table; it found a warm welcome with those many U.S. political audiences who regarded the family as the first battleground of civic politics. U.S. political theory has not gratified their tastes nearly enough. Indeed, thanks to its passage through the Presbyterian Enlightenment, U.S. political theory has tended to avoid on principle the harmonious imagery of family circles that Romans—emperors, popes, and traffic engineers alike—have used with such long success in organizing and administering vast and disparate territories. The family circle is too Papist, too *ancien régime*, for many in the United States. Nonetheless, for many citizens of New York state in 1982, the Great White U.S. political allegories of the past—John Winthrop's image of Massachusetts as "a city set upon a hill," Jefferson's creation of a God who is also a civil-rights lawyer, Lincoln's portrait of the fight for the union as a heavenly battle between good and evil, Roosevelt's figure of the president as a cardsharp issuing a fresh deal—all seemed theoretical and bloodless, hypocritical and harsh, next to Cuomo's vivid reinvention of a powerfully humble old idea.

From the hostile and isolated Cyclops masturbating in a dark hole, it is a long step to the vision of the nation, people and government together, as one large family. One circle around another, Cuomo's vision generalizes intimate family relations in the Sunday Feast, placing around them the image of a vast patriarchal government that treats its citizens as children and its officials as parents. Cuomo's vision reflects the struggle of immigrant Italian culture to deal with the very specter of isolation that has haunted Europe at least since Odysseus visited the Cyclopes and discovered to his horror that they had no laws.[29] The immigrants found themselves, their fellows, only too readily, only too awesomely, planted alone. Immigrant Italians, in short, have needed to confront again the psychological barriers to city building.

The Italian United States has long been seeking the laws of its own development, its passage from the mythic enclosure of Italian America into the civic space of the United States. Immigrant enclosure inside the Polyphemus family still recurs widely. Fear of strangers leads to acts of violence against strangers, as concerned U.S. Italians would see, to their surprise, still occurring in Howard Beach, New York, and in Bensonhurst during the 1980s. The strict mental enclosures of Italian American life have been the allegorical burden of many a Mafia film, from *The Godfather* to *Mean Streets*. These narrow confines amounted to deep grooves where immigrant Italian daily practice had cut the furrows of daily repetition. A constitutional practice of scarcity had partially determined the ways immigrant Italians constructed neighborhoods for themselves to inhabit. One must linger over the stories of Demetrio Lyba (takes place in the 1920s) and Vinnie Martana (the 1940s and

1950s) or the wall of Mr. Michelangelo (1920s) to assess at fair value
how deep was the groove, how high were the walls. It says something
for the collective heroism and cognitive energy that must have been
required to produce the ecumenical politics of *Christ in Concrete*.

Thinking and speaking his way out of this self-enclosure gave
Mario Cuomo the insight and power that lifted him to the first rank of
his profession. During what was called "the Forest Hills controversy" in
the 1960s, Cuomo's ability to speak for the Italians of Corona, effectively to represent how the world looked from inside their enclosure,
came from his own direct experience living inside a family enclosure,
leaving it for the cosmopolitan world of legal history, and returning to it
daily in the self-conscious performance of his public duties as a Neapolitan son and Italian American *paterfamilias*. The insight and power that
Cuomo gained made him a negotiator famous enough to run for office in
a citywide election (which he lost) and to run again in the subsequent
statewide election that made him governor of New York State. Cuomo
found ways to align the two audiences to whom he was appealing: the
audience inside the circle and the larger audience outside, where some
were looking directly at the circle and everybody inside it, whereas many
others were not in the least interested but still needed to be addressed in
terms that did matter to them, needed to be addressed from inside the
actual fortified circle, not from a platform of platitudes but from inside a
position that loomed substantially on their own horizons:

> Corona [Cuomo writes] was one of the disappearing vestiges
> of the ethnic pluralism that made New York City the great-
> est city in the world. It was tucked away in an infrequently
> traveled area of the borough about a mile and a half north of
> the Long Island Expressway. Unless one was looking up rela-
> tives or searching for a really authentic Italian American
> pastry shop, the chances of passing through the villagelike
> Corona were minimal. It was an old neighborhood; any
> home less than twenty years old stood out as a recent devel-
> opment. Some of the houses were constructed of cinder
> blocks; most of them were frame, small and neat. Many of
> them had been built literally by hand by the occupants or
> their immigrant forebears. Practically all of them had a yard
> with a fig tree or a grape arbor or both. Almost everyone in
> Corona was Italo-American and, except for the newest gen-
> eration, spoke Italian, with all its regional variations. There
> were three boccie courts where paunchy Italian grandfathers

played on weekends year round and in almost all kinds of weather. The two local Catholic churches were jammed with women each Sunday, many of them wearing the familiar black mourning costumes out of respect for loved ones who might have died ten years before. . . . In some cases the people occupying a house had been preceded by two generations in the same structure. Family ties had been intensified by numerous neighborhood marriages, so that almost everyone could be called "cousin."

For the most part, when they returned to their homes after a day's work, the Corona people left the outside world totally. There was little interest in political and social matters. The local assemblyman and state senator were nice boys from good families who had done well for themselves and for whom their vote was automatic.[30]

This is Cuomo's own account of the neighborhood whose interests he took on in 1966, when the New York City Housing Authority was proposing to tear down four-and-a-half acres of the neighborhood to make way for housing that would accommodate 509 low-income tenants. "Enraged," writes Frank Cavaioli, "this working-class neighborhood hired Mario M. Cuomo, a lawyer who was also an adjunct professor at St. John's University, to protect their community against bureaucratic encroachment."[31]

Periphrastic analysis:

- *Commentary:* Cuomo presents the portrait of a Cyclopean isolation. Just as Homer's Cyclopes had no assemblies, so in Corona, "There was little interest in political and social matters." More important, Cuomo presents himself as master of the situation, one who can see it both from inside and from outside: "Unless one was looking up relatives or searching for a really authentic Italian American pastry shop, the chances of passing through the villagelike Corona was minimal." He reassures the reader that, although speaking from within, he is hip enough to know how it looks from outside.
- *Pomp:* Cuomo constructs his portrait of Corona using a series of exclusionary practices that taken together amount to a system of ritual barriers: houses, yards, boccie courts, and most people speaking Italian and marrying their cousins. The

summary impact of all these protocols is a social vision almost entirely modulated by rites of mutual recognition, a ceremonious society. Cuomo's diaries themselves, apparently written in the intervals of struggle with the idea of early divulgation (Cuomo published his *Campaign Diaries* less than two years after taking office), show a straightforward willingness to monumentalize himself in private, a trait he shares with other such heroes of Italian history as Julius Caesar and, especially, Niccolò Machiavelli, who once wrote that after his long day riding through his fields on a horse, he would bathe and then dress himself in the toga of a Roman senator before entering his study to write down the results of his conversations with the texts of Titus Livius.

- *Explanation:* Although the people of Corona appear on the stage of public life to be speaking a class-bound language that is interpreted by others as meaningless or even dangerous nonsense, Cuomo, the cultural translator, claims to render the message as a form of sweet reason. Indeed, this is what afterward happens in this story. The Housing Authority persists in wanting to "urban renew" a hundred of these handmade Corona houses to make way for the new project. But Cuomo, patiently and relentlessly explaining the situation, manages to negotiate the incursion down to only two houses. Without precisely denying the undiscussable motives in play, Cuomo changes the theme to things that run close to it, without touching it.

Speaking for an inner circle to a rippling expanse of outer circles made a resonant position for an immigrant's son such as Cuomo, who lived close enough to the immigration that he still spoke to his mother every morning on the telephone in Neapolitan. Cuomo won his great audience by thinking very attentively from both inside and outside the minds of storekeepers such as his own father, immigrants who worked day and night to build their businesses, at the same time, given the Darwinian rituals of the real estate business, that they became a formidable obstacle to members of other groups who wished to share community space. Cuomo succeeded in representing his father's circle. Stand and look at this, he would say, pointing to his wife and children, naming his father's neighborhood and his own university law school, not hiding from the fact that both his first name and his last name ended in vowels.

His achievement at performing this rhetorical act of periphrasis qualified him for high office: its vision amounted to using an immigrant enclosure as a fresh instrument for constructing a stable social order. Cuomo could ask, because he had discovered the principle for himself, "What is there in our society more important than the rule of law? What has meant more to this country?" For those outside the circle, Cuomo meant to assert that immigrant Italians did not see themselves apart from the law. And he answered his own question by explaining to those outside the Italian circle something of how his question concerning the rule of law sounded when one asked it from inside the circle: "Of course there have, from time to time, been abberations [sic]—but over all [sic] the direction of the Law is forward and upward toward the light. Over all [sic], our Lady of the Law has proven stronger than the sins of her acolytes."[32] A Catholic Family vision of the Law. "Our Lady of the Law" is too Christian Democrat a figure to appeal to a U.S. audience. But the Italianographic circle that transforms familial isolation into a scheme of universal recognition attracted wide admiration. Cuomo's recognition of the antique and hard-won truths that belong to such a figure found grateful attention in U.S. political discourse. Sense and nonsense are cognitive problems and political problems at the same time. It may even be that the churches of the U.S. civil religion may yet assume a brighter coloration, more personal set of faces and figures, and that government of the father, by the mother, and for the children shall not perish from the United States of America.

Concentric History

Cuomo's innovation exemplifies how periphrasis can be an act of civilization. His achievement in the Forest Hills controversy stood on his ability to widen the conversation so that it included a major circle that others were not traveling. Jimmy Breslin, with admirable concision, analyzed the strategy this way: "Class before Color, Mr. Cuomo insists."[33] Moving the conversation onto that wider ground was the key to successful mediation in this situation. Class, in the contemporary United States, had been a far less explosive theme than color. People could respect a conversation that referred itself to established positions and interests more readily than one that directed itself to the less rational, less negotiable, issues of race hatreds, where the worst aspects of class exclusions expressed themselves most absolutely outside the reach of reason. Cuomo displayed here a degree of originality that surprised more than one observer. "Class struggle" by 1981 was a notion without much force in the United States. Reagan's election and his successful union-busting had turned class conflict into an old trade-union piety without any organized marchers behind it. But race still stimulated plenty of anger and organized resistance. Thus Cuomo's periphrastic policy of not uttering the dangerous word—in this case the word *color*—had a diplomatic value. Avoiding a debate about color and race in the circumstances of Corona and Forest Hills counted as periphrasis degree zero. In other circumstances, one might have expected class as a theme to constitute a series of flash points. But it turned out that people could more readily be brought to talk about class calmly than about those racial divisions, which in U.S. civil discourse often de facto took the place of class divisions. *Color*, not *class*, was the dangerous word. Early in the process of mediation, Cuomo informally visited black homeowners in Hollis, Queens, and found that they were as opposed to the idea of scatter-site housing in their neighborhood as was anyone in Forest Hills or Corona. Once he was able to move the discussion onto the less intensely charged grounds of class attachment to property values, Cuomo was able to begin to make progress in negotiations. People were more willing to admit to love of property than to ethnic or racial prejudices.

The drawing of wider circles around a center is the physical act of periphrasis. Cuomo breaks the isolation of the immigrant Italian family by making it the model for a wider notion of family. The immigrant Italian writer characteristically begins there, with the circle of single vision. Tina De Rosa's image for this act of framing is concise:

> The late sunlight glanced gold off the large hooped earrings. It was a perfect summer evening. With the earrings scrubbing at her neck, Carmolina watched the blue light that seemed like a curtain blowing behind the world. No one noticed yet that she was wearing Mama's earrings. Her mother sat across the street on a bench; she was sitting in the perfect blue light hunched over, her hands over her bare knees, her cotton dress was pulled up over her knees. The skin on her knees was dry and red. Mama ran her hand through her thick hair. She wore no nylons. Her legs looked thick and worn. She let her hands fall again between her knees, her back was a slope. She brushed dirt off one knee.
>
> Carmolina unclipped one earring and held it up to her eye. Through the golden hoop she watched Mama sitting

next to Grandma. She squinted where the sunlight sliced sharp off the golden edge. Inside the earring, Mama and Grandma were small. She could turn the earring any way she wanted; she could make them bigger and smaller.

Inside the earring, Mama and Grandma fanned themselves; Grandma with a newspaper, Mama with the skirt of her dress. It was too hot, even for summer, they would say.

Their mouths moved; Carmolina watched the quiet mouths through the earring.[34]

De Rosa wishes to make these ordinary lives eternal.[35] In her act of consecration, the narrator returns to the single circle of vision, the place at the start where the act of creation and the act of memory are the same act: the monocle of inward vision, the Cyclops of intimate recollection, and begins again from there. The golden earring is the very image of a magic circle, a hoop that in this instance signifies both the subjection of women and at the same time the power that comes from framing the story and writing it down. The narrator not only records the isolation of the dead within her golden hoop of memory, but also records Italy, a large collaborative project engaged in by all who would make themselves Italians by whatever means they find available, a project especially belonging to those who have made themselves Italians in the act of leaving Italy.

CHAPTER 8

A Literature Considering Itself

The Allegory of Italian America

"E la poesia si costituisce come esercizio di fronte
alla morte."

—Luigi Ballerini

A literature may be defined as a combination of what it is and what it
thinks it is. Persons interested in Italian American writing have largely
concerned themselves with the first half of this definition. Bibliogra-
phers, archivists, linguists, chroniclers, and anthologists have been successfully at work, often against very formidable obstacles, for two
generations and have at least laid down the secure foundations of a literary history.[1] But we have had very little contribution to the theoretical
debate implied by the second half of my definition. What does Italian
American literature think that it is?

A Few Preliminary Problems

Readers experienced in this kind of inquiry will recognize the difficulties
in the question as I have posed it here. "Can a literature think?" is the
first problem, and "Can this one think?" is the second. A literature can
think. The way a literature thinks is its intertext, its weaving, from generation to generation, new fabrics that contain what everyone will recognize to be bits of old familiar patterns. The number of tales in the
Decameron calls delicately to mind the number of cantos in the *Comedia*. The conversation of Virgil in the *Comedia* is a reminiscence of
prophecies long since superseded. This weaving, despite its random
appearance, actually does constitute real thinking about real situations.

139

Dante's appropriation of Virgilian voices has notoriously served purposes of authority and of political vision, or, to put it differently, has
given to the Italian foreground a shape we can still recognize. This
revising of the past points to the particular value of the ways that a literature can think. A literature can harmonize sharp historical disso-
nances—in the manner, for example, that the long baptism of Virgil and
Statius in Italian literature recuperates the heritage of paganism for the
purposes of Christianity. In a similar fashion, we have seen how U.S. literature, constantly reviving the contractual metaphors of the Old Testament, finds new means to think of the North American continent as a
Promised Land, and this tightly woven intertext serves to repress the old
familiar doubts about whether the white European has any right to
appropriate these territories at all. Not only can a literature think, but
also it can think to considerable purpose.

But can Italian American literature think? Some critics, to be sure,
have argued that what it can do is think its way into the U.S. tradition,
so that an open question certainly exists about whether this literature
possesses a distinct and effective intertext of its own.[2] Then one might
pause for a long time over the relations between Italian and American
literary traditions within the Italian American intertext. Experts have
forcefully argued, for example, that Italian American writing is a document of the interaction between two cultures.[3] Indeed, we have no
reason to stop at just two. Deciding precisely how many ethnic,
regional, prenational, and national encyclopedias contribute to the
stock of motives and figures available to a literature that could call itself
both *Italian* and *American* might be difficult. Cataloging these would be
interesting. Following the predictable confrontations among cultures so
diverse and even antipathetic as these might be painted could be endlessly amusing. Nonetheless, although I would be the last to deny the
possibilities of enlightenment in a contrapuntal ethnography, such an
approach would evade the burden of literary work, which is precisely to
discover how to answer those needs that only literature can meet by
providing both ontological orientation and historical authority.

These are needs, although only a cultural cataclysm such as a mass
migration can allow them to be felt as such by a whole people. We may
often forget, but great literatures do flourish in answering actual social
appetites. Perhaps a lingering heritage of the Arcadians, but we still
tend to separate the intertextuality of a piece of writing from its direct
social utility. Doing so, however, is always a mistake. No area of literary
history more suffers from such separation than does that large intersec-
tion of scripture and interpretation, which goes by the name *allegoresis*.

Even to pronounce the word is to call up the names of schoolroom divinities such as Macrobius and Origen, or pedagogical gems such as the famous distich of Nicholas of Lyra:

> *Littera gesta docet, quid credas allegoria,*
> *Moralis quid agas, quo tendas anagogia.*[4]

But allegory belongs neither to its historical heroes nor to its heroic pedants. Before all else, allegory is the method that literature offers to deal with the cultural dissonance produced by historical process.

No one has ever understood this capacity better than the two great virtuosi of the method, Saint Augustine (A.D. 354–430) and Dante Alighieri (1265–1321). Augustine needed allegory to resolve the violent disharmony of the Hebrew Testament with the Christian, and Dante employed allegory to reconcile Christianity with the Roman antiquity that Augustine had done so much to reject. Neither of these projects was an idle academic amusement. Each represented what the enterpriser in question saw as a pressing historical necessity. Nor could it have been otherwise because allegory, when employed thus with the fullness of its power, exacts enormous mental and emotional effort. It also requires the commitment of long generations of such effort. The virtuosi represent, as it were, peaks along a continuous range. Allegory, if it successfully answers a historical requirement, calls into play a long and collective literary enterprise. A great allegory is no less a communal work of art than a great cathedral.

Furthermore, in producing a great allegory, a literature defines its own history. This effect, although often overlooked, is fundamental. It explains the striking exhaustiveness we seem to find in the works of our virtuosi—the sense that subsequent Christian literature never quite managed to subsume Augustine, or the recurrent fear that Dante, in inventing Italian literature, had somehow used up most of its possibilities in advance. Neither suspicion is justified, but both reflect the enormous historiographical force of allegory, which generates an energy of its own beyond that belonging to other kinds of textual power, a way of continuing to grow and to explain things that had not even begun to exist when the allegory assumed its canonical form, so that at the end of Rousseau's confessions there seems to stand the figure of the Bishop of Hippo, and it was always easy to imagine Dante lingering in the doorway of the opera house where they were singing *Nabucco*.

Italian American writing—particularly when it focuses on the myth of an Italian America—is still discovering the shape and strength of its allegory. It has the aspect of a great ring or endless circular path, where readers return to a past they have left behind and then leave it behind all over again. This is the method of the Christian revisiting the Hebrew Bible. This is the method of Dante, seeing all things under many aspects as he wheels around them on the axis of Hell. An American future revisits an Italian past that was itself once the future. The Italian American vision grows out of the innumerable, even involuntary, returns that characterize immigrant Italian narrative as it registers its own passage through time and as it discovers and develops its own characteristic themes. The gradual appearance of this textual complex gives to this young tradition the explanatory power that grows from revisiting the same texts or the same themes repeatedly across the years. The allegory of Italian America is still learning its own capacities. Through it we begin to comprehend a future whose projectors mean to generate a literary history no less corrosive, no less definitive, than what Augustine and Dante represent for us now. How will they do this? *Littera gesta docet*: let us begin with what the letter of this text teaches.

Gesta Italoamericana

After Columbus and Vespucci, the continents of the Western Hemisphere acquired a European identity. They were called the *Americas*, and if an Italian was the reason for that, as immigrants believed, then the Italian presence in America shares all of the contradictions built into the project from the outset. To understand these, one must recognize that from the start it was a literary enterprise. Columbus, forging ahead with the unwavering conviction of the consummate autodidact that he was, had misread his maps and was convinced he had found Japan. Vespucci realized that a continental mass existed between him and East Asia and he, as he says, "lightly" called this the "New World," correcting the misconstruction of Columbus with a new and powerful interpretation: this bold metaphor invented a theoretical space into which Europeans, among others, have been pouring ever since. Some have argued that Vespucci's figure of speech would revolutionize the conception of the cosmos. Even more than that, the expression *Mundus Novus* suggested that a human universe could be created as the double of the one Europeans had left behind.

This is just what happened. The New World quickly fell under the heavy hand of the Old World. Within a few years of Columbus's discovery, Rodrgrigo Borgia, Pope Alexander VI, would take part in the dismantling of the Americas as if they had been Italy herself. It was a touching irony that eventually these same Americas would teach the art of colonial resistance to Garibaldi, who would return to march across Italy as if it were a slender Brazil. Italian American writing begins, then, in a theoretically divided space, a space divided by the theory of the explorers and doubly divided by the worldly powers that sustained their enterprise. We should not be surprised, then, to find that Italian American writing recognizes the total disconnection that such a space imposes.

All'Italia

Dal nuovo mondo, la remota sponda
Da un Italo Navarca a noi concessa;
La nostalgia profonda,
Che nel laco del cuor geme repressa,
A te trasmetto quale
Figlio devoto; terra mia natale.

I miei vagiti primi, il Coccigliano
Castello s'ebbe, in umile dimora:
Nel bel suolo toscano
Che della tua bellezza il serto infiora.
Con le altre doti incluse
Che natura, o mia Italia in te profuse.

E bambinello ancor, sempre correndo
Da fiore a fiore come farfalletta
Che i petali suggendo
Felice va; sovra la molle erbetta
Giocarellavo lieto
Quale agnelletto vispo e mansueto.

Ma, volgendo l'eta, speme sicura
Non dava il pane al morso quotidiano;
Per la coscienza dura
Della tua prole, un manipolo insano
D'ingordi: i suoi diritti
Di padroni, imponendo ai derelitti.

E misero e negletto, ahimé imbarcarmi
Per altri lidi, fu forza maggiore;
Per non assoggettarmi
Ai sanguisuga del proprio sudore:

Ai torvi pescicani
Che su le tue ricchezze hanno le mani.

Così, fintanto che da quei sinistri
Nemici, non avrai la polve scossa;
Famelici ministri
Ti roderanno oltre la pelle, le ossa.
Lasciandoti disfatta
Quale carogna, marcia e putrefatta.

Deh! Italia salva tu se pur ti preme
L'immensa schiera dei reietti figli;
L'umil falange geme
Lontan da te in incogniti perigli.
Soccorrila e imparziale
Concedi a norma il bene tuo sociale.

To Italy

From the New World, the remote shores given to us by
an Italian navigator; the deep nostalgia which repressed
sighs in the depth of the heart, this I pass on to you
as a devout son, O my native land.

In a humble house, Coccigliano Costello knew my first
cries: in the beautiful Tuscan land which is considered the
crown of your beauty. Along with the other gifts
which nature lavished on you, O my Italy.

When still a child, always running from flower to flower
like a butterfly which goes happily sucking the petals, I
used to play merrily on the soft grass just like a lively and
docile lamb.

But, with the passing years, there was no longer
certain hope of earning daily for daily hunger due to the
insensitive conscience of an insane and greedy bunch of
your own progeny who has chosen to impose master's
privileges on those weaker and poorer wretches.

Poor and neglected alas, I was forced to leave for other
shores in order not to subject myself to the bloodsuckers of

my own sweat, to the cruel sharks
who control all your riches.

So, until you have eliminated those sinister enemies
hungry ministers will devour not only your skin but even
your bones, leaving you destroyed just like a carcass, rotten
and putrified.

For pity's sake, O Italy, if you really care, save this
immense group of rejected children, this humble army cries
far from you in unknown perils. Help it and impartial grant
it just social conditions.[5]

This poem of the Canadian immigrant Vittorio Nardi, let us admit, is
not in full command of its own tradition. The blunt invocation of Leopardi in the title is scarcely sustained by the awkward use of anticlerical
pastoral in stanzas three through six.[6] Why read it, then, one may
inquire, to which the reply is that its very weaknesses exhibit with considerable force the painful complexity of the immigrant Italian's literary
situation, where the loftiest ambitions are forever smashing against the
walls of a reality altogether of a humbler kind. This complexity grows
directly from the fact that America remains for the immigrant an Italian
inscription; further complexity derives from the implied requirement
that, to attain the almost divine status implied in this inscriptional identity, the poet must assume as his own an *italianità* that, precisely for
him, is impossible to claim without a certain appearance of (at best)
bravado.[7]

At the same time that Nardi plainly attributes to Italy the
responsibility for the social disaster of migration, he reveals, almost as
if by accident, the pure emotional force that, for me at least, saves the
poem from its own shortcomings: *"l'immensa schiera dei reietti figli."*
This image of a vast wave of abandoned and rejected children
explains the recurrence in the poem of the sad verb *concedere*. That is,
Nardi's hobbled ode reduces and concentrates all Italian history, the
Renaissance discovery of America no less than the long chronicle of
exploitation of the poor, into this one simple memory of rejection.
The poet Emanuel Carnevali, with a similar notion, if a keener sense
of humor, after returning from his difficult years in America, writes,
"O Italy, O great shoe, do not / kick me away again!"[8] Nothing could
be plainer.

That recollection has a long half-life, like the bitter aftertaste of
burnt coffee, and it characterizes much immigrant Italian chronicle,

narrative, poetry, and song. The theoretical prospective Vespucci laid out still radiates a great hope, certainly, a great opportunity, but at the same time it carries the memory, a persistent refrain, of sharp and inconsolable loss. Only one who recognizes the central mythological role that the memory of such loss has assumed can understand the characterizing bent of Italian American discourse. Africans were transported to America as slaves; Anglo-Saxons remember coming in search of religious freedom. These experiences shape their founding myths, even if some Anglo-Saxons came as prisoners in chains or others came as transporters of Africans. The founding myth for the Italians is this memory of how the rich expelled the poor into the world the great Cristoforo discovered and that the great Amerigo first recognized it for what it was.

That is, this New World has turned out to replicate some of the less lovely features of the Old World. The Milanesi will tell you, "*Da Roma in giù comincia l'Africa.*" Northern Italians fear the South, regarding it as the source of various ills and weaknesses that racial myth associates with Africans and Semitic tribes.[9] The stigma associated with Southern Italians has followed them to the United States, where we shall see that it has become by a striking and improbable paradox the source of deep historical strength.

Before we look at the nature of this strength, however, we should consider the difficulties immigrant Italians needed to face in developing a discourse of their own entitlement in the millennial European project called *America*. These new arrivals in no way could identify themselves directly with the ruling peoples. The Anglo-Americans had resisted the entry of the Irish Catholics. But now these groups began to cooperate in the definitive marginalizing of the Italians, who found themselves forming, as they still do, a part of the vivid and highly decorated frame of American society, along with the blacks, the Latinos, and the Eastern European Jews. Naturally, a society as mobile as that of the United States always has room to absorb some members of these border peoples into the operating centers, but much larger proportions remain, as before, to a greater or lesser degree visibly tattooed with their tribal or racial otherness. For Italians this exclusion has been less rigid than for blacks or Latinos, but more rigid than for Jews and Irish Catholics.[10] In short, to the regional and class divisions of Italy has been added in the United States the machinery of ethnic boundary markers. The borders are such that Italians who cross them must do so at the risk of losing their own possibilities of historical self-awareness.

Allegoria Divina

Not surprisingly, many Italians have refused to pay this price. What have they done instead?

At this point one may observe the cognitive engine of allegory industriously at work—almost, as it seems, on every street corner; that is, one might expect that a device with so noble a literary lineage would live best in academies. But this has not been the case. Italian Americans have found the answer to their dilemma within the models that their own tradition provided. Garibaldi La Polla understood this when he made the hero of his novel *The Grand Gennaro* an immigrant who had left nothing behind in Italy but bad debts and bad memories. Gennaro Accuci became in Italian Harlem not merely a successful businessman but, more consequentially, a builder of churches and a leader of processions. La Polla's vision of the meaning of life in Italian Harlem has been successfully adapted by the historian Robert Orsi in *The Madonna of 115th Street: Faith and Community in Italian Harlem, 1880–1950.*[11] What both of these mythographers outline is a habit of thinking that one may call *processional*, a habit that produces a visible event in which the contradictions of the communal life become the materials of a public ritual. To appraise the full weight of this enterprise, one must return to La Polla, whose narrative understands precisely what is at stake for his hero in the melée of Italian Harlem, 1880:

> Gennaro Accuci actually found a place in this confusion, and sent for his family. But he did not send for his family before he had succeeded in what he called, and all his fellow immigrants called, "making America." "Making good" is an approximation, but without body and expression. Something both finer and coarser clings to the expression. There is the suggestion of envy on the part of the user and also of contempt. For it means that a nobody, a mere clodhopper, a good-for-nothing on the other side, had contrived by hook or crook in this new, strange country, with its queer ways and its lack of distinctions, to amass enough money to strut about and proclaim himself the equal of those who had been his superiors in the old country. And if one said of himself that he had made America, he said it with an air of rough boasting, implying "I told you so" or "Look at me." Although he knew that his spectators would be inclined to

despise him for the word, he threw out his chest. And yet
there were comfort and solidity, the double fruit of egotism,
in its use, and he used it, even roared it out, and laughed.
(pp. 4–5)

The recurrent parades that Gennaro leads, like the annual feasts of the
Madonna that Orsi describes, do not serve merely to communicate
secret feelings or to consolidate community. They also serve, quite literally, to make America, to celebrate a triumph. Gennaro, as bluntly as
any conquistador, intends to invent both himself and this continent
along the lines of a European ambition. That is, like every consequential
European, this hero comes to the United States not merely to escape
something, but also to demonstrate a hypothesis. He has a theory of
America; and his career is, in effect, a series of experiments designed to
test and to apply that theory. Gennaro is willing to do anything, to
labor as hard as imaginable, to commit whatever treason, to give life to
his imaginary self in its imaginary America. This projected place has a
precise architecture and social structure, replicating the pyramid of
nobles and *galantuomini* that Gennaro recalls from Italy—all just as it
was, except, of course, that now he is installed at its apex. He succeeds
in his ambition, but the machinery of the plot insists also that he shall
die as the price of this flawed triumph.

   That he must die is not surprising because what Gennaro has
accomplished in making America is to become a god. This is the allegorical destiny of Italian American heroes, to endure ritual death and
processional reidentification in the process of becoming divinities.
Emanuel Carnevali wrote that during the crisis provoked by the very
bitter life of an immigrant, he believed himself to be divinized by his
sufferings and wild imaginings. "I believe absolutely now that I was the
Only God" (p. 176). His *Autobiography* lays out the emotional prob-
lematic of the immigrant Italian with a clarity that only makes one wish
that more readers had ever examined it. Nonetheless, the only two Italian American novels to have entered the ordinary syllabus of American
literature advertise in their titles exactly the same impulse to divinity:
Christ in Concrete and *The Godfather*. In their diverse ways, these two
works demonstrate that the force of this writing has sprung from its
adaptation of the collective allegorizing engaged in by Italian migrants
in America. In di Donato's *Christ In Concrete*, the immigrant bricklayer
Geremio falls from a scaffolding and is buried in concrete. It takes two
days to recover his body. As we have already seen, because he dies on
Good Friday and his body is exhumed on Easter Sunday, the migrant

community weaves a long funeral discourse in which Geremio is first compared with and then becomes the risen Christ. Twenty years after *Christ in Concrete*, di Donato published *Three Circles of Light* in which he attempted to come to terms with other, less presentable, facts about Geremio's death. The scaffolding collapses because the contractor has skimped on materials. Geremio, the foreman, it turns out, had known of this and so had been complicit in his own death. But the eloquent honesty of *Three Circles of Light* has gone mostly unnoticed. What attracts readers is the divinity of *Christ in Concrete*. A similar logic has led most readers to prefer *The Godfather* and its film version *The Godfather, Part I*, to the moralizing sequels *The Godfather, Part II*, and *The Godfather, Part III*. In Puzo's novel, the identification of Don Corleone with the myth of God the Father is all but complete and carries only a light dusting of irony, often mistaken for satire. Although we find a good deal of ironic, even bitter and sarcastic, social commentary in *The Godfather*'s attitude toward American hypocrisy, we find little actual satire in this novel. We are expected to take its heroes very seriously indeed. Don Vito Corleone's divine stature comes directly from the sufferings and loyalties that he sustains. His one true son, Michael, himself becomes a godfather in the moment he avenges his father's losses. All this is perfectly well portrayed in their various ways by both the novel and the film. The film sequel, which aims to portray a spiritual emptiness and hollowness in the Corleone family's victory, has rather less resonance. What gives *The Godfather* its power as myth is not the moral stature of the Mafia, but the stature of the immigrant who has "made America"—who has, in effect, paid the price of making real the theoretical continent. Michael's wife, Kay, sees him as the reader is meant to see him, at the end of the novel:

> He reminded her of statues in Rome, statues of those Roman emperors of antiquity, who, by divine right, held the power of life and death over their fellow men. One hand was on his hip, the profile of his face showed a cold proud power, his body was carelessly, arrogantly at ease, weight resting on one foot slightly behind the other. (p. 437)

The temptation is to read this divinization as a straightforward *embourgeoisement* of the poor migrants.[12] This it is, but that ought not obscure the persistence of religious feeling that allows Italian American literary tradition to assign this status almost reflexively to its dead heroes. Here, for example, on the other end of the political spectrum, is the conclusion

of Daniel Gabriel's "narrative longpoem" on the anarchists Nicola Sacco
and Bartolomeo Vanzetti:

> but who could say
> their death was not
> a kind of defeat?
> defeat to this tyranny?
> who could say
>
> they were not killed
> definitively?
> their bodies
> burned magnificently,
> their spirits
> quenched by
> another fire,
> simply: act, memory,
> eternity.
> not so simply,
> but through the
> persistence of the two,
> the case, the trial,
> passion and memory
> they are
> like singing birds
> forever singing
> over the landscape.
> they are a metaphor
> of something bolder,
> of an unknown—
> and are sending,
> even as we breathe,
> a stitch of light
> to generations
> not yet born.[13]

The Daniel Gabriel who published this work in 1983 was a younger
poet, displaying a thorough awareness of all the devices of distancing
and irony that a well-trained late modernist was likely to find stained in
his marrow, and so the straightforward monumentality of this ending is,
accordingly, all the more striking. This part of the text bears the subtitle

"Metapoem (9)," although perhaps at first it does not seem to articulate a metapoetics, but rather to echo a simple elegiac line. In fact, the crucial point, towards which the poem carefully labors, is the statement "they are metaphor" because the metapoem recognizes that such a metaphor is precisely a figure of which we have need, not to celebrate a simple passage, but rather to make sense of a violent confrontation.

Tropologia Olimpica

To die into theory is to become a divinity. This is something that narratives of Italian America recognized before their metapoetics did—recognized it, not just as efficacious, but as essential to the project. To the protagonists of the discourse, if not to its explicators, no other role was open to Italian Americans in the American imagination except that of divinities. Frank Sinatra, Rudolf Valentino, Madonna. The first historian these divinities have had refers to himself in his book title as if he were not a writer of fiction but a writer who reports the miracles of divinities—an evangelist; he appears in his own title: *Valentino and the Great Italians According to Anthony Valerio*[14] mingles daydreams and divinity with something of the proportions but nothing of the effect belonging to magical realism: in Valerio's prose even the gods of Italian America spend most of their energy on the simple problems of daily life. The contrast between the ordinary and the divine is a reliable source of humor in Valerio's series of narratives. The self-consciously heroic Italian Americans saw from the start that they would need to assume the burden of divinities. Most of the other roles had already been colonized by others. The Puritans had preempted the role of moralists, the Jews were the heroes of the Diaspora in all its tragic complications from the ghetto to the Holocaust, the Native Americans were the indigenous spirits, the inheritors of African slaves had acquired the franchise as leading victims of U.S. hypocrisy. In this context, the Italians entered the imaginary U.S. economy by claiming and occupying specifically the divine space that Columbus and Vespucci, Verrazzano and Cabot had opened for them, that of the primeval progenitors or projectors of the very ontology of the New World, Italian gods that U.S. Europeans such as Morgan and Carnegie had imported along with Italian paintings, statues, and fragments thereof.[15] In 1775, the first U.S. Navy had four ships. Three of them were named after Italians: the *Andrew Doria*, the *Cabot*, the *Columbus*.

Thus it has been that the cultural implications of Italian American myth have been more than a little constricting. The martyred bricklayer

and the omniscient gangster entered directly into American myth. Demi-
urges of sexuality such as John Travolta and Madonna Ciccone have no
difficulty of access. But who is the archetype of the Italian American
intellectual? Is there a Saul Bellow or an Irving Howe? This figure is
going to take time to develop. U.S. Italians can point with pride to
Helen Barolini and Frank Lentricchia, Fred Gardaphe, and Louise De
Salvo. They can point with pride, but do they? The development of a
genuinely attentive readership is a necessary condition for the production of public intellectuals that are actually known to the general public.
In the meantime, active U.S. Italian players working before the general
public appear not to have paused too long pining over the polite society
of U.S. readers from which they feel excluded. Rather, the most successful strategy has been to capitalize on achievements of accomplished
divinity. Thus, to protest the foreign religion that masqueraded as
Catholicism, the poet Elaine Romaine writes the following:

> You were always irish, god
> in a church where I confessed
> to being Italian.
>
> But then St. Anthony
> had a feast and lights ringed
> the street as sausage and peppers
> steamed in booths, gambling wheels spun
> as the tenor held his stomach, pushing
> a note higher. Behind a booth my brother
> pitched pennies with a priest, rolling
> deep fried bread sprinkled with sugar
> in his mouth. The processions began.
> My father and his brothers shoulder
> the statue through the crowd, hymns
> and feast bless the air.
>
> And all the sights of you, god,
> were wine-filled.
> For these sins we took communion
> the next morning, sleeping on each other
> in the pews until the altar bell rang
> and we filed up to the railing,
> opening our mouths, for your blood
> and flesh. O god,
> god, I confess nothing.[16]

This is religious warfare on an Olympian field—no intervention of priests or even theologians, but simply one god against another, hegemony established in the jumbled demotic *ecclesia* of the streets where the procession and the feast fill the sensorium.

We confront here an extraordinary morality, if it is a morality at all. The historians of Italian America have only begun to notice the power of this myth to command belief. Thus, although the allegory of Italian America is everywhere present, its tropology is difficult to detect: its deepest believers do not quite realize how profoundly much it is an allegory, does what an allegory does. They simply believe in themselves. "Who's better than me?" as DeLillo's Bronx Italians obsessively ask at every turn.[17] Mistaking these self-regarding divinities for the familiar stereotypes of the Nietzschean Italian who can do anything and feel no remorse would be easy. A similarity indeed exists between these divinities and those older caricatures. But the difference is that these gods have suffered and have died. When they have awakened (in the essays of Camille Paglia, say, or the novels of Mario Puzo, where the writers are fully aware of making large claims), these gods have found themselves in possession of their names and powers, and in possession, too, of their theoretical selves, made real by death and grown clear in retrospect.

In the tropology, the motive power of this particular allegory stands forth: this is the place where the family ideology decides to take itself altogether too seriously. In the novels of Rocco Fumento and Charles Calitri, writers who emerged in the 1950s, Gene Mirabelli and Joseph Papaleo, writers who emerged in the 1960s and 1970s, the Italian American family has become an epic solitude.[18] It spans the ocean, it travels among cities, but it hangs onto the myth of its own self-sufficiency.[19] This tenacity requires high-energy expenditures. Immigrant Italian families in reality are not self-sufficient, let alone divine in their powers. Their very existence is a form of elaborate social project: like other card-carrying natives of modernity, U.S. Italians all live within, they all are completely formed and molded by, the international trade and communications networks that initially produced their situation. Each U.S. Italian—each single person on his or her own—forms a monad of permanent imperial salience, no matter where that person may wander. No U.S. Italians live entirely free of Italy's influence and reputation, for example, even though many of them have little command of any languages spoken on the Italian peninsula (unless we include English).[20] Italians in the United States often know very little of Italian history, geography, economy, or sense of collective purpose.[21]

But they live subject to its effects nonetheless. The very notion of an Italian American, with all its mythological powers and all its abysmal shortcomings, is an Italian export, continually produced and reproduced in the international trade network with major switching stations in peninsular Italy, a country that still does thriving business producing *italianità*, exporting time-tested commodity fetishes that all U.S. Italians, even ones that change their names and become corporate executives, recognize as vital elements in the Italian American identity they continue, somehow, to share: food, clothes, travel. These traditions of conspicuous consumption have broad enough appeal that one would be hard put to find a U.S. Italian who did not own any imported oils or cheeses or shoes or sweaters or souvenirs. The link does not confine itself to goods and services, however. It also includes politics. Italian political life affects the reputation of Italians everywhere in the world, and the world includes the United States. The effect may arrive through a maze of indirections, but it is nonetheless powerful. Italy the Fascist enemy. Italy the poor destroyed enemy nation. Neither of these Italys helped U.S. Italians gain respect in the United States in the 1940s and 1950s. Italy of the 1960s miracle; Made in Italy of the 1970s and 1980s, Clean Hands Italy of the 1990s—each notable success of Italy's assists U.S. Italians to gain power and prestige in their English-speaking homeland. Thus U.S. Italian families are not independent of their political and economic points of origin. Rather, the international trade networks that brought Italians to the United States are markedly more capacious than they were a century ago; the scale and opulence of these networks guarantee that U.S. Italians still live in visible, measurable relationship to their points of origin. And their points of arrival are even more powerful. They are not independent of U.S. life any more than they are of Italian politics. Bill Tonelli emphasizes how very American have become the various Tonelli families he finds all over the United States. You cannot distinguish them from their neighbors in the apartheid suburbs of Northern California and Southern Wisconsin. Thus, however much Italian American allegorists hold to the myth of Italian American self-sufficiency, it seems to have the character of willful pretense, about halfway between a pious hope and an outright lie.

The allegory of Italian America, in the moment it recognizes its imperial demands, also begins to learn of its status as an imperial product. Among peoples who have these old family connections to trading empires in Europe, producing a myth of divine self-sufficiency may assume many forms and is a fairly common habit. Old Virginia landowners, opulent New York patroons, radical Boston Protestants still maintain among their bourgeois descendants romances about the divine originators who founded their families and settled their real estate. Their style is different, but the myth still functions to justify their entitlements. Those who inherit the guilt of empire also inherit absurd, free-floating self-confidence.

Anagogia Cartografica

It has been something of a puzzle what to make of this peculiar security, and U.S. Italians have watched bemused as Italian American food, manners, and families, transfigured with celestial light, have become the playthings of advertising and the poetry of political speeches. Bemused but untouched. Unquestionably, theirs has appeared at times to be an unnatural calm. Social scientists and journalists have not seen in it any reason to rejoice; such persons have always approached U.S. Italian reality with the nervous apprehension that their training teaches them to mistake for close attention. Uneasy and (it seems) unloved, they are great seekers after noise and pretense; they want definitive action; they look for solutions with riddles attached. But we have every reason to think that poets and novelists among the Italians in the United States are passing through a period of energetic assimilation. Understanding that the crisis of great strife associated with the migration has finally drawn to a conclusion, these writers have recognized the vast access of grace and power that the dying migrants have left as their nimbus.

Thus it is that Italian America often seems to produce among some contemporary writers a meditative and glistening front at exactly the moment that others would be hauling out the stakes and spikes and tommy guns. Novels and poems these days may include visions of transfigured grandmothers:

> "We used to eat these," she said, bending over and plucking a dandelion from the green lawn. "We used to like these very much. A simple weed. We cooked it with garlic and olive oil and a few flakes of red pepper. We ate weeds and we were happy."
>
> My grandmother waved her arms above her head in some private choreography now, bending over and brushing her ankles in a delicate sweep, a graceful rythmic [sic] gesture.

> She was humming the tarantella again, she separated
> from us and whirled and whirled, moving one hand to her
> eyes as if shading them from some brutal Italian sun.[22]

This whimsical Shakespearean goddess inhabits a nursing home in
Carole Maso's poetic narrative *Ghost Dance*. Nor is her antique presence really unusual in its almost unbearable enclosure of a distant divinity. The heroine of Helen Barolini's *Umbertina* is a Calabrian
grandmother whose life the narrator very fully imagines, all the while
making it clear that the grandmother spoke no English and the narrator
no Italian, so that the entire recollection is a charged imagining rather
than a history, not a record but self-consciously a myth.

Quo tendas anagogia. Our analysis ought to tell us what this literature sees in its prospect, floating somewhere, it may be, just a step
ahead of its vanishing point This has to be a question of realizing possibilities that were written into the paper continent at the opening of its
career as an utopia for Europeans who wanted to try again. Thus, the
aspect of Italian America least understood by its many students and
critics is its sense of time. For its most devoted inhabitants Italian America is America, exactly as old as Vespucci's figure of speech. A sense of
common purpose extends over not years but generations, not decades
but centuries. "Our grandfathers built these buildings," an Italian
American college administrator said to me, pointing to the campus of a
great American university. "Now we want to work in them."[23] Such
bone-bred wisdoms of possession persist without needing any clearer
case to put. Not only do they persist, but also specifically in their lack
of an articulated argument, they retain the power to rest like gods on
their own peculiar abstract authority. Their having as yet no settled
hierarchy reflects merely the slow revolution of calendars they feel. The
burden of their theoretical inheritance, their chart of primeval luster,
has become as well the privilege of a starry equanimity. It almost seems
the name of a permanent disappointment, one might say, all these
clouds of prestige that so rarely seem to alight on the actual lawn. The
temptation to which I am in the act of not yielding any longer would be
to outline a history of the future of this name, *America*, knowing that
however it differs from its past, it will carry something of the same
impossible removal, will remain a sacrament of loss so pure as to give
to each remaining thing, each stone and every flowering vine, its own

shimmering position in the general and expanding edifice of divinities impaled on a theory, persistently imprinted in the map.

The Literary Criticism of the Imperial Gods

Italian America becomes a myth, a source of literary power. Some of its writers believe in it, others are obsessed with it and want to erase it as if it were a sign of their own guilt or unacceptability or both. But most U.S. Italians who write recognize the myth as part of the circumstances they inherit, not only their limitations, but also their historical stock in trade. Italian American literature becomes the name of an enterprise.

It also becomes at times the field of a Buried Caesarism that Italian Americans can easily share with other Americans. This literary history is a club where entrance is granted only to those who meet strenuous commercial standards. Gay Talese published in the *New York Times Book Review* in an 1993 essay provocatively titled, "Where Are the Italian American Novelists?"[24] This essay generated a great deal of controversy among Italian American writers, dozens of whom wondered aloud why Talese had chosen to ignore the importance of their achievements. Although Talese had mentioned some Italian American novelists, he had faulted most of them for their failure to achieve dominating positions. This use of domination as an aesthetic qualification is itself a form of internalized rejection, no doubt, but Talese was the only Italian American writer with access to the front page of the *New York Times Book Review,* so people could not help taking it seriously. They could not help being puzzled by it, too.

The roots of Talese's puzzling argument can be found in his famous analysis of Frank Sinatra, published twenty-seven years earlier.[25] Talese presents Sinatra as taking the place of a great Italian American novelist. Talese portrays the great singer as an imperial character, a man with the money, the energy, and the power to do "*anything* he wants." With his endless power and notorious willfulness, Sinatra comes across as an Italian American Nero. At the opening of the article Sinatra is suffering from a cold, whose impact Talese outlines with mock-epic particularity:

> A Sinatra with a cold can, in a small way, send vibrations through the entertainment industry and beyond as surely as President of the United States, suddenly sick, can shake the national economy.

> For Frank Sinatra was now involved with many things
> involving many people—his own film company, his record
> company, his private Airline, his missile-parts firm, his real-
> estate holdings across the nation, his personal staff of
> seventy-five—which are only a portion of the power he is
> and has come to represent. (p. 19)

Talese also places Sinatra where one might have expected to find the
great Italian American novelist. Italian American boys could not write,
he claims: "they were strong with song, weak with words, not a big
novelist among them: no O'Hara, no Bellow, no Cheever, nor Shaw."
On the other hand, they could express themselves in bel canto, and they
could see their names in lights, "but none could see [his name] better
than Frank Sinatra." Talese's Olympus is Caesar's Palace. In the Rome
of the Caesars, Nero, who fancied himself a poet, was crowned with
laurel. No one outside the emperor himself imagined Nero a great poet,
but power and money were the credentials in question. No one ever
took Sinatra for a novelist, but Talese makes of his dominant position
the evidence that he was the voice of his generation. During the time he
wrote this article, Talese was developing Caesarism as a way of describing American and Italian American reality. In his study of the Bonanno
family, *Honor Thy Father*, Talese wrote a lucid outline of Salvatore
Marranzano's Caesarist Mafia structure. In a study of the *New York
Times*, titled *The Kingdom and the Power*, Talese explained the great
newspaper in these terms: "[it] was a timeless blend of past and present,
a medieval modern kingdom within the nation with its own private
laws and values and with leaders who felt responsibility for the nation's
welfare but were less likely to lie than the nation's statesmen and generals."26 He might have been describing Don Corleone's alternative
world, which also had its own laws and felt itself morally superior to
the people running the nation. With these standards, understanding
why, even twenty-seven years later, Talese did not think much of the
great writers of the Italian American tradition—John Fante, Pietro
di Donato, Helen Barolini, Maria Mazziotti Gillan—is not difficult. Not
a private airplane among them, not even a *New Yorker* sale. As an
insider in the imperial American literary institution (*New York Times,
Esquire, New Yorker*, the land of first-line publishers and million-dollar
advances), Talese was in a position to observe it and to criticize it, but
he was still inclined to adopt its standards when judging literary
achievement. After all, doing otherwise would have been surprising.

That institution has prized and promoted him and his work. How can he seriously doubt its wisdom?

Most Italian American writers have grappled with the Kingdom and Power, whether that of the United States or that of ancient Italy, and indeed in Italian American writing, the two are often hard to tell apart. The issues are often the same. In this literature, the myth of Italy and the myth of America often meet in the mirror.

CHAPTER 9

The Italian American Sign

At some time in the past thirty years, the term *Italian American writers* no longer signified writers—not even, in some cases, scholars of Italian Americana—who could speak, understand, write, or read any of the languages usually called *Italian,* whether national or local. And the dialectic of dialect moved into a phase where *Italian American* came to signify most often persons whose native language was English, whereas the expression *Italian American writer* came to signify people whose literary educations had been conducted in the majority language of the United States. At this moment, the Italian American was faced with the full force of what *Italian* had long meant in the English language and what it currently meant in the Anglo-American language.

Italian as a Theatrical Form of English

Italian immigrants discovered on entering the English-speaking world that public rôles that allowed them to speak Italian already existed for them. Every student of immigration history will recall that in the daily life of the U.S. port cities where so many immigrant Italians settled, the ice cream vendor, the singing waiter, the coloratura soprano all played recognizable public rôles, and played them in Italian. Not everyone remembers, however, that during these years, another public use of Italian became well known in the very places where the King's English celebrated itself as the King's English; that is, on the Shakespearean stage.

First in London and afterward in New York and throughout the United States, presenting Shakespearean plays acted in Italian by famous actors was for some years in vogue.[1] The French actress Rachel started the tradition of playing Shakespeare in another language in the 1830s. But her successor in this practice was the Italian Adelaide Ristori, who performed many parts in Italian. Ristori most famously

161

played in Italian the sleepwalking scene from *Macbeth* to packed houses paying very high prices from Boston to San Francisco. At one point, the actor Tommaso Salvini even experimented with playing the part of Othello in Italian while the rest of the cast spoke English.

The parts Ristori, Salvini, and, later, Ernesto Rossi played capitalized on two notions: first, that the originals of Shakespeare's plays were often Italian;[2] second, that Italians were an intrinsically theatrical people, operatic in daily life, and were consequently capable of transporting a theatrical audience into a wonderland of emotion that English-speaking people believed that they could feel and understand without necessarily comprehending a single word that was being spoken.

In the United States, the Italian Sign had numerous aspects, well established before the Great Migration, that have proved enormously durable and have gone far to shape the role of Italian speech in the English language. Many of these arise from theatrical traditions: in English-speaking countries, the opera stage is a kind of lunatic zone, where untrammeled self-expression reigns, contrasting sharply with Anglophone codes of self-restraint; similarly, in English-speaking countries, the Shakespearean theater provides audiences with a vivid representation of Italians as a people who speak in English poetry.

Such theatrical traditions harmonized well enough with other traditions, also very well established by the mid- to late-nineteenth century, traditions in some cases dating back to the Renaissance, of Italy as the school of elegance and civility:

> You have swarved nothing at all in this discourse from the dutie of a perfect Courtier, whose propertie it is to do all things with careful diligence, and skillfull art: mary yet so that the art is so hidden, and the whole seemeth to be doone by chance, that he may thereby be had in more admiration."[3]

Thus the voice of Italy in sixteenth-century England. For the Elizabethans, Italy was the place that produced the best examples of how to practice courtesy, diplomacy, politics, and other arts that conceal their purposes. Virginia Woolf in *Orlando* presents the classic portrait of this chronotope. Her Elizabethans make Renaissance Italy into a permanent province of the English imagination—and, one might add, into a permanent resource for the English sumptuary appetite. This view has had many adherents since that time. The entire English Renaissance, as we know, is interwoven with Italian texts, from Chaucer's early translation and adaptation of Boccaccio to Spenser's of Ariosto and Milton's of Tasso. Elizabethan and Jacobean playwrights made of Italy an ideological theater for staging intellectual, political, military, dynastic, ecclesiological, soteriological, and eschatological inquiries, debates, and conflicts. Scholars now avoid the phrase *English Renaissance,* instead using the new name *Early Modern England,* which better suggests the power of persistence that the cultural innovations of that time have displayed during the following centuries. The greatest Renaissance effect in Early Modern England was the Reformation. It worked a revolution in the Church of England that has not been revoked, despite many efforts to re-Romanize that institution. The English invention of America as "a city built upon a hill" or an exemplary Protestant community has continued to have profound effects on American literary imaginations.[4] And the English practice of treating Italy as an aspect of its own civilization has only grown in material force and transatlantic consequence with the years.

The United States of America was conceived, designed, and built by leaders who, like other Englishmen of their rank and moment, had acquired a comprehensive understanding of Italy as the source of Roman politics, Milanese armor, Florentine banking, Venetian architecture, and Neapolitan music. Jefferson, Washington, and other planter aristocrats of the slave states established for the United States a perdurable currency of Italian material and intellectual culture. The mid-nineteenth century saw the rise of many capitol domes and tetra-style porticoes in the large cities of the nation, and the post–Civil War period only increased the proliferation of such constructions.

Thus immigrants who possessed Italian craft skills found a well-established market. Stone-carving, ornamental plastering, and violin playing, for example, were all thriving trades in U.S. cities, where the Italian Renaissance had become a permanent backdrop to the life of the new republic. Theatrical expectations belonged to the same luxury market, no doubt, as the arts of architecture and decoration, but the mode of belonging was different. The Renaissance backdrop implied a foreground rich in types drawn from Reformation anti-Romanism: poisoners, cozeners, ambitious Jesuits.

Thus, even before large numbers of Italians lived in U.S. cities, Italian speech already raised a large set of preconceptions there, as it did in other Anglophone countries as well. In the heteroglossia of daily life, these preconceptions arose at every turn.

The Italian Sign

The Italian Sign in English, before the Great Migration, was composed of a signifier, almost always connected with worldly pleasures or theatrical spectacle, and a signified, almost always suggestive of uncontrolled passions or vices.[5] The socially attractive was joined by convention with the socially abject.

Centuries of comfortable use established this signifier in the academies, galleries, and opera houses of the English-speaking world. Its signified had an equally vigorous and self-reinforcing history in the anti-Catholic pamphlets and preachments of the Protestant world, and during the Great Migration it added new dimensions among the police and the criminal anthropologists of the New World and the Old World alike.

This old economy had put out fresh roots and branches in post–Risorgimento Italy, which invested the Italian Sign with a degree of imperial ambition that the new nation struggled to satisfy. Federico Chabod has left us some stunning chapters on the ironies attendant on the governance of a bankrupt federation that felt the need to place itself on the same level with world empires past and present.[6] To choose the most dramatic example, the necessities of the new Italian Sign in the 1870s and 1880s included the construction of a new capital on the ruins of ancient and Renaissance Rome. The founders of the new kingdom called their new capital *Terza Roma*, the Third Rome, an exercise in monumental hysteria with few parallels even in Italian history, rich in monuments as that history may be. The two most famous piles are the *Vittoriano* (1885–1911) and the *Palazzo di Giustizia* (1889–1910), each in its way so ugly and conspicuous as to make an unforgettable mark. Worth noting, however, is that the construction of these pharaonic follies began during the early years of the Great Migration (1880–1924). The relation between these extravagant signifiers and the lives of the Italians spreading out into the world is suggestive, if not exactly exemplary, of the workings of the economy of the Italian Sign. The louder Italy boasted of its imperial mission, the more abundant evidence the world saw of its failure to educate, to feed, and to give fruitful labor to its people at home.[7]

In the United States, the Italian Sign functioned with considerable effectiveness. Henry Wadsworth Longfellow, Charles Eliot Norton, James Russell Lowell, and the other Brahmins who founded the Dante Society of America in Cambridge in 1881 were institutionalizing the profound American respect for Italian genius. Stanford White, J. P.

Morgan, and the others who projected and endowed the American
Academy in Rome in 1896 were ensuring for the United States a permanent supply of architects, artists, and scholars with deep personal
knowledge of ancient and Renaissance Rome. All of this activity meant
that Americans had a large investment, financial as well as aesthetic and
moral, in the Italian signifier. This made it more likely, and certainly
much easier, that they should be acquainted with the other, less attractive, aspects of the Italian Sign. During these same years, the Italian
immigrants in New York and Boston and other U.S. cities were heirs to
the entire encyclopedia of undesirabilities that formed the other, the
indissociable, half of the signature of Italy in the world.

Consequently, the Italian Sign in the United States had very little
trouble assimilating the Italian immigrants to its economy.[8] The American Renaissance had what appears in retrospect a fated meeting with
the Great Migration.

The American Renaissance[9]

The Great Migration was not accompanied by a withdrawal from
things Italian in Anglo-America. Indeed, the opposite occurred. The late
nineteenth century was a time of unparalleled Italianate splendor in U.S.
cities. The American bourgeoisie had an apparently unquenchable
appetite for trecento poetry (Dante, Petrarca), quattrocento painting
(Raffaello, Leonardo), and cinquecento architecture (Palladio, Serlio).
This period saw the rise of the Metropolitan Opera House and the Metropolitan Museum of Art in New York, as well as the appearance of
similar temples to ancient and Renaissance art in Brooklyn, Philadelphia, Louisville, Chicago, Boston, Worcester, and Springfield, Massachusetts, among other places. In Boston, Isabella Stewart Gardner built
a museum to her own Italophile passions. These varied tastes in Italian
signifiers were not unconnected with one another, and the American
propertied class often employed them as an entire system of "monuments of its own magnificence." These tastes enjoyed their greatest
moment of synthetic spectacle during the World's Columbian Exposition in Chicago in 1893, which exuberantly realized a grandiose architectural scheme based on Renaissance models. The contemporary
architectural critic Mariana Griswold van Rensselaer wrote, "No other
styles could have served so well as these allied yet not identical Renaissance styles in giving the architects a chance to build in agreement with
each other and yet to meet special practical needs and express individual tastes."[10] Van Rensselaer insisted, somewhat implausibly, that

"despite the fact that these buildings are not just like the ones we need to shelter our daily lives and works, their aspect ought to prove that Renaissance forms of art are the best for current use" (p. 73). Her argument meant to reassert the clarity of the Renaissance against the then current "strong leaning, sentimental rather than reasonable, toward Gothic fashions, inappropriate alike to the intellectual temper and to the practical needs of our time." This anti-medievalism shows that the critic's Renaissance tastes were not merely aesthetic but depended on a determined identification with the historical forces of the early modern period. This identification with Renaissance ambitions runs rather deeper than one might expect. Meaning to encourage her readers to visit the fair in Chicago, she wrote that they would be beholding "one of the most beautiful sights and, considering its genesis, the most wonderful sight, in the world—a sight the character of which, I am unafraid to say, has not been paralleled since the Rome of the Emperors stood intact with marble palace, statue, terrace, bridge, and temple, under an Italian sky no bluer than our own" (p. 69). "Of course," she added, as if suddenly catching her balance, "our Fair is a small place compared to imperial Rome. . . ." The litotes is too late and too little. During the Gilded Age in the United States, the identification with "Rome of the Emperors" is, of all Renaissance motives, the most seductive aspect of the Italian Sign. One thinks of the decisive scene in Henry James's *The Portrait of a Lady,* the moment in the Roman palace when Gilbert Osmond, the fortune-hunting Italophile American who marries Isabel Archer, forbids her to visit her dying cousin in England. Osmond is sitting at his drawing table, absorbed in a painstaking drawing of a Roman coin, in many ways the archetype of Italian signifiers.

As the Gilded Age progressed, the attachment of the American rich to the Italian signifier grew increasingly intense, producing absolute monuments to Renaissance extravagance such as Morgan's library on East 36th Street, built in the manner of a Medici villa, or the Federal Reserve Bank on Liberty Street, an orgy of rusticated stone on the model (and scale) of the Florentine Signoria.

All this investment in Roman and Renaissance splendors meant that the American city and the American mind had a good deal of Italian signifier to behold, and inevitably, it came along with an equal proportion of Italian signified that needed to be to dealt with. Now this made for a difficulty. The United States was still a vigorously Protestant country in the nineteenth century, and, well before the arrival of actual Italians, it had been working diligently to find places to put the material that insisted on arriving in the same crate with the Roman statuary and the Pre-Raphaelite Madonnas. Protestants were happy with these items as tokens of their own greatness but had trouble managing the physical realities and sometimes the ideological contents of the art in question. The material presence and the intellectual burthen of this art were often deeply disturbing to the American moral imagination. The Italian signified included a profound apprehension of the weaknesses of human nature and of the criminalities that enter a conversation under the name of History. All the seven deadly sins might come out of the ground with a Roman statue. Roman glory might bring along with it the history of Roman depravity and Catholic oppression.

Why should the meaning-maker and the meaning made be so tightly interwoven? Henry James, from the early *Roderick Hudson* to the late *The Golden Bowl*, frequently builds a plot on the notion that when one buys a desirable Italian signifier an undesirable Italian signified may come along with it. Gilbert Osmond's obsession with the Roman coin belongs to his fierce devotion to *convention,* in the most oppressive sense of the word, and James's novel dramatizes the strength of this bond. In Ferdinand de Saussure's theory of the sign, convention alone keeps a signifier attached to a given signified. The Italian practice of convention (including the judicious use of convents), Henry James so acutely makes clear, is one of the very things that attracts the American with aristocratic pretensions. In this example, a degree of overdetermination joins the elements of the Italian Sign. Not only is it the product of a conventional bond, as Saussure would say, but it is also a Sign, as Henry James is at pains to specify, whose very theme is convention.

Along any good residential street of the American Gilded Age, the Italianate signifier abounded floridly enough in the precincts of brownstone mansions that its need for a signified might seize on any handy object of projection. And the streets themselves were full of Italians, not only of desirable Italian signifiers such as the virtuoso violinist Niccolò Paganini or the Shakespearean actor Tommaso Salvini, but also of undesirable Italian signifieds, poor and dubious personages whose manner, whose physical persons, whose inarticulate intensities all made them perfectly plausible agents of vice, ignorance, violence and depravity.[11]

A Protestant attachment—even a Puritan attachment, as in Nathaniel Hawthorne's *The Marble Faun*—to the desirable Italian signifier found itself connected to the undesirable signified with a degree of conventional force that functioned quite independently of actual conditions in the streets of the United States—conditions, however, that it was easy to imagine prevailing in the streets of Little Italy. One was aware of the prior fact that the streets of Italy itself were captives to a similar conventional bond. In the United States the economy of the Italian Sign worked somewhat differently, although the effect was remarkably similar. Among the most popular and successful writings in Italian during the years of the Great Migration were the crime novels of Barnardino Ciambelli, *I misteri di Mulberry, I misteri di Bleecker Street,* and many others.[12]

The Great Migration

We have examined (in chapter 4) the commonplace that many immigrants never felt themselves to be Italian at all until they left Italy. This commonplace has many implications, particularly for the immigrants' discovery, long and often painful as it was destined to be, of the actual structure of the Italian Sign as it existed in the world outside Italy. It was not automatically evident that the existence of a panorama of brilliant Italian signifiers such as the American Renaissance cityscape would operate as rigid convention returning the Italians from Italy to that set of undesirable conditions perpetually associated with the Great Migration.

In Italy itself, connections between the desirable signifier and the undesirable signified, theoretically real enough as they may have been, often did not present themselves with any clear outline or seem to have any clear impact on the daily lives of Italians. Regardless of class origin, any Florentine may kneel before the bejeweled wonder-working image of the Assunta. The walks and parks of Rome belong to everyone, as if these were the very pleasances that the Senate and people of Rome had inherited from Julius Caesar. Many continuities invisible and visible give a sense of social coherence to Italian life. The political and commercial fabric of *comuni*, the intricate root-and-branch systems of *parentela*, profound attachments to ancient places and to inherited roles—all these factors have often served to keep the contradictions of the Italian Sign at a considerable distance from the consciously lived experiences of people in Italy. The Italian Sign only became visible as such when a person left those places and attachments behind, when the local and personal and familiar suddenly resolved themselves into the national and international, so that a person was no longer *fiorentino, genovese, napoletano, barese,* or *palermitano,* but definitively and irreducibly Italian. And then began the adventure of discovering just what that actually meant in the world.

The Italian American Sign

This discovery becomes a basic and continuing condition for the creation of an Italian American literature in the English language. Although the new condition may impose on any immigrant Italian innumerable necessary shocks and adjustments, for a writer many of these changes can remain muted as long as discourse goes forward in the dialect of *Corriere della Sera* and *Il Messagero*.[13]

The Italian Sign becomes the Italian American Sign when American English can fully participate in producing and reproducing the conditions of undesirability that the American Renaissance requires in the Italians of the Great Migration.

Writers experience and express the discovery of their new condition most sharply when they begin to operate in the language and discourse of the American Renaissance, which carries with it a powerfully overdetermined conventional bond subtending the condition of the Great Migration. Accordingly, the English language, for the first writers who enter it bearing the Italian Sign on their backs, was not always a hospitable ambient. Many immigrants wrote as if their arrival in the English-speaking world had given them a new kind of bitterness. "The red plague rid you," as Caliban says to Prospero, "for learning me your language!"[14] One of the earliest Italian Americans to publish verse in English, the revolutionary poet Arturo Giovannitti, clearly transfers his enormous resentment of the immigrant condition onto the language that has institutionalized that condition. His poem "To the English Language" is spoken from within the Italian American Sign, where the immigrant Italian signified needs to overcome his incapacities to effectively deploy the powerful American signifier:

> To the English Language
> Athlete, builder of towers, digger of chasms,
> O navigator of all the great seas, escalator of all the heights,
> I have put my hands in your hands to grapple with you,
> And I have understood you, your strength and your anger,
> You the deed that has become word.
> O abandoned foundling of a thousand orgies of men and
>   gods
> Picked up night after night upon all the doorsteps of the
>   earth,
> Beggar and burglar, law giver and pirate, lavisher of gifts,
>   hoarder of booties,

Raw, rugged, unharmonic, miserly collector of music,
Unloved worshipper of all the graces,
You shriek, you moan, you growl, you rustle, you roar,
Aye, and you sing, too, but you are unhappy,
For you cannot weep and be holy.
Bestial like all flesh arut and in pain, all-enveloping like the
     fog,
All-hiding like the clouds,
All-stirring like the wind,
You are neither of the earth nor of the skies, but just thyself,
     unknowable and lonely like death.
How I would love you, O fierce One, were you not so
     untiring and cruel and so grasping and selfish a denier
     of truth!
But I admire you in awe and I acclaim you;
For you and I are strangers, but we meet often,
You and I are enemies, but we have a habit of truces
And often feast and get drunk together, at the same table
     with the flesh of the same quarry from the gourd of
     the same song.
Like two rival hunters after the chase.[15]

"You the deed that has become word." In Giovannitti's poem, the English language and the oppressive system the immigrants need to negotiate become the same thing.

Caliban's image of a red plague is remarkably apt for the response of many Italian Americans to the combination of signifiers and interests that pressed down on the Great Migration. Not a few were the Italian American intellectuals who gravitated to that extreme form of the Italian signified that is represented by violent politics. Gaetano Bresci, the silk-worker anarchist who returned to Italy from Paterson, New Jersey, to assassinate King Umberto I during the boat races at Monza on July 29, 1900, was not the most notable of these radical activists. There were many such, particularly after the Lawrence strike in 1911.

But the most famous Italian American revolutionaries were the two anarchists, Nicola Sacco and Bartolomeo Vanzetti, who in 1920 were arrested for a robbery and murder in the holdup of a Brinks truck in South Braintree, Massachusetts. Vanzetti, by far the more eloquent of the two, made clear that his entire life amounted to an utterance in the hostile language of a hostile society. He regarded his arrest as a badge of honor. He wrote to his father in 1920, urging him to speak of it: "Do not be silent, silence would be shameful."[16]

In an interview given after he had been sentenced to death in 1927, Vanzetti spoke to Philip D. Stong of the North American Newspaper Alliance in words that have achieved an undying fame, memorably presenting the deeds of his life as having an eloquence he could have achieved in no other way:

> If it had not been for these thing, I might have live out my life talking at street corners to scorning men. I might have die, unmarked, unknown, a failure. This is our career and our triumph. Never in our full life could we hope to do such work for tolerance, for joostice [*sic*], for man's onderstanding of man, as now we do by accident. Our words—our lives—our pains—nothing! The taking of our lives—the lives of a good shoemaker and a poor fish peddler—all! That last moment belongs to us—that agony is our triumph.[17]

Vanzetti portrays his own life as precisely what Giovannitti calls a "deed that has become word"—in this case the English word of an Italian immigrant in the United States. Vanzetti's eloquence in English was not accidental. He understood its life-and-death importance in his situation, and he struggled mightily to master the language during the seven years he spent in prison before his execution.

The trials placed Sacco and Vanzetti firmly in the signified half of the Italian Sign: they were, in the opinion of the nativist Judge Webster Thayer, good examples of everything undesirable about Italian immigrants. In Vanzetti's last speech before sentencing, he made it clear that he understood how the economy of the Italian American Sign had placed him where now he found himself:

> This is what I say: I would not wish to a dog or to a snake, to the most low or misfortunate creature of the earth—I would not wish to any of them what I have had to suffer for things that I am not guilty of. But my conviction is that I have suffered for things that I am guilty of. I am suffering because I am a radical and indeed I am a radical; I have suffered because I was an Italian, and indeed I am an Italian; I have suffered more for my family and for my beloved than for myself; but I am so convinced to be right that if you

could execute me two times, and if I could be reborn two
other times, I would live again to do what I have done
already. I have finished. Thank you."[18]

Louis Joughin and Edmund M. Morgan, who studied Vanzetti's development as a writer, have analyzed his contribution in terms that deserve
to be cited:

> Vanzetti . . . indubitably wrote literature. Within a relatively
> short time he extends the scope of his vocabulary and also
> enlarges his understanding of single words. He makes mod-
> erate progress in the idiomatic complexity of the language,
> and shows surprising vigor in the construction of imagina-
> tive phrases which lie between the domains of neutral speech
> and crystallized idiom. However, it is Vanzetti's mastery of
> the English sentence which unquestionably establishes his
> right to a place among the creators of our literature. His
> grammar is at times faulty, and his uncertain phonetic basis
> occasionally causes him trouble. But in cadence, in the total
> rhythmic force of English prose, Vanzetti comes very close to
> mastery. (p. 500)

Sacco and Vanzetti's execution in 1927 was a world event to be sure,
but it was also a turning point in the history of the Italian American
Sign. Among the tens of thousands of protestors in Union Square the
night of their electrocution was the 16-year-old bricklayer Pietro
di Donato. After the execution took place, he crossed the street and
entered the New York headquarters of the Communist Party.
Di Donato's joining the party was a definitive moment in his career and,
accordingly, in Italian American literary history. The Communists gave
the young bricklayer—who had not attended school since age twelve
when his father died—an education in politics, history, and literature.
Summers spent at Communist Party of America camps in the country
gave di Donato the benefit of intellectual conversation and introduced
him to the leading themes of modernism in arts and letters. The effects
of this radical schooling are evident throughout *Christ in Concrete,*
where one sees what di Donato has assimilated from his exposure to the
lessons of modern experimentation in the arts. Clearly he has been a
student of futurism, of Joycean stream-of-consciousness, of collage and
montage. Di Donato's translation of Abruzzese dialect into English

prose has, among its other purposes, an attack on the sign that has kept the Italian immigrant subordinate to the Italianate culture of the American bourgeoisie.

It was not, in di Donato's case, a question of transforming immigrant manners. It was a question rather of transvaluing them. To his dying day, di Donato played the working-class hero, using strong language and dressing more as a bricklayer than as a writer frequently invited to deliver himself in university seminar rooms. Indeed, in those places, he often dramatized his own distaste for authoritative discourse. He might have been speaking as Caliban: "You have taught me language; and my profit on't / Is, I know how to curse" (I, ii, 365–66).

That level of frustration grows out of his failure to complete the transvaluation. *Christ in Concrete* has a utopian program built into it. It means to represent the intellectual order of the workers' camp and the communal ethic of the tenement feast as occupants of the superior position, so that the Great Migration in effect takes precedence of the Renaissance. It intends to be a revolutionary gesture, but in the actual event its fortune was not good. Shortly after publishing *Christ in Concrete,* di Donato found himself facing the draft. Rather than fight in World War II, he declared himself a conscientious objector, an act of resistance that effectively sidelined his career for the next two decades, marooning his utopia in the pages of his masterpiece.

Revolutionaries use their deeds as words. In di Donato's enterprise, that strategy aims to reverse the order of the Italian American Sign, changing the position of the immigrants. No longer the inarticulate signified, they acquire the role of the signifier, the articulate masters of the Sign. This maneuver focuses on the political reality that anyone can aspire to speak and on the structural reality that a signified is also another signifier in a subsequent Sign. Di Donato, for all his verbal powers, rested the force of his argument equally on the actual grim exploitation to which his writing stood witness. For the reversal he postulated to have an effective life beyond the revolutionary novel, an actual change of situation would need to take place.

Reconstructing the Italian American Sign

Writers are, of course, more accustomed to using words as deeds than the converse. Words are difficult weapons to use effectively, however, when meaning to undermine a regime profoundly rooted in the very structure of language. As long as the Anglo-Americans are able to sustain a cultural dominance that Italian Americans must recognize as a form of the Italian Sign, then escaping the underlying conventional structure of that Sign is very difficult, if not impossible, for Italian Americans. Such a situation means that the Americans prepossess the desirable signifiers that belong to the Italian Sign and project on the immigrants and their descendants the qualities that belong to the undesirable signified. The structure of this semiotic machine inevitably produces resistance in writers who find themselves effectively silenced by it. These writers need not be revolutionaries in the strict political sense, but they may instead insist on their right to command the sign of their condition. Some Italian American writers turn their attention to the weakest point of this dominance—the cultural pretensions of the Americans.

Many immigrants were not the inarticulate and uneducated undesirables that met conventional expectations. Often an Italian immigrant with a good classical education can find plenty of holes in the façade of American culture.[19] The first Italian American writer to achieve a serious literary reputation in English, the immigrant Emanuel Carnevali, for example, writes with considerable bitterness concerning the fabric of American civilization:

> O altars of a little comfort, altars of a dyspeptic god gone
>   crazy in America for lack of personality
> (hamburger steak, Irish stew, goulash, spaghetti, chop suey,
>   and curry!) O lunch-room counters!
> O tripods of a little secure religion, tripods of a little secure
>   beauty! O kitchen fires!
> O bedraggled romances, O alcoholic ladies in crimson and
>   green mists, O
> women so cheap and ingratiating, O sacrifices for you,
>   ladies, of all the flesh and all the brains! O saloons!
>
> My malediction on the cowards who are afraid of the word
>   (the word is a kind sweet child, a kind sweet child!)
>   Malediction on the sacrifices of the dumb and deaf!
>
> Hesitating everywhere, hesitating fearfully,
> The few poets, they who weigh with delicate hands,
> Walk in the unfrequented roads,
> Maundering,
> Crying and laughing
> Against the rest.[20]

Like much of Carnevali's writing, these verses depend for their critical authority upon his peculiar position among immigrants as master of the Italian—indeed of the European—signifier. Carnevali scrutinizes America and Americans through the eyes of one who has seen something better. In his autobiographical writing, he chronicles his education in the "best" *licei* and the "best" *collegio* in Italy. From this position he scrutinizes without mercy the critical divagations of the dictatorial Ezra Pound:

> There is a word which one associates with Dostoevsky's works—Sorrow; as we think of Walt Whitman the word may be Joy; for Mr. Pound the word is Irritation. Irritation inspires him and he inspires irritation in his readers. Here he had made a translation of Laforgue in which Mr. Pound achieved a thing worthy of observation: he was true to the letter (almost) of the original and at the same time had betrayed and desecrated it. Laforgue's satires are veiled by a delicate and almost humbly haughty modesty, and they have a sorrowful humble way; this becomes boisterous in the translation, reminding one of what Billy Sunday did to Christ. (p. 118)

Carnevali's critical self-possession rests on a familiarity with European literary modernism. Not every American writer in 1921, whether immigrant or native, will have read Laforgue, much less have had so firm a grasp of his paradoxical stance. Indeed, Carnevali evokes Laforgue's "delicate and almost humbly haughty modesty" as a metonym for his own strategies of surprise. Throughout his work, Carnevali evidences his mastery of the European Sign as a qualification allowing him to undermine its American appropriators. He not only demonstrates his ability to deploy the European and Italian signifier, but at the same time he dramatically lives out the undesirability of the Italian signified. Indeed, one might say that he caricatures that undesirability. He is variously poor, wheedling, lascivious, ungrateful, schizophrenic, and unkind. He presents a complex front at all times, as if he were the contradictions of the Italian Sign, all joined together and up and walking about in New York and Chicago. In sum, Carnevali presents himself in postures quite as paradoxical as those of the self-deprecating Laforgue.

Thus it is that Carnevali does not, repeat not, restrict himself to his mastery of the desirable Italian signifier. To do so would be an act of pretension, and he would thereby render himself awkwardly vulnerable

to all the evidence of those many Italian undesirabilities that attach to
him. Such undesirabilities richly abound in the American cities he fre-
quents. Carnevali's willingness to place this contradiction in the foreground of his self-portrayal gives him his powers of self-deprecation. He
can take down the pomp of Americans who appropriate the Italian signifier but neglect to address the numerous Italians who humbly stand,
as it were, in the courtyard among the inarticulate signified. Ezra Pound
emerges from Carnevali's pages as a self-deluded fraud talking mainly to
himself:

> Men are forces within the world and when they become con-
> scious one hears an exaltation or a complaint; and these are
> signs of life. Ezra Pound has estranged himself, and this is
> our resolution: He cannot talk to us. By us, I mean readers,
> artists, and shoemakers. We—and I stand together with all
> the fools he so hopelessly curses—acknowledge that there
> are many things the matter with us; but we realize that he is
> not really interested and we consider his talk an intrusion.
> (p. 120)

The moral authority that Carnevali achieves by presenting himself as
reader, artist, and shoemaker helps him to discredit the American
appropriation of the Italian signifier, an act he paints as crude and self-
deceptive. The Anglo-American reconstitution of the Italian Sign evidently lacks any of the ancient usages that in Italy blunt the edges and
defeat the cruelties built into that arrangement.

   Carnevali constructs an Italian American position that belongs not
only to the American signifier, but also to the American signified. A
writer cannot master the Italian American Sign without coming to terms
with the American sign.

The American Sign

The American Sign, as Carnevali encounters it, has a profound linguistic dynamic. Mastery of English is the key to the American signifier,
which constitutes itself an American Sign specifically by its ability to
subordinate other languages, other systems of signifier. Language
inevitably has a dialectic force.

   That is to say, like any Italian American writer, Carnevali has
entered the social and cultural order of Anglophone America, an act
with familiar consequences. "I am not as my fathers were—broader

means and nobler influences have fallen upon me."[21] These are the words, uttered in 1826, of the Cherokee Buck Watie who had taken the name Elias Boudinot and entered a Christian seminary. In this position, Watie/Boudinot speaks as an Indian but gives important evidence of what the English-speaking world has taught him to desire. He tells his white audience that the Cherokees wish to establish a printing press and a seminary; they wish to learn English, sensible as they are of the many advantages that can flow therefrom. The lamentable history of the Bureau of Indian Affairs is the closest thing we have to a history of the American Sign in its coming-to-be. By the end of the nineteenth century, Native Americans had established a role of barbaric speech into which wave after wave of immigrants found themselves involved. Carnevali, in his mastery of the American Sign, quite spectacularly demonstrates his ability to generalize this position. He tells the story of a fellow tenant in a West Side rooming house in Manhattan. The cleaning woman strikes this man's door with her broom at two in the afternoon, and he comes out of his room in a white fury, saying to Carnevali, "I gotta fon the dictionary book, see?" This obscure utterance becomes the occasion for some comic dialogue that ends with Carnevali's recognition that the man wanted the dictionary "because he wanted to throw it at me."

> It was the damn broomstick had awakened the man and all his night with him, his night darker for his ignorance of English. . . . One day he passed my door—the Pole—for he was a Pole—shouted
> "No can shleep. Some people make noise. I fix." (p. 122)

Then, parenthetically and without warning, Carnevali places himself inside the darkness of this man's ignorance, and dramatizes for the reader the predicament of the person in New York who knows no English:

> (You pass in the street and look sideways, and down, and sideways. Hardly you lift your eyes from the broken sidewalk before you. As far as to see the sky your head never twisted. And a mother points you out to her child—ah, look at the bogey man! They are against you, all they who know English. They enjoy knocking at your door, they who won't see how much you need your sleep, and you must get angry at yourself because you know these creatures who go to

vaudevilles, and put on queer neckties on Sunday morning,
you know they're awake, making a noise they have a right to
make, being more beautiful than you, knowing English.
What was it came to you and revealed itself? What were the
new things? The wife you married in Poland is dead one year
now, two months after the wedding, and that new thing for
you was the shape of eternal misery. All are against you.
When you open your eyes you see a broken sidewalk, broken
with its own tragedy and not your own. If you would sometimes lift your eyes you would see a sky that can't possibly
have anything to do with you. . . .) (pp. 122–23)

Both inside and outside, the narrator Carnevali—who never speaks of
his own difficulties while learning English, who indeed seems not to
have experienced any—shows here by reflection that he understands
profoundly the position of the linguistic outsider, at the same time
demonstrating his own silent overcoming of such difficulties.

Carnevali publishes his work in *Poetry* and in *This Quarter*,
alongside writers such as Ezra Pound, James Joyce, Carl Sandburg,
William Carlos William, Ernest Hemingway, Kay Boyle, and Marianne
Moore. He demonstrates a mastery of English, transcending itself as a
mastery of international culture, which has become a lodestar for Italian American intellectuals.

Professing English

Professing English turns out to be one of the best-traveled roads to mastering the Italian American Sign. As a road of development, it enters the
institutional dialect of national languages by way of the English departments, which are its best-established disciplinarians. Many an Italian
American writer has gone as far as acquiring a doctorate in English or
American literature as part of the vital equipment for a career of literary
work that is not necessarily going to confine itself to scholarly contributions. Sandra Mottola Gilbert, Fred Gardaphe, Josephine Gattuso
Hendin, Frank Lentricchia, Arthur Clements, Louise De Salvo: these are
a few well-known writers whose entry into the Italian American language has carried with it the passport of a doctorate in English language
and literature as part of a career devoted at least equally to the production of work in fiction, poetry, or memoir. Such writers often display a
formidable grounding in international literary culture. Sandra Gilbert is
one of the founders of women's literary history in the United States and

is also a distinguished poet; Fred Gardaphe is a leading historian and
critic of Italian American literature who is also a gifted writer of fiction;
Josephine Gattuso Hendin made her reputation as a critic and historian
of American fiction before publishing her highly praised novel *The
Right Thing to Do*; Frank Lentricchia made his name as a literary theo-
rist writing in dialogue with leading thinkers on both sides of the
Atlantic and has published several novels in recent years; Marianna De
Marco Torgovnik is the author of an important study of primitivism in
the arts and has published a prizewinning memoir; Arthur Clements
began his career as a critics of seventeenth-century English verse and
later became a widely published poet; Louise De Salvo was a well-
known Woolf scholar before making a name for herself as a distinguished memoirist. This career pattern has the air of a deliberate
strategy, worthy of a long-meditated purpose. Acquiring university credentials, which are in fact a form of legal entitlement to speak English
in public, takes a long time.

Some writers, although not professional academics, frame their literary work with a mastery of the tradition of American Italophilia. This
is a variant of the Ph.D.-in-English strategy, and it does not always
require a graduate degree. For the writer who can use it successfully,
this strategy allows for travel that needs less institutional baggage. The
best-known, the pattern-setting, practitioner of this strategy is the poet,
editor, columnist, lecturer, television host, professor, writers' conference
director, and translator of Dante Alighieri, John Ciardi (1916–1986).
Ciardi first made his name as an American poet very much in the English department tradition of American poetry, an epigone of John
Holmes, Archibald MacLeish, Louis Untermeyer, and Robert Frost.
Ciardi put himself forward as a virtuoso of the iambic pentameter line,
which he believed to be "the norm of English metrics." His virtuosity
came "less out of a strict observance of that line, than out of a sensitively trained memory of it with wide variations in the number of light
beats in a foot."[22] That sensitively trained memory was a claim even
more powerful than Carnevali's self-mockery, although it could and did
often lead the poet into speaking with more authority than others found
comfortable. Nonetheless, it provided a remarkable degree of entitlement. Ciardi never stopped insisting on his qualifications as an American (not Italian American) poet. His friend Archibald MacLeish
commented on the paradoxes of this career in 1971, when Ciardi published his autobiographical sequence *Lives of X*, a work containing a
higher proportion of Italian material than Ciardi was conscious of
previously having used. MacLeish expressed "thanksgiving to God for a

live rhythm of English again, begotten by an Italian on the stale roots up in this North-East corner where things still grow and smell and rustle but with no rage in them." And he asked Ciardi, "But I wanta know: how did a writer of your origins come to the Anglo-Saxon the way you have?"[23]

Ciardi's strategy was, basically, to build on this mastery of "the Anglo-Saxon" as a leading theme of his career. This not only freed him from the stigma belonging to "a writer of your origins," but at the same time it allowed him to enter Italian literary culture through the American door. His translation of *The Divine Comedy* became a standard text in American colleges and universities, with an oblique reference to the translator's linguistic background as the son of immigrants but with considerable emphasis on his scholarship and on his mastery of American English prosody. Ciardi rested so strongly on this mastery that he often forgot the outline of his own trajectory. After reading the galleys of his *Selected Poems* in 1983, he wrote to a friend, "I'm a bit surprised at how heavily Italo-American it is."[24]

Ciardi preferred to rest his position on credentials that had more to do with the American Renaissance than with the Great Migration. This allowed him subsume the national/imperial *italianità* he derived from Leopardi and to speak firmly with the amused loftiness he acquired in a year (1956–1957) at that temple of American Italophilia, the American Academy in Rome. He wrote a famous poem "S.P.Q.R. A Letter from Rome" articulating this position. The epigraph is "Sono Porci Questi Romani," ("These Romans are swine"). These are the first three strophes:

It does for the time of man to walk here
by the spoken stones forgotten, a criss-crossed empire
sticking its stumps out of cypress. Not a name,
though stone-carved, but what a name
is plastered over it. Not a god in town
but watched his temple changed into a quarry.

And could smile: "Let them change Heaven and Earth
if they can: nothing changes the Romans.
Men as they were, beasts as they were, they are.
Their God across the Tiber has stone arms
stretched from his dome like crab's claws. Can claws hold them?
A thousand Kings have held Rome; none, the Romans.

Who knows the goats better than the goatherd?
We piped their lambing from burnt rock
and made a people of them. Rank and graceless
they are a people yet. And ours. All arches
are one to them. Whatever name is on them,
they read their own. Exactly as we give it."[25]

The voice is that of the gods themselves, and the self-assurance belongs
to that of the current imperial masters, the Americans, snug and smug
on the crest of the Janiculum. It is an aside to Ciardi's American readers: "We are all Caesars here together."

The poem so perfectly embodies Ciardi's tactic of appropriating
the lordly appropriators that it came as a particularly bitter shock to
him, one he never tired of recounting, that after the poem appeared in
The Atlantic, Robert Lowell wrote him an admiring letter "to say it was
the best Italian American poem he had read. As if he wrote Am and I
wrote It-Am" (Cifelli, 438). Ciardi never quite worked out the formula
for the position he had so brilliantly devised. He was forever complain-
ing that there was no "Am-It aesthetic," as indeed there is not. But
there was, as the praises of friendly Anglo readers such as Lowell and
MacLeish made it evident, such a thing as an Italian American semiotic
and, consequently, the possibility of an Italian American position. There
was, indeed, for a poet who prided himself on his memory and his ear
for echoes, no escape from the historical pressures that call forth such a
position.

There is no end of ways to respond to such pressures. The critic
Fred Gardaphe constructs a history of Italian American narrative that
uses Vichian historiography as a way of accounting for the possible contributions of Italian American writing to American literature:

> I suggest that we are now witnessing the descent of Anglo-
> American literature into a *ricorso.* Having moved through a
> *corso,* from the *vero narratio* (telling it like it is) of its earli-
> est writers, evidenced by oral traditions and autobiographies,
> through the mythic period (or the mimetic), which is histori-
> cally characterized as the period from the American renais-
> sance through high modernism, American literature, as
> traditionally defined, has reached its period of decadence. It
> has become, in John Barth's phrase, a "literature of exhaus-
> tion." According to Vico, the next stage of cultural history

will be a descent into barbarism. While such a descent is
inevitable, it can be delayed by a return to the culture's fundamental principles, its roots. What is enlivening American
culture at this time, and delaying its descent, is the rise of the
artists and intellectuals of America's other-cultural components. These writers are like Vico's plebeians (the powerless),
who struggle for the laws and the benefit (the power) of the
patriarchs (the ruling class). The contemporary struggle for
inclusion by minority cultures into the mainstream of the
dominant culture parallels the political struggle that Vico
sees in the movement from aristocratic rule to a popular
democratic liberty.[26]

Mastering the Italian American Sign in this manner always means
simultaneously identifying with the "minority culture" aspect of the
Italian signified at the same time that one lays claim to the "divine"
aspect of the Italian signifier in the form and manner that this signifier
is possessed and deployed by the American Renaissance. The fancy
footwork required to achieve this degree of double-sidedness sometimes
confused Ciardi himself. Gardaphe's lucid outline shows the advantage
to be gained by appropriating not only the poetic power of the Italian
signifier, as Ciardi did, but also its theoretical sophistication. Ciardi,
ever concerned to make himself clear to the general audience of the *Saturday Review*, where he wrote a weekly column, or to the vast audiences he commanded at colleges and universities all over the country,
avoided the complexities of continental theory and restricted himself to
familiar common-sense Anglo-Americanisms that Archibald MacLeish
and other midcentury American poets he admired could recognize and
approve. This approach kept Ciardi from seeing the true extent of even
his own Italian American poetry, much less from recognizing the contradictory positions occupied by writers who needed to make a claim on
the Italian signifier at the same time that they needed to negotiate the
disabilities that came along with the status of the Italian immigrant, the
Italian signified par excellence. Gardaphe uses Vico to map the surprising effectiveness of Italian American autobiography as a machine for
revising and reinvigorating the standard American autobiography that
is constitutional to American literary history.

    Gardaphe, accordingly, is able to propose a myth of complemen-
tary American decline and Italian American ascent. The notion that Italian immigrant autobiography could revise American national myth was
first introduced by William Boelhower, whose studies in this arena have

given Italian American writing a claim on the very heart of American studies.[27] Boelhower, an American who has taught at the universities of Trieste, Venice, and Padua, married to a Venetian and living on the Lido, exemplifies the kaleidoscope of possibilities that are hidden in the expression *Italian American*. Ciardi and many others who have considered the question that this expression poses have had difficulty escaping the conventional bond that ties it to a specific kind of immigrant culture, a chronotope bounded on one side by the forensic anthropologist and on the other by the American Renaissance. But in the present case, as elsewhere in this book, we are driven to see the interaction of languages and places, of cultures and civilizations, as endlessly various.

Dialect and Dialectic

Whenever two languages interrupt one another in a discourse, questions of relative power arise, and, we can also say, questions of signification. One language can mean—can imply the existence of—another. A language's definition can include its subordination of, or to, another language in a given situation. An Italian language calls itself a dialect as part of the dialectic of centers and peripheries, of historical authorization and deauthorization. Similarly, an Italian American language is the site of decisive engagements among the protagonists who speak in it.

Such a conclusion leaves open, as indeed it should, the question of how to invent an Italian American literature. The fields of possibility are limited only by the chances of history, incalculable and not to be discussed. The writer who enters the contention continually reexamines the dynamics of the Italian Sign, the American Sign. On these fields, the writer's own powers and fortunes of combination are the decisive engagements. Without endorsing Boelhower's or Gardaphe's conclusions, seeing that their arguments focus effectively on the conventional bond that casts the Italian American as the shadow of the Renaissance is possible. Disrupting that bond means in effect rearranging the diagram of the Italian American Sign.

Interruption can be both aggressive and amicable, even amorous, at the same time. Giovannitti's "To the English Language" is not only an attack, but also a *strambotto*, a ritual insult, full enough of real animosity, to be sure, but at the end a way to seal the pact that joins poets across boundaries of convention and of language. "Like two rival hunters after the chase."

This Italian speaker of English is transformed through struggle. His subordination becomes an embattled equality, and this is the

beginning of a genuine field of literary possibilities. The writers we have
examined in this book have all passed such moments. Many of the early
Italian American writers in English dealt with this struggle. Some
embraced a kind of embattled self-subordination. Constantine Panunzio, for example, in his *Soul of an Immigrant,* gives the impression that
an Italian, if he tries, can be more of an Anglo-American Protestant
than even someone born to that condition.[28] Panunzio's solution has
had a limited appeal, but in recent years other writers have taken up the
question from distinctly more secular positions. Louise De Salvo's memorable essay "A Portrait of the *Puttana* as a Middle-Aged Woolf
Scholar" gives a thorough survey of the contradictions that greet an
immigrant granddaughter who aspires to the authority of a literary
scholar in English.[29] Similar themes inform every page of Marianna De
Marco Torgovnick's memoir.[30]

Today, Italian American writers aim to revisit Italy to transvalue
their Italian signifieds. Even in English, such a journey always implies
revisiting the economy of the Italian Sign itself, because the English-
speaking Americans with every trip to Herculaneum and every drink at
Cipriani's, have made the desirable Italy so very much their own that
they have continued to give new charms to the old signifiers and new
undesirabilities to the old signifieds.

Many strategies have been employed in the struggle to interrupt
the workings of this old economy of conventions. There is the strategy
of immigrant historiography. Some Italian Americans have simply recat-
egorized the immigrant past and its humble protagonists, making those
persons quite as much objects of historical pomp as the kings and ministers who usually attract such ritual attention. Many examples of this
kind of work exist, of which perhaps the best known is Robert Orsi's
The Madonna of 115th Street, which focuses on the cult of the
Madonna di Monte Carmelo in Italian Harlem, using a thickness of historical detail itself so excellent as to imply a similar excellence in its historian's academic formation.[31]

Others have wrestled with the persistence of an old semiotic
mechanism. Such writers continually point to the progress Italian
Americans have made in social status. This is the strategy of protest.
Italian American organizations—the Commission for Social Justice of
the Order Sons of Italy in America; the National Italian American
Foundation (NIAF); UNICO National, the Italian American One-Voice
Committee; and the American Italian Defense Association among
others—have taken part in a steady drumbeat of protest and complaint

ever since Paramount Pictures announced in 1970 that it was going to make a movie of Mario Puzo's best-selling novel *The Godfather*. No amount of protest seemed to lower the intensity of interest in this film and in the others that followed it—the two subsequent *Godfather* movies, as well as *Mean Streets, Goodfellas, Analyze This,* and many others. As recently as 1997 the National Italian American Foundation sponsored the publication of a volume of essays whose subtitle bravely suggested that the vogue of such films was over: *Beyond the Godfather; Italian American Writers on the Real Italian American Experience*.[32] All this right-mindedness seems, however, largely to have failed of its object. In 1999 HBO unveiled its new dramatic television series *The Sopranos*, a work that gives entirely fresh depth and detail to the old Italian American Sign, so much so that Camille Paglia, at a NIAF symposium on the subject, praised *The Godfather* because of the dignity it accorded to its gangsters, in contrast to the working-class stereotypes that populate *The Sopranos*. Why is it that protest has made so little impact here?

Or why is it, one might also ask, that Italian American social progress, the motorized column of commuters streaming out to the suburbs every night, the famous stockbrokers and corporate CEOs with Italian American names, the prizewinning actors, composers, and playwrights, the fashionable painters and even literary critics have so little interrupted the production of Italian undesirables on American screens? Commenting on these films, Pellegrino D'Acierno has written that Italian American culture attracts so many undesirable meanings that it has become in effect a floating signifier—one that is with no steady conventional connection to a given signified.[33] *Floating* seems too strong a word to use for a signifier that continues to reinscribe the economy of mastery and subjugation, of desirables and undesirables, that one reads in the Italian Sign as the immigrants learned to experience it. Perhaps *omnivorous* would do better. Regardless, something unaccountable is certainly taking place here. The firmer a grasp Italian Americans achieve on the desirabilities of the Italian Sign, the more vividly they appear to evoke the opposing representations.

Here we see the machinery of the Italian Sign reasserting itself in the progress of the Italian American Sign. As Italian Americans shop at Prada and Gucci, as they spend their summers in Tuscany and the Veneto, as they learn to cook with wood fires and balsamic vinegar, their mastery of the Italian signifier has required the renewed presence of the Italian signified. Seen in this light, the American triumphs of

Fellini, Antonioni, Bellocchio, Bertolucci, and other Italian cinematic
masters in the 1960s seem to lead directly to Coppola's successes of the
1970s. More Italian desirables means more Italian undesirables.

We also have a strategy of acceptance. Some writers choose simply
to inhabit the semiotic space of the Italian American signified but to do
so more richly. Here I place Tina De Rosa, whose *Paper Fish*[34] treats
immigrant daily life as the recurring occasion of a highly charged poetic
prose. Don DeLillo, after publishing almost nothing on this subject, in
his vast novel *Underworld* painted a portrait of the Italian signified in
its grittiest East Bronx incarnation—gangsters, hustlers, and sad little
apartments.[35] The novel sets this portrait deep inside a much larger
panoramic vision of the contemporary world as itself a kind of underworld, a hell of missed chances and misbegotten intentions. The effect is
to make the Italian signified appear part of a general worldwide condition, almost in the manner of an old fashioned internationalist.

DeLillo's reservoir of high-mindedness has preserved him from
protest. Who could object? His Mafia is not so much itself as it is a case
in point, a synecdoche for the reckless ecology of global capitalism.

Some writers approach this circumstance as a dilemma calling for
an analysis of the Italian Sign. In Fred Gardaphe's *Italian Signs, American Streets,* the Italian Sign "is one signifying *italianità,* or the qualities
associated with Italian culture" (p. 20). This allows him to develop a
general strategy for dealing with the dissonance between the Italian sign
and the American street. Anthony Tamburri's investigation of the *Semiotic of Ethnicity* in Italian American writing aims to separate expression
from content (Peircean terms, roughly parallel to the Saussurean signifier and signified), emphasizing that these two are always joined by an
interpretant, which seeks to naturalize their connection. Any utterance,
he says, "will always be polyvalent, its combination will always be
rooted in heteroglossia and dialogism, and the interpretive strategies for
decoding it will always depend on the specificities of the reader's inter-
texual reservoir."[36] Where Peirce puts *interpretant,* Saussure places *convention.* I have followed Saussure as a way of emphasizing the
persistence of the discursive yoke that brings together the desirable and
the undesirable in every instance to complete the Italian or the Italian
American Sign. The interpretant in the case of the Italian Sign is the set
of political, economic, and cultural forces that have collaborated to
keep Italy, so often during its history, a net exporter both of persons
and of value-added goods. In the case of the Italian American Sign, the
interpretant is the American Renaissance appetite for those same value-
added goods and its contemporaneous need for Italian immigrants to

import the cheese and carve the marble blocks their appetites required, as well as to work the mines and populate the railroad gangs who labored to generate the wherewithal that could purchase all this delectable matter.

Another kind of acceptance characterizes the saga of the most famous Italian American waste management consultant: Tony Soprano. David Chase has bluntly inhabited the entire shadowland of the Italian American signified. This shadowland is perhaps best thought of as the unconscious way of life that children internalize when growing up, what Pierre Bourdieu calls a *habitus*. Bourdieu writes, "The *habitus*— embodied history, internalized as second nature and so forgotten as history, is the active presence of the whole past of which is the product."[37] Chase's characters live in a habitus defined by images, desires, acts, and styles of expression that exploit, exaggerate, and caricature the massive history of indignities that belong to the workings of the Italian American Sign. Tony Soprano, as he examines the paintings on the psychiatrist's waiting-room wall in the opening of the first episode, carries this entire habitus in his very physical attitude. An entire history is buried in his body.

CHAPTER 10

The Imperial Sopranos

"Our souls were in our names."[1]

One fragment of Italian stubbornly attaches itself to even the most assimilated Italian American body: the family name. Many no longer use that name itself, of course. Peter Lazzara's daughter Bernadette took her father's first name instead of his last and went into show business as *Peters*.[2] Sandra Mottola married Eliot Gilbert after graduating from Cornell in 1957, and became a major feminist critic as Sandra M. Gilbert (coauthor of *The Madwoman in the Attic*).[3] Salvatore A. Lombino obtained his father's permission to adopt an American pen name and signed dozens of books *Ed McBain* and *Evan Hunter,* as well as *Curt Cannon, Hunt Collins, Ezra Hanson* and *Richard Marston*.[4] But the ancient mark remains legible. People still tell these stories on themselves, even when the name change has proved itself effective. The old names reappear in personal and family narrative long after they have disappeared from birth certificates and title pages. The creator of *The Sopranos* likes to say that he is the grandson of a man who changed the family name from *DeCesare* to *Chase*.[5]

The family Caesar continually returns in this series, like an embodied ghost or a hysterical symptom. *The Sopranos* ripples with imperial Latins. When Paulie Walnuts and Silvio Dante are trying to coerce a Hasidic Jew to give up his share in a motel, they beat him mercilessly, but the man refuses to yield. They are amazed by his willingness to suffer. He explains his behavior by citing the nine hundred Israelites who resisted the legions at Masada, how they died rather than submit. "Where are the Romans now?" he asks, scornfully. Tony Soprano replies, "You're looking at them, asshole"[6] (I, 3).

When Tony Soprano admits to his crew that he has been visiting a psychiatrist because he has been passing out from anxiety attacks, one of them immediately points out, by way of defense, "Julius Caesar was an epileptic" (III, 3), thus elevating Tony's weakness to a proof of Julian stature. This theme in *The Sopranos* is neither minor nor merely decorative; rather it runs directly to the heart of the process that frames the entire series.

David Chase invites viewers to read the series as a fable of his personal psychoanalysis, an invitation that many have taken up enthusiastically.[7] Fragments of his own history appear in every episode. Livia Soprano, Tony's mother, resembles Chase's mother in many details, as he has been at pains to make explicit in interviews. Chase's own teenage daughter plays Hunter Cacciatore, best friend of Tony's teenage daughter Meadow Soprano. When Tony Soprano's Uncle Junior appears in the first episode, Chase's own uncle, also known as Uncle Junior, plays another gangster in the same scene. Tony and Carmela live in a house in North Caldwell, not far from where David Chase grew up. Chase has, of course, not led the career of a mob boss nor of a waste management consultant, as Tony calls himself. But Chase has carried the mark of a Buried Caesar. This is the connection that makes the psychoanalysis work, not so much as an autobiography, but as a rhetorical device. The audience of *The Sopranos* has its own Buried Caesars, a vast field of embodied histories, some of them American, some of them Italian—and all of them, it would seem, able to find themselves in this remarkable fable.

Much of the appeal is straightforwardly psychoanalytic. Chase's personal investment can be said to play on what head doctors used to call an *onomatomania*, an unconscious obsession with a name and all that it means. In this case, two names: *Cesare* and *Soprano*. To identify with the hero of this series means to recognize in oneself both a Caesar and a *castrato* or male soprano. A Caesar here is a sign of the overcompensating ambition of the man who feels himself secretly a *castrato*. A Caesar is the sign of aggressive *italianità,* whereas the *castrato* is a sign of a singer who has lost his tongue, an Italian who has lost his language. And Tony is both of these. Sitting at a sidewalk table dispensing justice in front of Satriale's Pork Store, Tony's is a Caesar, a worthy descendant of Salvatore Marranzano or Michael Corleone. But sitting in Dr. Melfi's office, Tony is a man who recounts dreams of his penis being carried away by birds.[8]

Losing one's name before one is born has the character of infantile circumcision—an irreparable loss, suffered before one can stop it. The series is preoccupied with mutilation and feminization. When Tony decides to get really serious with the reluctant Hasid, he threatens to cut off the man's penis, announcing to his crew, "We're going to finish his circumcision." There are two male characters named Pussy. At the end of the second season, Tony dreams of Big Pussy Bompensiero in the form of a talking fish. Pussy the fish admits to Tony that he has been singing to the FBI (II, 13). The fish theme continues in the third season when Paulie Walnuts brings in a novelty item, a "Big Mouth Billy Bass" mounted on a plaque. This fish, when touched, sings "YMCA," a gay disco anthem of the 1980s (III, 7).

Psychoanalysis glides into cultural and social history here. This investigation is a psychoanalytic archaeology in which the subject is an opera singer. *Soprano* refers obliquely to the canonical Italian gangster of the movies, who is named not only for Julius Caesar but also equally for the singer *Enrico Caruso*: *Cesare Enrico Bandello*, the hero of W. R. Burnett's 1929 novel *Little Caesar,* known then and afterward as *Rico*. "Mother of Mercy, is this the end of Rico?" cries Edward G. Robinson, dying at the end of the film.[9] Rico did not in fact end there but became instead the template for subsequent gangster characters, and in 1970 his name was attached to the draconian conspiracy law that the federal government has in subsequent decades used to incarcerate gangsters, the Racketeer Influenced and Corrupt Organizations Act, known from Day One as the RICO law. The RICO law has in effect fucked all the gangsters, and they speak of it that way. At the opening of the second season, Uncle Junior is living under a RICO indictment and makes the much-quoted complaint, "Federal marshals are so far up my ass, I can taste Brylcreem" (II, 1). At the end of that season, Pussy speaks to the FBI man Skip Lipari of evidence that can be used as "RICO predicates." Later in the same episode, Tony says, "I have predicates up the ass, a fucking RICO case." (II, 13) The logic of the position is the homophobic logic of gay contagion: fucked by a singer, they all become singers.

Tony's psychoanalysis is operatic in many ways. Stylistically, its mode is hysteria: Tony often exaggerates his feelings, and he very frequently shouts or weeps at moments when calm consideration would serve him better. But more important, he "sings" in the sense that he tells this doctor many things that his oath as a Mafioso forbids him to reveal. His circumlocutions and careful avoidances of actionable admissions increasingly have the effect of a shabby charade that fools no one. He is preoccupied that he will be assassinated for his transgressions in Dr. Melfi's office. Rightly so. Uncle Junior is furious when he hears from Livia Soprano about her son's therapy. But, as it turns out, other members of the gang have become singers in the same sense. When Tony admits to Paulie and Silvio that he has been seeing a shrink, both of them shrug and confess to having done the same thing. "I had some

issues," Paulie says, by way of explanation. In *The Sopranos* the femi-
nizing of Caesar is not only the premise, but it is also the problem, the
plot, and the appeal. It is the process that David Chase has devised for
reconstructing the Buried Caesars that constitute so large a topic in Italian American cultural history.

Burnett crystallized the tradition of such Caesars in *Little Caesar.*
How he came to do so is of interest. For the 1958 edition of the novel,
he wrote a new introduction recounting the process of germination that
resulted in this work. He had begun to write a novel to be called *The
Furies,* inspired partly by Al Capone and partly by a sociological study
of the gangster Sam Cardinelli (pp. 16–18). Burnett had—naively, as he
tells it—concentrated on the gangster's moral psychology. But then he
met a young Italian American named John, "the pay-off man for the
biggest mob on the North Side," who gave him a more "practical" out-
look. "I was under the impression that murder—or, as John would have
said it, a rubout—was morally wrong and the murderer was bound to
suffer pangs of conscience and remorse." John disabused him of such
notions. "Was I kidding? Do soldiers in a war suffer stuff like that?
What was the difference if a guy rubbed out Germans or 'impractical'
business rivals?" (p. 20).

> In short, I gradually and painfully acquired from John an
> entirely new and fresh way of looking at the world. It was
> not a pretty way; it was more than a little frightening; but it
> was certainly "practical" and was later taken over lock,
> stock, and barrel by all the tyrants—all the little Caesars—of
> Europe. . . .
>
> I am sure that the title had a lot to do with the book's
> success. . . . Well . . . when I was halfway through the book I
> started to have qualms. Rico, the leading figure, began to
> take on nightmare proportions in my imagination and I
> couldn't help wondering if I was on the right track after
> all—I was afraid I was giving birth to a monster. But then a
> consoling thought came to me—out of the blue or the sub-
> conscious, as you prefer—my leading figure, Rico Bandello,
> killer and gang leader was no monster at all, but merely a
> little Napoleon, a little Caesar. (20, 22)

That is, these gangsters are not only criminals, but they are also military
leaders. They represent the force of a subaltern population struggling to
attain power. This transformation dramatizes the situation of the Italian

American gangster, who now becomes a protagonist in social struggle, an actor in history. Burnett provided this gangster with a genealogy that has become canonical in American culture.

In Burnett's formula, four historical figures are embodied in the Italian American: Mussolini ("all the little Caesars of Europe"), Napoleon ("merely a little Napoleon, a little Caesar"), Cesare Borgia (Burnett cites Machiavelli in the novel's epigraph), Julius Caesar (the most resonant patriarchal icon in imperial history), as well as the famous teller of Renaissance tales Matteo Bandello. All of these figures persist in the colonial narrative of Italian America, and they resurface on Chase's set, like revenants rising through a trap door on an operatic stage. No one can write a Don Juan story without a Stone Guest. The Italian American story always has at least one Buried Caesar. Such Caesars belong to the imperial/colonial imaginary where much of Italian American history has been lived, and the place where American readers have looked to find that history.

Located on Sixty-Second Street in Bensonhurst is an Appia Granite Company. If there were an Italian American via Appia to go with it, one might dig up Albert Anastasia and Joe Colombo among the Roman dreams along the roadside. One would also find the chief Buried Caesars of Italian America, the very ones Burnett names: *Benito Mussolini*, the dictator whose *buon'anima* haunts the colonial imaginary; *Napoleon Bonaparte*, the outsider as a pattern lunatic; *Cesare Borgia*, the Italian evil genius; *Julius Caesar*, the dictator whose ghost haunts the American empire.

Benito Mussolini

One of "the little Caesars of Europe," no Italian made a larger issue of reviving an epic Rome than Benito Mussolini, and no corpse has more resonance in postwar Italian American history than his.

In 1928–1929, Il Duce was a topical reference to W. R. Burnett and to Mervyn Le Roy, who directed the film *Little Caesar*. In subsequent Italian American memory, Mussolini is much more. He dramatizes most vividly the problem of a colonial culture. Italian Americans found that Mussolini spoke powerfully to their predicament.[10] Fascism as an imperialist gospel was a triumph of signifier over signified, a violent campaign of overcompensation for a history of perceived humiliation. Such overcompensation is an old story in Italian politics. People began to grow passionate about Rome, for example, in the mid-fourteenth century, forty years after the Popes had abandoned it for the more sensible, more centrally located, and far more secure seat of Avignon in Southern France.[11] In subsequent centuries, Renaissance ideology would grow from a powerful sense that Rome's glorious past had come to shame its ignominious present. The same theme drove the Risorgimento, from the poems of Leopardi down to the Pelion-upon-Ossa style of the *Vittoriano*. By 1923, when Mussolini assumed office, the long history of humiliation in Italy had acquired new chapters among the Italian colonies in the factory towns of New England and at the ports of entry in New Orleans and New York. Mussolini's heroics soothed the permanently damaged self-esteem of those who had left Italy forever only to find that they carried its long history of woes and sorrows on their skins like scars.

The fall of Mussolini, for these reasons, would have hit many Italian Americans hard in any case. They would have needed to give up their belief in the glorious present and future that many had found comforting for so long. But by the time of Mussolini's death, the war had already removed such beliefs as comforts. No anodyne could soften the bitter truth that Italy had become an enemy nation. On June 10, 1940, when Mussolini declared war on the British Empire, Prime Minister Winston Churchill was asked how His Majesty's Government ought to treat the thousands of Italians who had settled during the past three generations in Great Britain. Churchill replied, "Collar the lot."[12] Italians were rounded up and interned. Many were shipped to Canada and Australia. On July 2, 1940, *H.M.S. Arandora Star*, carrying German prisoners of war and hundreds of British and Scottish Italians to concentration camps in Canada, was attacked by the German U-boat *U47* in the North Sea. Many passengers, including German and Austrian Jewish refugees, went down with that ship. Four hundred forty-six Italian men, most of them subjects of the British Crown, were lost at sea that night.[13] In December 1941, three days after the attack on Pearl Harbor, Mussolini declared war on the United States, an act with severe repercussions for the millions of Italians then living there. In 1942 hundreds of Italian Americans in California were arrested and placed in concentration camps.[14] It had now become difficult and dangerous to be Italian in the English-speaking world. Gay Talese movingly describes the agonized balancing act that his father performed in the WASP-dominated community of Ocean City, New Jersey, during the war. A Calabrian immigrant who had studied tailoring in Paris, Joseph Talese ran a successful business in tailoring, fur storage, and dry cleaning (which he always called "French dry-cleaning"). Talese *père* aimed to be a pillar of the community, donating generously to the church and taking conspicuous part in civil defense organizations. At the same time, he worried perpetually about his two brothers in the Italian army, and his mother who was still living in Calabria, exposed to the dangers of invasion and occupation. Joseph Talese was a cultivated man who studied Italian and Italian American history and was conversant with European high culture, from Italian opera to French painting. During this period, he was especially sensitive to the racist slurs Americans routinely bestowed on Italians. He strove to conduct his business in a dignified posture, always beautifully dressed and serious in manner. When a customer, in a dispute over a dry-cleaning problem, called him a "dago," he went after the man with "a long, heavy pair of scissors that were customarily used for cutting thick material or fur skin."[15]

However, many Italians could still cherish pride in the much-advertised achievements of Fascism and hope the war might not end too disastrously for Italy. But the actual fall of Mussolini was a defeat that went beyond something disappointing or humiliating and became instead a moment of indelible national shame. Nothing could erase from memory the spectacular public violation of the corpses of both Mussolini and his mistress Claretta Petacci on April 28–29, 1945. Roy Palmer Domenico's summary conveys the horror of the events:

> Shot at Giulino di Mezzegra on the shores of Lake Garda, [Mussolini's] body was brought back to Milan. The corpse and those of fourteen companions were hideously beaten, trampled, and spat upon until they were barely recognizable as human beings. Photos of the dead Duce reveal something inhuman: caved-in eyes, twisted, misplaced features. He had no face left. Beaten and blood stained, the bodies were then hanged upside down at a gas station facing the enormous dusty Piazzale Loreto, where the Fascists had publicly executed fifteen partisans some months before." [16]

Nonetheless, the redeeming spirit survived among those whom Italian history had marooned in the colonies. Mussolini's ignominious fall did not stop postwar Italian Americans from attempting to raise Caesars who might overcome centuries of abjection both in Italy and Italian America. The most energetic and resonant attempt was Mario Puzo's 1969 novel *The Godfather*. Puzo aimed to restore a paradoxical dignity to the body of an Italian American Caesar. Santino "Sonny" Corleone, Don Vito Corleone's eldest son, provides the occasion. When the Don is incapacitated after an attempt on his life, Santino takes over

as heir apparent. The first thing he does is compile a list of people to be
killed. His younger brother, Michael, returning to the Family (always
capitalized in this novel), finds it "chilling to see the list of names [San-
tino] had scribbled down, men to be executed, as if he were some newly
crowned Roman Emperor" (p. 93). But Santino's reign is as brief as it is
bloody. Thanks to the treachery of his brother-in-law Carlo Rizzi,
Sonny is gunned down in the mob war he has insisted on fighting. Don
Corleone accompanies the body to the funeral home and speaks to the
undertaker, Amerigo Bonasera:

> "I want you to use all your powers, all your skill, as you love
> me," he said. "I don't want his mother to see him as he is."
> He went to the table and drew down the gray blanket.
> Amerigo Bonasera against all his will, against all his years of
> training and experience, let out a gasp of horror. On the
> embalming-table was the bullet-smashed face of Sonny Cor-
> leone. The left eye drown in blood had a star-fracture in its
> lens. The bridge of his nose and his left cheekbone were
> hammered into pulp.
> For one fraction of a second the Don put out his hand
> to support himself against Bonasera's body. "See how they
> have massacred my son," he said. (p. 258)

Bonasera, the first person to appear in both the novel and the film, is a
key character. The undertaker's art expresses the need to restore dignity
to bodies that history has mutilated.

Bonasera's art is an emblem of the purpose of the narrative, which
turns on Sonny's "massacre" (where the Italian *ammazzare* peeks
through the English of the dialogue) and on his failure as a Caesar. This
failure attacks a central belief for the characters in this book. Michael's
chilling announcement to Carlo Rizzi—"You have to answer for Santino" (p. 435)—is the culmination of the many-armed revenge plot that
he summarizes in the words, "I want to square all the Family accounts
tonight" (p. 436). This squaring of accounts in fact makes Michael a
new Caesar, as his wife is startled to discover, when the Dons formally
acknowledge his supremacy: "Kay could see how Michael stood to
receive their homage. He reminded her of statues in Rome, statues of
those Roman emperors of antiquity, who, by divine right, held the
power of life and death over their fellow men" (pp. 438–39). This
moment of vindication is repeated at the end of Francis Ford Coppola's

1972 film *The Godfather*. By that time, however, certain elements of the project had already begun to seem suspicious.

A real-life attempt to raise the ignoble Caesar had taken place in the few years that intervened between the novel and the film. In spring of 1970, Joseph Colombo, the leader of what had been known as the Profaci Family (afterward known as the Colombo Family), responded to the investigations of federal prosecutors by claiming discrimination. He organized an Italian American Anti-Defamation League and held a rally in Columbus Circle on June 29, 1970. Although many scoffed at a civil-rights movement led by a known gangster, among Italian Americans existed a strong feeling that the federal government was targeting them unjustly. Forty thousand people turned out to protest with Colombo. A year later, while preparing for a second rally at Columbus Circle, Colombo was shot in the head. His bloodied body became the object of considerable speculation. He survived until 1978 but never regained consciousness. The conclusion of this story was not encouraging. Colombo did not succeed in stopping the federal government's move to perpetuate the degradation of the Italian American Caesar. Colombo's protest tried to ignore the colonial economy of force that supported it, the underlying contradictions that produce a Caesar in the first place.

Such contradictions are a steady feature of Italian and Italian American political life. According to the classic formulation of Antonio Gramsci, Caesarism is the result of a situation in which the forces of violence reach a sate of abstract equivalence: "One might say that Caesarism expresses a situation in which struggling forces balance one another in a catastrophic way; that is, they balance one another in such a way that the continuation of the struggle cannot lead to any conclusion except reciprocal destruction."[17] Mussolini's Caesarism was a direct result of a policy of blind self-contradiction: the attempt to overcome a slave's history by declaring oneself a master. Mussolini aimed to present Italy, a nation that had been for centuries colonized by other European powers, as if it had become a major power, one that could colonize others. Mussolini did not invent this policy. It first great practitioner was Francesco Crispi, who as prime minister in the 1890s led Italy into a disastrous invasion of Somalia. Crispi believed that war and empire were the ideological elixirs that could give to the colonized Italians a sense of national purpose. The Mafia ideology, as practiced by Joseph Colombo and preached by Mario Puzo, attempted something similar. It addressed the problem of Italian subordination in the United

States by constructing a version of the world in which Italian Americans are in charge. Its ideology is Caesarism, even as its reality is criminal marginality.

The Godfather II (1974) moved the chronicle of the Mafia Caesar into a bleak algebraic landscape where its inherent contradictions lay open to the naked eye. The film strongly responded to the inherent deception and quasi-Fascist *romanitas* of *The Godfather* itself and of Mafia grandiosity as it had expressed itself in Joseph Colombo's delusional career. Michael Corleone appears in this film as an emperor whose triumphs gradually isolate him from all human relations: he divorces his wife, terrifies his children, and orders the murder of his weak-willed older brother Fredo. Triumphant but isolated at the end of the film, he might be the Emperor Claudius, alone in a room with his family ghosts and his fears of assassins.

Napoleon Bonaparte

When Burnett writes that Rico is "no monster at all, but merely a little Napoleon," he evokes the gangster's self-justification: he is a soldier— and by extension, revolutionary, an insurgent, an emperor in the making. Burnett at the same time refers casually to a crowd of images that associate themselves with the name of Napoleon when it is uttered in connection with Italian immigrants.

Small and dark. Napoleon belongs to the history of how Europeans think of Italians. He is the emperor of contradictions. On the one hand, he signifies a glorious ambition. As the first man to be crowned King of Italy in many centuries, Napoleon was so ubiquitous in Italian culture that pieces of him are buried everywhere in the collective Italian memory, even in Italian America. On the other hand, Napoleon signifies total abjection. Almost since the beginning of hostilities between the United Kingdom and *la République Française* in the 1790s, it has been normal in Anglophone culture not only to belittle Napoleon but also to do so in racial terms. Carlyle faithfully reflected English conversation on the subject when he referred to Napoleon as "a dusky-complexioned taciturn boy."[18] The name *Napoleone,* with its suggestion of *Neapolitan*, has long carried racist freight among speakers of Italian and English alike. The man Napoleon was proverbially short. It is a pleonasm to call someone a *little* Napoleon when there is no *large* one. Not only short and dark, Neapolitans were also considered congenitally inferior: "Steerage passengers from a Naples boat show a distressing frequency of low foreheads, open mouths, weak chins, poor features, skew faces, small or knobby crania, and backless heads."[19]

Worth watching. The immigrant Neapolitan/Napoleon leaves Italy an object of interest to police anthropologists. In the United States, anthropologists give way to psychiatrists. *Napoleon* is a periphrasis for a person with delusions of grandeur, and *Neapolitans* are also considered to be prime candidates for the attentions of mental health doctors:

> Before the boards of inquiry at Ellis Island their emotional instability stands out. . . . They gesticulate much, and usually tears stand in their eyes. When two witnesses are being examined, both talk at once, and their hands will be moving all the time. Their glances flit quickly from one questioner to another, and their eyes are the restless, uncomprehending eyes of the desert Bedouin between walls. Yet for all this eager attention, they are slow to catch the meaning of a simple question, and often it must be repeated.[20]

When Tony Soprano enters Jennifer Melfi's office at the beginning of the first episode of *The Sopranos*, David Chase places his whole saga firmly under the professional gaze that has framed the entire tradition of Italian American gangster narrative. It is an epic cycle of lunatics. Throughout *Goodfellas,* the Scorsese film that David Chase calls his "Koran," wasted bodies proliferate in a counterpoint with a rising tension of male anxiety and criminal insanity. The chief bearer of these two syndromes is Tommy DeVito, played by Joe Pesci as a monumentally insecure tough guy, always ready to savage and kill anyone, even the innocuous teenage bar boy Spider (Michael Imperioli), whom he imagines to be doubting or challenging his male primacy. "Napoleon," says Silvio Dante, comparing Bonaparte with Tony Soprano, "he was a moody fuck too" (I, 12).

The surveillance industry. The myth of congenital inferiority combines with a reputation for social dysfunction, ensuring for Italian immigrants a permanent place under the eyes of the surveillance industry. Generations of social workers and psychiatrists have devoted themselves to keeping these immigrants under control. Such characters figure in the novels of Garibaldi La Polla, where the Baptist missionaries teach the Harlem Neapolitans to brush their teeth and go to Sunday school, and in the autobiographical fiction of Mario Puzo, where the Boys'

Club social workers give the Tenth Avenue Neapolitans two weeks in the country among the Anglo middle class every summer while, back at home, the mental health police tie up their father in a straitjacket and lock him away forever in an asylum. During World War II, hundreds of Italian Americans lived under the watchful eyes of the War Department in internment camps. After the Apalachin meeting in 1957, when the FBI rounded up dozens of gangsters at a meeting in the mountains, the level and scope of surveillance expanded. In more recent decades, the RICO law has allowed for an entirely new level of intrusion. James Goode in *Wiretap: Listening in on America's Mafia* presents transcripts based on "years of audio tapes from bugs and wiretaps permitted under a statute that allows FBI agents under court order to break and enter and install transmitters to record private conversations of suspected criminals. Hundreds of court orders for such wiretaps [have been] issued."[21]

The Sopranos explores surveillance as a narrative device in every conceivable way. The opening sequence is shot, in effect, over the shoulder of James Gandolfini as he drives from the Lincoln Tunnel to his home in suburban North Caldwell. The members of the Soprano Family go through all the comic rituals of avoiding surveillance while using the anonymous pay telephone that previous Mafia films have made canonical (the boss Big Paulie Cicero in *Goodfellas* is the occasion of much comic byplay on this theme). The entry of the surveillance mode has offered endless opportunities for showing Caesar in his nightgown. Mafiography now often employs a mode of constant humiliation even when representing moments of spectacular dominance. In *The Sopranos*, one boss suffering from constipation actually expires of a heart attack while sitting "on the crapper." One might almost say he died of ignominy.

With its usual intricate intertextuality, *The Sopranos* sends up the art of the FBI–surveillance narrative. The feds follow the gangsters as if they were fans dogging movie stars. *The Sopranos* makes the most of this government-sponsored voyeurism, referring itself often to the vast literature that federal agents have produced for those who would like to share their experiences as mobster watchers. On one occasion, *The Sopranos* shows federal snoopers focusing an enormous amount of energy on placing in the basement of the Soprano house a microphone concealed in a gooseneck lamp. This lamp refers to perhaps the most famous episode in the by-now long history of FBI men who monitor the private conversations of gangsters and then write books about what they hear. In *Boss of Bosses, The Fall of the Godfather: The FBI and*

Paul Castellano, former agents Joseph F. O'Brien and Andris Kurins tell the story of some remarkable discussions that took place within earshot of a bug they had placed in the kitchen telephone of Big Paul Castellano's famous house ("The White House") atop Todt Hill in Staten Island. Castellano had fallen in love with the family's Colombian maid Gloria Olarte. After some hesitation, she accepted his advances, but, as the agents learned, Castellano suffered from impotence. His lovemaking always ended in frustration. So he decided to rectify the situation with a penile implant. The former agents provide the following transcript of the moment when Castellano informed his lover of the heroic step he was about to take:

> "Operation?" said the maid. The word scared her.
> "They put a rod in."
> She said nothing.
> "They make a cut, down here . . ."
> She averted her eyes and cringed. "No, don't tell Gloria."
> But the Godfather was full of bravado that night. "No big deal. They make a cut, then they take a small drill and make a tunnel. The rod goes in, and then, *zhup,* it works just like a . . . like a gooseneck lamp."
> "Gooseneck?" said the maid. "What ees gooseneck?"
> "Gooseneck," repeated the Godfather. He found it was a difficult thing to explain. "Like, flexible. But not too flexible. Like, you can make it turn up, or you can make it turn down."[22]

The word scared her. She averted her eyes and cringed. But the Godfather was full of bravado that night. He found it was a difficult thing to explain. How do the former agent–writers know these things? Because they have only telephone tapes to go on, they must do a lot of imagining. They begin to transform the raw material of mechanical snooping into the voice of omniscient narrative. And the reader of *Boss of Bosses* may wonder, "Are these surveillance transcripts, or is this a novel?" Mafia narrative nowadays often focuses so obsessively on surveillance, real and imagined, that its point of view merges with that of the camera, the microphone, the narrator, and the audience.

Surveillance concentrates itself on the corpse of any Caesar, large or small. Paul Castellano's gooseneck lamp and the ducks who steal Tony Soprano's penis keep easy company with the scattered pieces of

Napoleon Bonaparte. A recent Google search turned up 242 entries for "Napoleon's penis," most of them recounting the story that the item in question was sold at auction in the 1980s for a large sum of money and that over the years it had shrunk and darkened to the size and color of a grape.[23]

Cesare Borgia

In naming his hero *Cesare*, W. R. Burnett calls up the image of the most vivid Buried Caesar of the Italian Renaissance. Three centuries before there was Napoleon, another figure terrified and startled all the dukes, monarchs, and viceroys who thrived and struggled in the rich states of fifteenth-century Italy.

Whatever Cesare Borgia may have been in actuality—and plenty of disagreement exists on the matter—he became a dark hero in the story of his time and place.[24] Protestant pamphleteers and historians found in him and in his father Rodrigo Borgia, Pope Alexander VI, mountains of evidence showing all that was wrong with papal institutions of the High Renaissance. Alexander VI was politically and territorially ambitious, and his son, whom he appointed Captain-General and Gonfalonier of the Papal States (commander of the papal armies), was the willing and effective instrument of papal expansionism. Call it farsighted protection of Italy against outsiders or call it gross rapacity, according to your predisposition, but the Borgias made themselves felt. In the end, history was not to favor them, to be sure, and the reputations that survived them were not good. Taken together, the lives of these two men were destined to become copybook samples of simony, nepotism, luxury, greed, hypocrisy, lust, incest, pride, violence, stealth, absolute immorality, and unquenchable ambition; they threatened all good order and were the sworn enemies of virtue. They stopped at nothing. Poison rings and masked assassins belonged to their normal bag of tricks, alongside more familiar forms of malfeasance such as selling church titles and benefices or buying the votes of cardinals in papal elections. The Borgias were destined to become the greatest villains of the Reformation. In the memory of English Protestants, Cesare Borgia was as much a devil as his great admirer, the Florentine secretary Niccolò Machiavelli, who immortalized Cesare's career in *The Prince*.

Machiavelli presents Cesare Borgia as the model of how a new prince ought to act. Borgia is also a key figure in the history of the dismembered peninsula that preoccupied Machiavelli, who presents Borgia as a man who might have overcome the destiny of Italy, once an empire and now a set of fiefdoms making foreigners rich. According to this reading, Cesare Borgia's career made it clear that with a firm purpose, an appropriated authority, a loyal army—as well as with unlimited daring, well-disciplined speed, and an unwavering courage—one might unify Italy. In all these particulars, we might say, Machiavelli's Cesare Borgia proved to be an avatar of Napoleon Bonaparte, himself the latter-day Caesar who would blaze a path for the unifiers of Italy who would follow him in a subsequent generation. Machiavelli's pragmatic arguments for the effective use of cruelty by a tyrant have come to seem like the beginnings of a rational approach to political calculus. But for centuries those same arguments supported the lurid reputation that still clings to his name. Even today, Machiavelli's reasoning can still astound one. Perhaps the single most notorious example of it occurs in chapter 7 of *The Prince*. Machiavelli tells how Cesare Borgia employed "a cruel, efficient man" named Remirro de Orca to subdue the city-states Borgia had conquered in the Romagna. "In a short time this Remirro pacified and unified the Romagna, winning great credit for himself." This, Machiavelli points out, was not a convenient development:

> Then the duke [Borgia] decided that there was no need for [Remirro's] excessive authority, which might grow intolerable, and he established in the centre of the province a civil tribunal, under an eminent president, on which every city had its own representative. Knowing also that the severities of the past had earned him a certain amount of hatred, to purge the minds of the people and to win them over completely he determined to show that if cruelties had been inflicted they were not his doing but prompted by the harsh nature of his minister. This gave Cesare a pretext; then, one morning, Remirro's body was found cut in two pieces on the piazza at Cesena, with a block of wood and a bloody knife beside it. The brutality of this spectacle kept the people of the Romagna at once appeased and stupefied.[25]

The Saint Valentine's Day Massacre, Albert Anastasia at the Sheraton barbershop, Joe Colombo at Columbus Circle rally, Joey Gallo at Umberto's Clam House, Carmine Galante in the garden at Mary's Italian American Restaurant, Paul Castellano on the sidewalk outside Spark's Steak House—these bloody spectacles were all meant to broadcast assertions and warnings that make sense in the secret language of the Mafia. They have an even more vital role in the operatic culture to

which *The Sopranos* has added its many contributions: Martin Scorsese
and David Chase have made a specialty of showing bodies cut and
bleeding in every conceivable situation.

Since Burnett, other Mafiographers have made a point of studying
Machiavelli's *Prince*. Michael Corleone's famous holocaust of his enemies at the end of *The Godfather* reflects Mario Puzo's understanding
of Cesare Borgia's similar act at the moment when he wished to consolidate his victories over the city-states of the Romagna. In one coup,
Michael dispatches all his enemies, just the sort of political theater that
Machiavelli recommends:

> So it should be noted that when he seizes a state a new ruler
> must determine all the injuries that he will need to inflict. He
> must inflict them once for all, and not have to renew them
> every day, and in that way he will be able to set men's minds
> and rest and win them over to him when he confers benefits.
> . . . Violence must be inflicted once for all; people will then
> forget what it tastes like and be less resentful. (p. 32)

Puzo, indeed, is said to have regarded the Borgias as the template of the
whole tradition:

> He swore that they were the original crime family, and that
> their adventures were much more treacherous than any of
> the stories he told about the Mafia. He believed that the
> Popes were the first Dons—Pope Alexander the Greatest
> Don of all.[26]

Puzo, according to his partner Carol Gino, worked for years on his
"Borgia book," a historical novel that she finished after his death and
published as *The Family*. He never completed the work himself because
he felt he could not afford to give that much time to a project he did not
believe would make money. But even as he continued to write Mafia
novels, he returned to this one as a constant source of fresh ideas:
"Although he would write several other novels in the years between,
each time he had difficulty writing, each time his creativity felt blocked
or he felt discouraged, he went back to the Borgia book for inspiration
or refuge" (p. 416).

Gino introduces her discussion of this matter with a remarkable
sentence: "Mario was fascinated with Renaissance Italy, and especially
with the Borgia family" (p. 415). She appears to regard the Borgia

family as a special case of which "Renaissance Italy" is the general condition. If this was Puzo's idea about the Renaissance, he was not alone.
Machiavellian schemers have long been a staple of Renaissance storytellers. When W. R. Burnett named his gangster Cesare *Bandello,* he
made reference to Matteo Bandello (1480–1564), the man of letters
whose *Novelle* became the primary popular source in France and England for knowledge of life in the noble courts of Italy during the late-fif-
teenth and early-sixteenth centuries. Bandello does not chronicle the
Borgias directly, but many other families whose doings are torn from
the same book of horrors. Bandello, through translations in William
Painter's *The Palace of Pleasure* (1566–1567), provided the source tales
for *Romeo and Juliet, Measure for Measure,* and *The Duchess of Malfi.*
Puzo's notion of the Renaissance as the natural ambient for the Borgias
is not an uncommon one and is regularly promoted by stage representa-
tions of Machiavellian characters:

> Typically, the Machiavel believes that he . . . is living in an
> unsettled age or in an age that he can easily unsettle. The
> wealth and privileges of the society are ripe for plucking, and
> it seems to him that advantage lies with those who are intel-
> ligent and resourceful enough to exploit opportunity. The
> dull will be at a disadvantage and so too will those cribbed
> and confined by religious or moral scruples; the complacent
> will be handicapped. The Machiavellian villain confides his
> schemes to the audience and boasts of his prowess. Some-
> times he triumphs; other times, when victory seems within
> reach, he falls suddenly and spectacularly. The audience
> watches his progress fascinated and vicariously enjoys his
> successes; however, if his moment of reckoning arrives, the
> audience may turn smug and enjoy his defeat.[27]

Puzo, in sum, draws on the self-renewing throng of murderer dukes and
poisoner cardinals and schemer lieutenants who populate Elizabethan
and Jacobean plays, characters who appeal to people with a sense of
living in uncertain times. Italian American Caesarism depends for its
effectiveness on the belief that not only the gangster but also the audience of the gangster, is living in an unsettled age. This is the underlying
premise of Nicholas Pileggi's narrative of Henry Hill in *Wiseguy:*

> [Henry speaks:] "To me being a wiseguy was better than
> being president of the United States. It meant power among

people who had no power. It meant perks in a working-class neighborhood that had no privileges. To be a wiseguy was to own the world."

. . . For Henry and his wiseguy friends the world was golden. Everything was covered. They lived in an environment awash in crime, and those who did not partake were simply viewed as prey. To live otherwise was foolish. Anyone who stood waiting his turn on the American pay line was beneath contempt. . . . To wiseguys, "working guys" were already dead. Henry and his pals had long ago dismissed the idea of security and the relative tranquility that went with obeying the law. They exulted in the pleasures that came from breaking it. Life was lived without a safety net. They wanted money, they wanted power, and they were willing to do anything necessary to achieve their ends.[28]

Puzo and Pileggi are working in the tradition of Matteo Bandello: these "Italian stories" (as Martin Scorsese calls them) address profound doubts and uncertainties that characterize the times in which they are set.

Such moments are favorable not only for the Machiavel or the Mafioso but, in Gramsci's terms, for actual Caesars who arise directly out of incoherent conditions. "Caesar, Napoleon I, Napoleon II, Cromwell, etc. Compile a catalogue of the historical events which have culminated in a great 'heroic' personality."[29] In effect, Puzo and Pileggi address the colonial version of this same theme: "Compile a catalogue of the historical events which have led to a *little* 'heroic' personality."

Little Caesarism occurs among colonizers who are themselves colonized. In this context, the very name *Caesar* expresses the confrontation of incompatible opposites. *Caesar* expresses, on the one hand, the colonizing imperative, the Italian who represents the expanding empire of Crispi, Giolitti, Mussolini; *Little,* on the other hand, indicates the colonized *abjectio,* the Italian who lives inside the guilty and diseased projections of the American empire with its larger forces and its more successful imperative.[30] Although these two positions struggle against one another, together they project the phantasm of an imperial leader who is at the same time hopelessly excluded from real power.

"Either Caesar or nothing." *Aut Caesar aut nihil.* This motto of Cesare Borgia's expresses the drive to power that has tormented Italian politics since the Middle Ages. It might just as well have been adopted by Cola Di Rienzo in 1348 as by Borgia in 1500. Its headlong exagger-

ation speaks to the place that this figure has long held in the iconogra-
phy of Italy's frustrations. As a summary of the motives that have
driven some Italian American gangsters, it explains the recklessness of
such doomed individuals as Joe Colombo and Joey Gallo.

Julius Caesar

After the assassination of Julius Caesar in Shakespeare's play, Mark
Antony gives a famous speech about the stab wounds in the dead dictator's body. It is the beginning of Caesar's long afterlife, wherein he
comes to resemble Osiris, a god whose corpse is eloquent, magical,
ubiquitous. Caesar's *disjecta membra* can be found almost anywhere.
Robert Venturi finds Caesar in Las Vegas.[31] Brutus meets him at
Actium:

> *Enter the* GHOST OF CAESAR
> Brutus: How ill this taper burns. Ha, who comes here?
> I think it is the weakness of mine eyes
> That shapes this monstrous apparition.
> It comes upon me. Art thou any thing?
> Art thou some god, some angel, or some devil,
> That mak'st my blood run cold and my hair to
> stare?
> Speak to me what thou art.
> Ghost: Thy evil spirit, Brutus.
> (4.3.275–282)

Like Great Caesar's ghost, Little Caesar too, from the start, has shown
to Anglo-America the face of its own evil spirit. In the 1920s, that evil
spirit was Demon Rum, the exasperated projection of America's
hypocrisy about the alcohol it craved and consumed. Along with alcohol came women, murder for hire, gambling, drugs, and eventually the
image of a large underworld empire. That image has grown in the popular mind as faithful dark reflection to America's ever-expanding global
ambitions.

Italian American Caesars have an old plausibility for Anglophone
audiences. Shakespeare's plays long ago accustomed these audiences to
Romans who were English-speaking Italians. This is especially the case
in *Julius Caesar*, where Antony and Octavius routinely go by the names
Antonio and Octavio.[32] And thanks to Shakespeare, these Anglo-Italian
Romans have proved irresistible to generations of film producers. The

Roman Empire is traditionally staged in an inverted minstrel show mode, where pale English faces conceal dark Italian hearts. On the Shakespearean back lots of Hollywood and Cinecittà alike, consuls and aediles, bloviating in speaking-coach British, pay heady lip service to ideals of civic responsibility and heroic self-sacrifice, at the same time that they practice a Machiavellian politics of remorseless ambition and pitiless revenge—stabbing, poisoning, garroting, beheading, disembow-eling, chopping, and cooking one another in casseroles. The evergreen popularity of this tradition had one of its extreme points in the *Master-piece Theater* series based on Robert Graves's novels *I, Claudius* and *Claudius the God.*[33] Here was an entire season of one-hour dramas showing several generations of the Caesar family with a backstage inti-macy previously available only to its physicians and coroners.

Caesarean bodies in the Shakespearean mode have resonances that reach to the heights of power in the English-speaking world. They form part of the mythology of the British royal family, another invention we owe to William Shakespeare, which has long sustained itself by a mix-ture of high and low representation. The pattern sample comes from the alternation between court and tavern in the so-called *Henriad,* Shake-speare's saga of the troubled Plantagenet family. Such alternation has been traditional—nay, canonical—down to the present in representa-tions of the British royal family. Loyal monarchists in the twentieth cen-tury have regularly and freely speculated on the bodily fluids of several heirs to the throne. They reveled in an orgy of abject speculation during the family's protracted expulsion of the fetishized body belonging to Diana Spencer, Princess of Wales. This process gathered in intensity during several years of much-discussed adultery, separation, and divorce, reaching its climax in the James Bond spectacle of high-speed collision under the banks of the Seine, followed by the slow-motion dead march along the streets of Westminster. Don Philip Tartaglia and Don Emilio Barzini at Don Corleone's funeral in Calvary Cemetery under the Kosciusko Bridge did not muster better poker faces than did the grim, vindictive royals as they sat before Diana's casket in Westmin-ster Abbey, listening to Elton John singing "Like a Candle in the Wind." In the United States, where there are no actual kings, Democratic presi-dents (Roosevelt, Kennedy, Clinton) have provided the sperm and lymph for speculative minds to ponder, and even, in November 1963, the savaged corpse of a Caesar. The Kennedys have become the cham-pion millionaires or Tribunes of the People in U.S. society, embracing the causes of the poor and the racialized. Jack Kennedy's body carried all the contradictory magic that belongs to a prince among paupers.[34]

His corpse, in retrospect, has come to belong more and more intimately
to the myth of magical pseudo-British sovereignty, where the Myth of
Camelot has kept company with the Eternal Flame and the Riderless
Horse, while the aura that Mark Antony gave to Caesar's corpse continues to radiate from the Warren Commission Report and its photographs
of Kennedy's shattered skull, its diagrams of the grassy knoll, its pint-
by-pint chronicle of the final minutes in Parkland Memorial Hospital.

A word about how this works. Just as *Caesar* is a name for political doubleness, so Julius Caesar's body was the meeting place of irrec-
oncilable forces. As Michael Parenti tells this story, Caesar was born to
a line of plutocrat patricians but earned the hatred of Cicero, Brutus,
Cassius, Metellus Cimber, and many other members of his class
because he set limits to their powers of appropriation at the same time
that he introduced entitlements, protections, and opportunities for
many in the less-privileged ranks of republican Rome. Hated as a class
traitor, the aristocrat Caesar died a death more appropriate to a revolutionary than to a patrician and distinguished military leader. His destiny implies a double vision, as Machiavelli himself points out in a
slightly different connection, when explaining to the Magnificent
Lorenzo de' Medici why he has dared to dedicate his treatise *The
Prince* to so august a personage:

> Nor I hope will it be considered presumptuous for a man of
> low and humble status to dare discuss and lay down the law
> about how princes should rule; because, just as men who are
> sketching the landscape put themselves down in the plain to
> study the nature of the mountains and the highlands, and to
> study the low-lying land they put themselves high on the
> mountains, so, to comprehend fully the nature of the people,
> one must be a prince, and to comprehend fully the nature of
> princes one must be an ordinary citizen. (*The Prince*, pp.
> 3–4)

Writing about Julius Caesar without considering a similar double perspective is impossible. Plutarch, Suetonius, Tacitus, Cicero—anyone
who writes about Caesar—must contend with his intense relationship
with the plebs or common people of Rome and their intense relationship with him. Shakespeare's staging of the funeral speeches of Brutus
and Mark Antony before the Roman mob remains today perhaps the
most vivid caricature of democratic process in literature. Caesar's fatal
belief in his own destiny grows directly out of his visceral relationship

with the people of Rome. In this, he is one with Napoleon, Mussolini, and Cesare Borgia, all of whom fell victim to their own demagoguery: all of them believed themselves exempt from the rules and limitations that bound ordinary leaders. All of them came to bad ends partly because of their faith in their own invincibility.

Mafia narratives call for a similar double perspective. These stories, particularly *The Godfather* and *The Sopranos,* are written on the fault line that joins immigrant poverty with American glory. From one angle, they present vaudeville caricatures of the dysfunctional underclass, characters who speak in Damon Runyon Brooklynese and pass long afternoons handicapping horses in the dim light of go-go bars where they brutalize their girlfriends in the back rooms. On the other hand, they tell dynastic fables of aristocracy, placing the Family above individuals and the Code above even the Family. The Family theme provides the immigrant gangsters an ideological connection with the great Roman aristocrats they so much admire. Cassius plays on the family pride of Brutus in convincing him to betray Julius Caesar, his greatest friend and benefactor. "Family values" have become a political slogan in the United States justifying all manner of crimes, from personal vendettas to class conspiracy, in the name of dynastic prosperity.

> A lot of the killing revolved around the family. . . . Endless vendettas. The family is the safekeeper of revenge. They keep the idea warm. They nurture it, they promote the conditions. It's like those sagas of crime in the movies. People respond to Italian gangster sagas not just for the crime and violence but for the sense of family. Italians have made the family an extremist group. The family is the instrument of revenge. Revenge is a desire that almost never becomes an act. It's a thing most of us are limited to enjoying in the contemplation alone. To see these families, these crime families, many of them blood relatives, to see them enact their revenge is an uplifting experience, it's practically a religious experience.[35]

In Don DeLillo's *The Names,* the Italian-family-as-extremist-group becomes an abstract model of the dynamics of revenge. The family serves as a model for understanding the focus of the action, a killing cult (not Italian) whose motives resemble a pure act of contemplation. With a Kabbalist concentration on the power of single alphabetic characters, this group chooses to assassinate people whose initials coincide with the name of the chosen site for assassination. The killers sometimes need to wait a long time for the victim to arrive at the place of execution. The destinations and persons chosen are obscure, and the only evident connection joining them is their initials.

DeLillo employs initials with a similar resonance in *Underworld,* his novel about the Italian family as an extremist group. This is DeLillo's fable of what the Mafia means in American society.[36] Published in 1997, it reads like a prologue to *The Sopranos,* which made its debut two years later. *Underworld*'s central character is Nick Shay, an Italian American who, like Tony Soprano, has pursued a career in "waste management." Nick, with a Bronx Mafia childhood to remember, has dropped his father's name Costanza and now goes by his mother's maiden name. "He left her for a time before I was born. That's why I carry her name, not his" (p. 105). "I live a quiet life in an unassuming house in a suburb of Phoenix. Pause. Like someone in the Witness Protection Program" (p. 66). Stories of name changes routinely draw attention to the original name: "My father's name was James Costanza. Jimmy Costanza—add the letters and you get thirteen" (p. 102). Underline the initials and you get Jesus Christ and Julius Caesar. Costanza is a target:

> He went out to get a pack of cigarettes and never came back. This is a thing you used to hear about disappearing men. It's the final family mystery. All the mysteries of the family reach their culmination in the final passion of abandonment. My father smoked Lucky Strikes. The pack has a design that could easily be called a target but then maybe not. . . . But I call it a target anyway and fuck the definitions. (87)

David Chase resembles Nick Shay with his changed name. Nick certainly reads like a model for Tony. After a childhood in which he inadvertently murdered a man, Nick has had a successful adult career as a consultant for Waste Containment, a corporation with a global purview:

> At Waste Containment I've become a sort of executive emeritus. I go to the office now and then but mostly travel and speak. I visit colleges and research facilities, where I'm introduced as a waste analyst. I talk to them about vacated military bases being converted to landfill use, about the bunker system under a mountain in Nevada that will or will not accommodate thousands of steel canisters of radioactive

waste for ten thousand years. The waste may or may not
explode, seventy thousand tons of spent fuel, and I fly to
London and Zurich to attend conferences on rain and sleet.
(p. 804)

As a waste executive, Nick does in earnest what Tony Soprano does as
masquerade (and metaphor—for a career, that is, of "wasting" people).
Nick not only chronicles the discarding of what once what integral to
the American and to the Italian, but he also maintains a methodical fas-
cination with what has been cast away:

They are trading garbage in the commodity pits in Chicago.
They are making synthetic feces in Dallas. You can sell your
testicles to a firm in Russia that will give you four thousand
dollars and then remove the items surgically and mash them
up and extract the vital substances and market the resulting
syrupy stuff as rejuvenating beauty cream, for a profit that is
awesome. (p. 804)

Thy evil spirit, America. Here the son of a Mafioso reflects in meticu-
lous detail how everything that used to be called sacred is now something to be traded in commodity pits. Nick, like Tony, is Caesar's ghost
rising in a junkyard.[37] For Tony, the mashing of body parts has not yet
achieved the postindustrial anonymity of the process Nick Shay
describes. When Furio and Christopher take apart Riche Aprile's body,
they do it in a butcher shop. They need a hose to clean the place afterward. In a Shakespearean moment worthy of *Titus Andronicus,* Tony
kills Ralph Cifaretto with his bare hands, then cuts off the man's head
and carries it out of the house in a bowling bag.

In Mafia stereotyping, the Italian name is the sign that transforms
the body to something terrible, something to be wasted. In *The Sopranos,* the process is returned to the roots of language: *the name itself* is
the thing that has been wasted. There is no *De Cesare.* The name
having been wasted, it haunts the story. Caesar reappears everywhere.
The family Caesar is continually dying and being buried all over again
in this series.

It becomes an emblem for the Mafia story itself, a Caesar that Italian Americans would like to bury and not to praise. They have worked
hard at becoming ideologically correct suburbanites, and they have
advertised their progress in this effort, but no mountain of Boy Scout
badges or college diplomas has been able to cover this corpse so well

that pieces of it do not keep reappearing in the most unlikely and unwelcome places. Why?

One might point out that, after all, the Mafia still successfully operates in the United States and in Italy alike. This objection, while cogent, would hardly explain why the Mafia theme continues to display the level of energy that *The Sopranos* regularly unveils, episode after episode. That a story is true does not mean that a story has any juice: we find accountants everywhere, indeed, we could not run our world without them, but few are interested in hearing about their adventures.

Second, one might explain the energy of the Mafia story by under-lining, as Guy Debord has done, that the Mafia's mode of operation is secret, and thus not only hard to get rid of, but also easy to imagine in every circumstance—shadow and silent partner to the universal specta-cle, infiltrating legitimate businesses, corrupting distinguished statesper-sons, controlling international shipping, commanding its own cadres of doctors and lawyers and priests. This approach gets us much closer to the problem posed by the popularity of this story. The spectacle of con-temporary life is not only universal, but also anonymous. Who is pro-ducing all these effects? The Mafia supplies the illusion of omniscient authorship. God may be dead, but the Devil continues to draw crowds.

Third, one might best explain the energy of the Mafia story by seeing it as the sudden revelation of Italian history in the United States—doubly resonant because it occurs at the place where American history and Italian history encounter one another. The ritual in question is the wounding and obliterating of bodies, the ceremony branding men as Little Caesars. Such a ritual is a moment of embodied history, *habi-tus*, where a set of ancient conditions produces a new set of conditions that reconstruct the past in a way that is both familiar and unrecogniz-able as such. This ritual lives in the half-light of social practice that the sociologist Bourdieu defines as the "principle of regulated improvisa-tions"; that is, the very reason that new ideas tend to look like old ones in social life. It is the very essence of ideological forgetting: "history turned into nature." "The 'unconscious' is never anything other than the forgetting of history which history itself produces by incorporating the objective structures it produces in the second natures of habitus" (Bowdein, p. 56). In short, the Mafia story works just below the line of conscious analysis, the wetlands of ideological reproduction. *The Sopra-nos* has a particular value for the student of this phenomenon because the new situation is always revealing the deep repetitiveness of the event. Every time the characters reveal themselves to be Italian in the worst sense of the word they also reveal themselves to be Caesars in the structural sense of the word. *The Sopranos* is a psychoanalytic discourse that aims to reveal history that is embodied silently.

Resistance to such revelation is the very texture of psychoanalytic process. For this reason, *The Sopranos* makes systematic use of witticisms. If a witticism is surprising, according to Pierre Bourdieu, it is because it "appears as the simple unearthing, at once accidental and irresistible, of a buried possibility" (p. 79). This process allows the buried history to enter the conversation under the radar of one's defenses—either as the analysand or, in this case, as a member of the audience.

We have good reason to dismantle the machinery of branding that operates in the story of the Buried Caesar. The question is not the gangster stereotype but the belief in a fallacious glory, one that stands on self-contradiction and self-deception. *The Sopranos* itself claims that to focus on the gangster stereotype amounts to avoiding the real issue, which is one of self-esteem. Why boast about Columbus, when you have your own achievements to claim (IV, 3)? In many episodes, Chase portrays his Italian American critics as themselves examples of brittle defensiveness. In such defensiveness, one hears the symptomatic throb of the Buried Caesar. Italian Americans have inherited the colonialist habit of claiming the glories of the long-dead—whether the Caesars or the Great Navigators—without pausing to consider the social meaning or moral impact of those glories. The result is often an empty and unlovely self-aggrandizement. Italian Americans may boast of long-ago splendors, but in fact they have made their way in America through a valley of sorrow and ashes. They have few grandiose triumphs to remember. Italian Americans did not conquer Gaul. They did not invade Somalia. And, if they had had a nation of their own, and if it had done such things, they would need to account for them. Italian Americans did not paint the Sistine Chapel ceiling. They did not invent the helicopter. The men who did those things were Florentine artists born before Columbus set sail for the West. Michelangelo Buonarroti and Leonardo da Vinci were men who worked for the pope and the duke of Milan. Italian Americans did not discover America. Columbus was a Genoese working for the king of Spain. Amerigo Vespucci was a member of the Florentine upper class who worked for the Medici bank and the king of Portugal. They were men whose loyalty was not to a nation-state but to money and power. If the Great Navigators had been Italian Americans, or even Italians, then Italian Americans might have inherited some of the booty they brought back to Europe. Fewer of them would then have needed to become rumrunners in Chicago and button men in the Bronx.

They would have been in a position to engage in the higher gangsterism
of the upstanding Massachusetts Puritans who made the slave trade into
the basis of a continental empire. But this was not the case. It is no surprise that, when the Italians arrived in America, they were not happy
with the welcome that met them. An unreflective and brute self-aggrandizement was often the result. Here, again, DeLillo forestalls Chase.
Here is Rosemary Shay, Nick's mother, thinking about the Bronx Italians who produced her gangster husband:

> The Italians. They sat on the stoop with paper fans and
> orangeades. They made their world. They said, Who's better
> than me? She could never say that. They knew how to sit
> there and say that and be happy. Thinking back through the
> decades. She saw a woman fanning herself with a magazine
> and it seemed like an encyclopedia of breezes, the book of all
> the breezes that ever blew. The city drugged with heat.
> Horses perishing in the streets. Who's better than me? (p.
> 207)

Such an attitude of thoughtless pride claims the power of a gangster
without admitting to the guilt that goes with it. *The Sopranos* disman-
tles the pretense. It represents the bitter truth of immigrant life as it continually revives itself even in the luxury suburbs, where any Italian
American doctor or lawyer or professor or stockbroker can be called a
Mafioso, where the achievements of today often bring into vivid relief
the stigmata of yesterday. More important, it represents the bitter truth
of self-contradiction and self-deception. The gangster has two families,
and his divided loyalties dramatically represent those of anyone who
leads a life of deception, accommodation, and hypocrisy.

Italian Americans need their writers. They need John Fante, with
his ironic dismissal of colonialist braggarts. They need Pietro di Donato,
to remind them that the true glories of Italian America grow from the
sufferings of people who endured the cruelties of bosses and the greed
of the rich. They need Garibaldi LaPolla to remember their first
encounter with the arrogance of American Protestant missionaries.
They need Maria Mazziotti Gillan, who speaks for all the Italian
women in black dresses and for all their daughters who had to wear
cheap clothes to school. They need Diane di Prima to demonstrate that
an Italian American life can glorify the simple, the poor, and the ordinary. They need Jerre Mangione to recall what growing up in two
worlds was like. They need George Panetta to remember what not being

white was like. They need Mario Puzo to underline the bitter truth that immigrants did not read Leopardi. They need Gay Talese to recall sustaining Italian pride in the days when Mussolini was invading Ethiopia and declaring war on the United States of America. They need Daniela Gioseffi to recall what speaking the language of the enemy was like. They need Helen Barolini to remind them what carrying an Italian name into the schools and colleges of the American bourgeoisie was like. They will always need Nicola Sacco and Bartolomeo Vanzetti to make plain that there was a time in America when you could die for the crime of being an Italian immigrant. They will always need Carlo Tresca to remind them that Italian politics have often been deadly in Italian America.

Italian culture is a system of prestige as old as written memory and as solid as a Roman coin. The Roman coin, as that immigrant's grandson Henry James once pointed out, is the symbol of an oppressive system as vast as a continent and as unbreakable as one of Plato's archetypes. Italian culture is a system of prestige that stands on the shoulders of untold millions of anonymous slaves and serfs, sharecroppers and prisoners, who cut and carried the huge blocks of marble, built and fought in the huge galleys, planted and harvested the rich crops, spun and wove the splendid fabrics, dug and died in the canals, had sex with and bore the children of, the Great Italy and the Great Italians. In this system of prestige, the rich are beautiful and the poor are invisible. In this system of prestige, the glories of literature and science belong to the rich. The poor cannot pretend to them. In this system of prestige, the rich are good and superhuman, and the poor are evil and subhuman by nature. In this system of prestige, the Italian Americans are like the poor, only worse. The Italian pyramid rests on the poor of Italy, who nowadays at least have a voice in Italian politics. The Italian pyramid also rests on the colonial Italians, who cannot speak a word of the language and would have no voice in Italian politics even if they could, but earn money in America and spend it on Pellegrino water and expensive trips to Rome and Florence. Every time an Italian American raises a hand to the elevate the glories of Italy, that Italian American risks sinking a little further into the mire that underlies the foundations of the old pyramid.

What can writing do?

The Italian *colonie*, old and half-forgotten, are now the writer's memory garden, where the tailor Joseph Talese is still advertising "French dry-cleaning" and the undertaker Bonasera still lays his hand on his heart when the American flag goes by in the parade. Outside the bread bakery, women in black dresses punctuate their conversations with gestures of their powerful hands. My grandfather comes in from the garden, whistling an aria and carrying a huge bouquet of escarole and tomatoes.

The past has encountered the present in Italian America. David Chase has placed the colonized mind in dialogue with the chances of time. Tony Soprano, unhorsed and unmanned, is able to recognize in his own economic interests the actual engine of his self-esteem. It does not depend on the trophies of someone else's victories. This is a powerful first step, always needing to be taken again. The blandishments of history, for any Italian, have a permanent attraction. *O mia patria, si bella e perduta.* Italy, that lost object of desire, continues to gleam on the horizon of Italian America. Supposing this star will ever set would be foolish. Nonetheless, Italians in America speak in a language that has its own concentrated force. English is a dialect all Italians must learn to speak if they want to do business with Italians not only in the United States, but in Australia, Canada, England, Scotland, and many other places as well. Italian Americans write in English, and they have money to spend. They are willing, many of them, to go on being Italian, but they probably want to do so more and more on terms that make sense to them. Writing in English leaves them immune to many of the old war songs. It allows them a distance of reflection.

It allows them a certain freedom of access. In Italian America, they have already dug up the Buried Caesars, dusted them off, and set them up in Las Vegas. "Pizzaland," a locale made famous in the opening sequence of *The Sopranos,* is effectively everywhere, as is the habit of looking at the old stereotype vaudeville gangsters not as a tragic insult but as a kind of regional comedy, a neighborhood one has left behind under the awnings of long ago. By now Italian America is thick with million-dollar houses and fertile with children in Ivy League colleges. Writing that answers to this condition struggles with its colonial beginnings. This always means raising Caesar from the dead if only for the space of an interview. Such confrontations are useful. In speaking to the Italian ancestors, Italian Americans have given America a way to consult the ancient Italian will to power—vast as it was, doomed, and full of meaning for the New World empire.

Notes

Preface

1. See Lawrence DiStasi, "How World War II Iced Italian American Culture," in *Una storia segreta: The Secret History of Italian American Evacuation and Internment during World War II*, ed. Laurence DiStasi (Berkeley, Calif.: Heyday Books, 2001), p. 307.

2. Nathaniel Hawthorne, *The Marble Faun, Or, The Romance of Monte Beni* (New York: Modern Library, n.d.), p. 4.

3. Pierre Bourdieu, *The Logic of Practice* (Stanford, Calif.: Stanford University Press, 1990), p. 56.

4. Mario Puzo, *The Godfather* (New York: Putnam, 1969), p. 92.

5. Vincenzo Ancona, *Malidittu la lingua: Damned Language: Poetry and Miniatures*, ed. Anna L. Chairetakis and Joseph Sciorra, trans. Gaetano Cipolla (New York: Legas, 1990).

6. This is the theory elaborated by Karen Horney in *Our Inner Conflicts: A Constructive Theory of Neurosis* (New York: Norton, 1945).

Introduction

1. Bill Tonelli, *The Amazing Story of the Tonelli Family in America: 12,000 Miles in a Buick in Search of Identity, Ethnicity, Geography, Kinship, and Home* (New York: Addison-Wesley, 1994), records Tonelli's trip to visit as many people as he could find who shared his surname, all over the United States. He summarizes his results in this memorable passage:

> [The Tonellis] really don't think much about their ancestry. Surrounded as Tonellis are by Americans (and even non-Americans) of every stripe and flavor, their pasts just don't have much to do with their presents. The tie has been severed; no aspect of their lives speaks to their sense of themselves as creatures of history. At some unobserved point, they (or somebody before them) made a crucial transfer—they stepped out of the story of their blood and into that of their country. That's mostly the work of real estate, the great transformer, for if they limited their associations

to individuals of similar provenance, they'd be very lonely people. They're Americans, and that's why their ancestors came here in the first place, I guess. (pp. 252–53)

2. On lynchings and anti-Italian discrimination, see Richard Gambino, *Vendetta: The True Story of the Largest Lynching in U.S. History* (Toronto: Guernica, 1998), pp. 129–41, as well as Sal La Gumina, *WOP: A Documentary History of Anti-Italian Discrimination* (Toronto: Guernica, 1999).

3. "Caesarism can be said to express a situation in which the forces of conflict balance each other . . . in such a way that a continuation of the conflict can only terminate in their reciprocal destruction." Antonio Gramsci, *Selections from the Prison Notebooks*, ed. and trans. Quintin Hoare and Geoffrey Nowell Smith (New York: International, 1971), p. 219; "*Si può dire che il cesarismo esprime una situazione in cui le forze in lotta si equilibrano . . . in modo che la continuazione della lotta non può concludersi che con la distruzione reciproca.*" Antonio Gramsci, *Note sul Machiavelli* (Roma: Editori Riuniti, 1977), p. 70. Connections between Caesarism and the Mafia run more or less implicitly throughout the essays in Luigi Barzini, *From Caesar to the Mafia* (New York: Library Press, 1971).

4. Goffredo Mameli, "Il canto degli italiani," in *Fratelli d'Italia: La vera storia dell'inno di Mameli*, ed. Tarquinio Maiorino, Giuseppe Marchetti Tricamo, & Piero Giordana, translation by Robert Viscusi. (Milano: Mondadori, 2001), p. 133. The entire text of Mameli's poem deserves study. For example, he writes, "*Noi fummo per secoli / calpesti, derisi,/ perché non siam popolo, / perché siam divisi.*" ("We were for centuries / abused and derided, / because we are not a people, / because we are divided.")

5. See Michael La Sorte, *La Merica: Images of Italian Greenhorn Experience* (Philadelphia: Temple University Press, 1985); see also Edmondo DeAmicis, *Sull' Oceano* (Milano: Garzanti, 1996).

6. Temistocle Solera, libretto, in *Nabucco (Nabocodonosor)*, ed. Giuseppe Verdi (Milano: Ricordi, 1970), pp. 242–53. English trans., Schiller Institute, *http://www.schillerinstitute.org/music/va_pensiero.html* [download March 3, 2003].

7. The most comprehensive publication to date in this arena is Francesco Durante, ed., *Italoamericana: Storia e letteratura degli italiani negli Stati Uniti 1776–1780* (Milano: Mondadori, 2001); see also Giuseppe Massara, *Americani* (Palermo: Sellerio, 1986).

8. Some texts by women authors come into this discussion, but separate histories of vision pertain specifically to women's writing. See Helen Barolini, ed., *The Dream Book: An Anthology of Writings by Italian American Women* (New York: Schocken, 1985); Mary Jo Bona, ed., *The Voices We Carry: Recent Italian American Women's Fiction* (Toronto: Guernica, 1994), and *Claiming a Tradition: Italian American Women Writers* (Carbondale: Southern Illinois University Press, 1999); Mary Ann Mannino, *Revisionary Identities: Strategies of*

Empowerment in the Writing of Italian/American Women (New York: Lang, 2000); Edvige Giunta, *Writing with an Accent: Contemporary Italian American Women Authors* (New York: Palgrave, 2002); Louise De Salvo and Edvige Giunta, eds., *The Milk of Almonds: Italian American Women Writers on Food and Culture* (New York: Feminist Press, 2002); Mary Ann Mannino and Justin Vitiello, *Breaking Open: Reflections on Italian American Women's Writing* (West Lafayette, Ind.: Purdue University Press, 2003).

9. See Rose D. Scherini, "When Italian Americans Were 'Enemy Aliens,'" in *Una storia segreta*, pp. 10–31.

10. Pier Paolo Pasolini writes, "*in Italy an actual national Italian language doesn't exist*" in "New Linguistic Questions," collected in *Heretical Empiricism*, ed. Louise K. Barnett, trans. Ben Lawton and Louise K. Barnett (Bloomington: Indiana University Press, 1988), p. 3 (italics in original).

11. Felix Stefanile, "A Fig Tree in America," *The Country of Absence: Poems and an Essay*, VIA Folios 18 (West Lafayette, Ind.: Bordighera, 2000), p. 23.

Chapter 1. English as a Dialect of Italian

1. Maria Mazzotti Gillan, "Public School No. 18: Paterson, New Jersey," *Where I Come From: Selected and New Poems* (Toronto: Guernica, 1995), p. 12.

2. Dante Alighieri, *De vulgari eloquentia*, in *Literary Criticism of Dante Alighieri*, trans. Robert S. Haller (Lincoln: University of Nebraska Press, 1973), p. 12, says that his new common speech should serve as "the vernacular of all the Latin cities against which all other Latin vernaculars are measured, weighed, and compared."

3. Maria Mazziotti Gillan, "*Growing Up Italian*," in *Where I Come From*, p. 54 (see n. 1).

4. Jerre Mangione, *Mount Allegro: A Memoir of Italian American Life* (1942; repr. New York: Harper and Row, 1989); Maria Laurino, *Were You Always an Italian: Ancestors and Other Icons of Italian America* (New York: Norton, 2000).

5. This remark is a chimera of Italian scholarship. Frequently cited, it never comes with a traceable source, and I have not found anyone who knows where to find it. It is sometimes credited to Massimo D'Azeglio's memoirs, first published in 1866, where in fact we do find a comparable sentiment:

> *gl'Italiani hanno voluto far un'Italia nuova, e loro rimanere gl'Italiani vecchi di prima, colle doppocaggini e le miserie morali che furono ab antico la loro rovina; perché pensano a riformare l'Italia, e nessuno s'accorge che per riuscirci bisogna, prima, che si riformino loro, perché l'Italia, come tutt'i popoli, non potrà esser ordinata, ben amministrata, forte cosí contro lo straniero come contro i settari dell'interno, libera e di propria ragione, finché grandi e piccoli e mezzani, ognuno*

nella sua sfera non faccia il suo dovere, e non lo faccia bene, od almeno il meglio che può. .... Il primo bisogno d'Italia è che si formino Italiani che sappiano adempiere al loro dovere; quindi che si formino alti e forti caratteri.

Massimo D'Azeglio, *I miei ricordi* (Torino: Giulio Einaudi, 1971).

6. Umberto Eco, *La ricerca di una lingua perfetta nella cultura europea* (1993; repr. Bari: Laterza, 1996), pp. 41–60, places this enterprise within the larger context of European linguistic history.

7. See Vittorio Spinazzola, "*Introduzione*," in *I promessi sposi*, ed. Alessandro Manzoni (Milano: Garzanti, 1981), pp xv–xix, for an account of the writing and rewriting of *I promessi sposi* and of its relation to Manzoni's language project. According to Maurizio Vitale, *La questione della lingua* (Palermo: Palumbo, 1978), pp. 446–47, the Minister of Public Instruction Emilio Broglio had charged Manzoni's Commission "*di proporre tutti i provvedimenti e i modi con quali si possa aiutare e rendere più universale in tutti gli ordini del popolo la notizia della buona lingua e della buona pronuncia*" ("to propose all the arrangements and methods with which it may be possible to assist and to render more universal among all ranks of the people the understanding of proper language and proper pronunciation"). Natalia Ginzburg, *La famiglia Manzoni* (Milano: Giulio Einaudi, 1983), and *The Manzoni Family*, trans. Marie Evans (New York: Arcade/Little, Brown, 1989), gives a group portrait of the Manzoni literary and aesthetic dynasty, extending from the novelist's grandfather Cesare Beccaria down through his son-in-law Massimo d'Azeglio, allowing the reader to reflect on themes that have been central to Italian intellectual and artistic culture from the late Enlightenment down to the present. The authority of the national language did not end with d'Azeglio and his generation, but even today resides somewhere out of the range of values that can be seriously questioned or doubted, and is still guiding Italian educational policy at the opening of the twenty-first century.

8. Or did their best to use it. See Hermann Haller, *Una lingua perduta e ritrovata: l'italiano degli italo-americani* (Firenze: La Nuova Italia, 1993), for a study of the language of *Il progresso italo-americano*, the leading Italian-language periodical in the United States for more than a century.

9. J. D. C. Atkins, cited in J. Crawford, ed., *Language Loyalties: A Sourcebook on the Official English Controversy* (Chicago: University of Chicago Press, 1992), pp. 48–51; cited in Lesley Milroy, "Standard English and Language Ideology," in *Standard English: The Widening Debate*, ed. Tony Bex and Richard J. Watts, (London: Routledge, 1999), p. 195.

10. Bruno Migliorini, *Storia della lingua italiana* (1961; repr. Firenze: Sansoni, 1962), pp. 6–8, summarizes this history.

11. See Richard J. Watts, "The Social Construction of Standard English: Grammar Writers as a 'Discourse Community,'" in *Standard English*, pp. 40–68, for a discussion of the methods English grammar writers employed to teach English grammar as conformable with Latin. In a typical maneuver, Daniel Duncan, *English Grammar* (London: Prevost, 1731) treats English

prepositions as forms of the Latin cases for nouns. One example: "As the Comparative Degree governs the Ablative in Latin, therefore Grammarians have made the particle *than*, that follows the Comparative in English, a sign of the Ablative. For that same reason the Prepositions *from, by, of, in, with, through, for*, &c. are deemed Signs of this Case, because the Latin Prepositions answering to them govern it" (cited in Watts, p. 53).

12. Cited in John Larner, "Chaucer's Italy," in *Chaucer and the Italian Trecento*, ed. Piero Boitani (Cambridge: Cambridge University Press, 1983), p. 25.

13. Anna Laura Lepschy and Giulio Lepschy, *The Italian Language Today*, 2nd ed. (London: Routledge, 1991), pp. 45–48.

14. Burton Bollag, "The New Latin: English Dominates in Academe," *Chronicle of Higher Education*, September 8, 2000, p. A7, writes that English "is increasingly becoming the language of higher education throughout the world. The development is being stoked by the growing integration of the world economy, with the United States, the one remaining superpower and the world's economic locomotive, at its head." The railroad imagery in this article about the Internet suggests a continuity of Anglocentric imperialism joining the nineteenth century with the twenty-first century.

15. Carlo A. Pescosolido and Pamela Gleason, *The Proud Italians: Our Great Civilizers* (1991; repr. Washington, D.C.: National Italian American Foundation, 1995); Gaetano Cipolla, *What Italy Has Given to the World* (New York: Legas, 1999); Arturo Barone, *Italians First! From A to Z* (Sandgate, Folkestone, Kent: Norbury, 1989) is an Italian-British version of the same phenomenon.

16. Eco, pp. 41–59 (see n. 6), explores the more extreme claims that Dante's innovation suggests.

17. See Reed Way Dasenbrock, *Imitating the Italians: Wyatt, Spenser, Synge, Pound, Joyce* (Baltimore, MD: Johns Hopkins University Press, 1991).

18. This is a rich theme for exploration. For a recent discussion, see Marianna De Marco Trogovnick, *Crossing Ocean Parkway: Readings by an Italian American Daughter* (Chicago: University of Chicago Press, 1994).

Chapter 2. *De vulgari eloquentia*

1. Dante Alighieri, *De vulgari eloquentia*, p. 3 (see chap. 1, n. 2).

2. This hypothesis was to be tested in a sociolinguistic atlas of Italian American languages. This chapter was, in a slightly different version, first written for the New York University Colloquium on Italian and Italian American languages, which met monthly for years in the late 1970s and early 1980s to discuss issues surrounding the project of such an atlas. At this point I wish to acknowledge its debts to the members of this colloquium, to Luigi Ballerini and Fiorenza Weinapple, the leaders of the project, who invited me to write the paper that eventually became this chapter, as well as to the other participants, particularly Giuseppe Di Scipio, Hermann W. Haller, and the late Robert Di Pietro.

3. That Daly's was a useful and important enterprise is maintained in Gaetano Cipolla, "Thomas Augustine Daly: An Early Voice of the Italian Immigrants," *Italian Americana*, 6 (1980): 45–49.

4. See, for example, his story "Mora Amore" in *From the Margin: Writings in Italian Americana*, ed. Anthony Julian Tamburri, Paolo A. Giordano, and Fred L. Gardaphe (West Lafayette, Ind.: Purdue University Press, 1991), pp. 102–9.

5. Frank Lentricchia, *Johnny Critelli and the Knifemen* (New York: Scribner, 1996), p. 17.

6. Nonetheless it remains an option. I have outlined some of the politics of this linguistic history in "Coining," *Differentia: Review of Italian Thought*, 2 (Spring 1988): 7–42.

7. Lou D'Angelo, *What the Ancients Said* (Garden City, N.Y.: Doubleday, 1971), p. 9.

8. *What the Ancients Said*, pp. 16–24.

9. *Italian American novel*: herein, a novel using Italian America, the English-speaking version of it, as a focus or a setting.

10. The significance of Italian names among immigrants in Great Britain has been even greater. See Terri Colpi, *The Italian Factor: The Italian Community in Great Britain* (Edinburgh: Mainstream, 1991), pp. 192–97.

11. Lawrence Ferlinghetti, for example, changed his name back to the paternal form from *Ferling*, which his brothers used. See Neeli Cherkovski, *Ferlinghetti: A Biography* (Garden Citym N.Y.: Doubleday, 1979), pp. 23, 82.

12. Garibaldi M. La Polla, *The Grand Gennaro* (New York: Vanguard, 1935), p. 3.

13. Robert Canzoneri, *A Highly Ramified Tree* (New York: Viking, 1976), p. 41.

14. Louis Forgione, *The River Between* (New York: Dutton, 1928).

15. Joseph Arleo, *The Grand Street Collector* (New York: Walker, 1970).

16. Rocco Fumento, *Tree of Dark Reflection* (New York: Knopf, 1962).

17. Mario Puzo, *The Fortunate Pilgrim* (New York: Atheneum, 1965).

18. Mario Puzo, *The Godfather* (New York: Putnam's Sons, 1969).

19. A good idiomatic performance is "*La luna mezzu i mari*," transcribed by Franco Li Causi, performed by Antonio Vasquez, Maria Lupo, Franco Li Causi, A. Principato, and G. Vaccara, on *Folklore Siciliano*, Cetra LPP 7.

20. These readers played an important role in the success of the book, as they would a few years afterward in the success of Richard Gambino's *Blood of My Blood: The Dilemma of the Italian Americans* (Garden City, N.Y.: Doubleday, 1974).

21. Arleo's novel and Puzo's were compared even when they were published, notably by Barton Midwood, in "Fiction," *Esquire,* Feb. 1971, 51

Advertising copy for *The Grand Street Collector* compares it to *The Godfather,* but the two books have very little in common, except that they are both about Italian immigrants in New York in the Thirties. Moreover, the intentions of the two books are diametrically opposed. *The Godfather* is essentially exhibitionist and makes its appeal to ignorance and fear, while *The Grand Street Collector* is essentially introspective and makes its appeal to reason.

In truth, the issues raised here are complex enough to merit separate attention. A good discussion of the difficulties with *The Godfather* is Giovanni Sinicropi, "The Saga of the Corleones: Puzo, Coppola and *The Godfather,*" *Italian Americana,* 2 (1975), 79–90. The most serious critics of Italian American literature have always tended to take Puzo's book very seriously indeed, beginning with Rose Basile Green in her comprehensive and indispensable study, *The Italian-American Novel: A Document of the Interaction of Two Cultures* (Rutherford, N.J.: Fairleigh Dickinson University Press, 1980), pp. 352–68, and continuing in Marianna De Marco Torgovnick, "*The Godfather* as the World's Most Typical Novel," *South Atlantic Quarterly* 87, no. 2 (1988): 329–53, Fred L.Gardaphe, *Italian Signs, American Streets: The Evolution of Italian American Narrative* (Durham, N.C.: Duke University Press, 1996), pp. 86–98, and, most recently in Chris Messenger, The Godfather *and American Culture: How the Corleones Became 'Our Gang'* (Albany: State University of New York Press, 2002).

22. The murder of Carlo Tresca is one of those overdetermined assassinations that confound historians who want things neatly settled. The Tresca problem is neatly set forth in Dorothy Gallagher, *All the Right Enemies: The Life and Murder of Carlo Tresca* (New Brunswick, N.J.: Rutgers University Press, 1988).

23. *Sbagliato: mistaken.* Puzo has no monopoly of blunt allegory, which is one of the simpler and sometimes more effectively comic ways of introducing Italian words into English sentences.

24. On di Donato's language, see also Giovanni Sinicropi, "*Christ in Concrete,*" *Italian Americana,* 3(1977): 175–83, and Daniel Orsini, "Rehabilitating DiDonato: A Phonocentric Novelist," in *The Melting Pot and Beyond: Italian Americans in the Year 2000,* ed. Jerome Krase and William Egelman (Staten Island, N.Y.: American Italian Historical Association, 1987), pp. 191–205. See also Robert di Pietro, "Language as a Marker of Italian Ethnicity," *Studi emigrazione,* 42 (1976): 202–18. A comprehensive bibliography on this subject is in Louise Napolitano, *An American Story: Pietro DiDonato's* Christ in Concrete, Studies in Southern Italian and Italian American Culture (New York: Lang, 1993).

25. "*Up, down*" is a rhyming sequence in standard spoken Italian: *su, giù,* as in "*Figaro su, Figaro giù.*"

26. Pietro di Donato, "Mister Nicky, The Floatin' Bricky," in *Naked, As an Author* (New York: Pinnacle, 1971), p. 109.

27. Jerre Mangione, *Mount Allegro* (Boston: Houghton Mifflin, 1942), p. 52.

28. This is of course a favorite locution. It and others like it helped ensure the popularity of George Panetta, *We Ride a White Donkey* (New York:

Harcourt, Brace, and World, n.d. [1944?]): for example, "Crine loud" for "for crying out loud," "Nuncha do gen" for "Don't you do it again," pp. 141–42; the same theme is treated in *Mount Allegro*. Michael LaSorte discusses "Italglish," as he calls it, in *La Merica: Images of Italian Greenhorn Experience* (Philadelphia, Penn.: Temple University Press, 1985), pp. 159–88. Michael James Eula revisits the theme in a brilliant article, "Language, Time and the Formation of Self," *Italian Americana: Cultural and Historical Review*, XVI, no. 1 (Winter 1998): 64–86.

29. The *Gone with the Wind* theme in Italian American Historiography specializes in linoleum floors, basil plants, and Parodi cigars. It holds that only the immigrants are fully Italian Americans, as if no one could ever be Italian again. Its most frequently cited large entry is Richard C. Alba, *Italian Americans: Into the Twilight of Ethnicity* (Englewood Cliffs, N.J.: Prentice-Hall, 1985), and its most frequently cited literary spokesperson is Dana Gioia, "What Is Italian American Poetry?" *VIA: Voices in Italian Americana*, 4, no. 2 (Fall 1993): 61–64; in this essay Gioia links the meaning of the *Italian* in *Italian American* to the Italian experience and expression of the immigrants. Disagreeing that much has been lost is difficult. Agreeing that new formulations, which continue to emerge, will not be rich enough to merit attention is impossible. The return of third- and fourth-generation Italian Americans to Italy, combined with the increasing depth of the liteary tradition developed by Italian travelers to the United States, has laid the foundations for a new international literature. A student of this literature would want to read Giuseppe Massara, *Viaggiatori Italiani in America (1860–1970)* (Roma: Edizioni di storia e letteratura, 1976), and *Americani* (Palermo: Sellerio editore, 1984), as well as Martino Marazzi, *Little America: Gli Stati Uniti e gli scrittori italiani del Novecento* (Milano: Marcos y Marcos, 1997), and Helen Barolini, *Chiaroscuro* (New York: Italica, 1997).

Chapter 3. *Il caso della casa*

1. This tetrad applies to the meaning-system of houses a series of distinctions of purpose strictly analogous to the four aspects of Italian American literary language outlined in the previous chapter. It makes sense, after all, that ritual powers of language should evoke ritual scenes appropriate to their natures. This theory of categories also may suggest other uses for the general theory of linguistic reciprocity upon which it stands.

2. Mario Puzo, "Choosing a Dream," *The Godfather Papers and Other Confessions* (New York: Putnam, 1972), p. 17.

3. Mario Puzo, *The Dark Arena* (1955; repr. Greenwich, Conn.: Fawcett, n.d.).

4. Mario Puzo, *Fools Die* (New York: Putnam, 1978).

5. The Freudianized immigrant may be visited at greater length in two excellent books: Andrew Rolle, *Italian Americans: Troubled Roots* (Norman: University of Oklahoma Press, 1984); León Grinberg, M.D., and Rebeca Grin-

berg, M.D., *Psychoanalytic Perspectives on Migration and Exile*, trans. Nancy Festinger (New Haven, Conn.: Yale University Press, 1984).

6. Italians were real estate heroes of slum renewal as early as 1905. Lord, Trenor, and Barnes, *The Italians in America* (New York: Buck, 1905), pp. 75–76, write of Italian Greenwich Village:

> Fifteen years ago this was one of the most notorious of the so-called slum quarters of the city, very largely tenanted by Negro and French families, and often glaring in its dissolute and riotous displays. Here the Italians began to settle about fourteen years ago, and their influx now dominates the section...the advance of the section has nevertheless been remarkable. Now whenever any real estate in the section comes into the market, it is eagerly bid for by Italian operators and builders. Hancock St. on both sides of Bleecker to Bedford now shows lines of tenements that would be a credit to any city. . . . The value of the real estate in this section has increased, and the quarter is, in the main of excellent character.

Cited in Donald Tricarico, *The Italians of Greenwich Village: The Social Structure and Transformation of an Ethnic Community* (New York: Center for Migration Studies, 1984), p. 3. In real estate narratives, the Italian immigrants were frequently pitted against the former slave population.

7. Guido D'Agostino, *Olives on the Apple Tree* (New York: Doubleday, Doran, 1940).

8. Raymond De Capite, *The Coming of Fabrizze* (New York: McKay, 1960).

9. John Fante, *The Brotherhood of the Grape* (Boston: Houghton Mifflin, 1977), p. 25.

10. Lorenzo da Ponte and Wolfgang Amadeus Mozart, *Il dissoluto punito ossia il Don Giovanni: Dramma giocosa in due atti* (1787) in *Mozart Werke*, Serie V, *Opern*, N. 18 (Leipzig: Verlag von Breitkopf & Hartel; repr. Ann Arbor, Mich.: Edwards, 1955), p. 17.

11. Jerre Mangione, *Reunion in Sicily* (Cambridge, Mass.: Houghton Mifflin, 1950).

12. Helen Barolini, *Umbertina* (New York: Seaview, 1979).

Chapter 4. Immigrant Ambitions and American Literature

1. Walt Whitman, *Leaves of Grass*, Facsimile of the first [1855] edition (San Francisco: Chandler, 1968), pp. iii, iv,v.

2. David Simpson, "Destiny Made Manifest: The Styles of Whitman's Poetry," in *Nation and Narration*, ed. Homi K. Bhabha (New York: Routledge, 1990), pp. 177–96. David S. Reynolds, *Walt Whitman's America: A Cultural Biography* (New York: Knopf, 1996), p. 326, writes "So powerful was [Whitman's] belief in the possibilities of cultural democracy in 1855 that he could assume an almost totalitarian stance: 'And what I assume you shall assume.' The 'I' of the 1855 edition asserts total control. . . ."

3. Christopher Duggan, *Francesco Crispi* (New York: Oxford University Press, 2002), p. 711.

4. *The Godfather Papers*, p. 25 (see chap 3, n. 2).

5. Pasquale Verdicchio, *Bound by Distance: Rethinking Nationalism through the Italian Diaspora* (Madison, N.J.: Fairleigh Dickinson University Press, 1997), pp. 21–51; Stefano Luconi, *From Paesani to White Ethnics: The Italian Experience in Philadelphia* (Albany: State University of New York Press, 2001), pp. 37–55; Ralph Cunsolo, "Italian Emigration and Its Effect on the Rise of Nationalism," *Italian Americana* 12, no. 1 (1993): 62–72.

6. William Boelhower, *Immigrant Autobiography in the United States: Four Versions of the Italian American Self* (Verona: Essedue edizioni, 1982), p. 31.

7. Luigi Fontanella, "Introduzione," *Son of Italy*, trans. Sonia Pendola (Mercato San Severino: Il Grappolo, 2002), writing as an Italian critic, finds it desirable but difficult not to treat D'Angelo as a "caso." At best, he admits, after decades of oblivion, D'Angelo's work has returned "*a incuriosire (ma ancora non più di tanto) la critica, sia pure quella interessata alla sociologia della letteratura e alla storia dell'emigrazione italiana in America. È già qualcosa*" ["to arouse the interest (though not yet very greatly) of criticism, some of it interested in the sociology of literature, some of it in the history of the Italian migration to America. That's already something"] (p. 12). Clearly, he is not convinced.

8. Pascal D'Angelo, *Son of Italy* (1924; New York: Arno, 1975).

9. William Boelhower, "Surviving Democracy," in *Social Pluralism and Literary History: The Literature of the Italian Migration,* ed. Francesco Loriggio (Toronto: Guernica, 1996), p. 133.

10. Giuseppe Verdi, *Aida*, libretto by Antonio Ghislanzoni (New York: Kalmus, n.d.), pp. 4–5.

11. See Antonio Gramsci, *The Southern Question*, trans., annot., introd. Pasquale Verdicchio. (West Lafayette, Ind.: Bordighera, 1995).

12. Carlo Dionisotti, *Geografia e storia della letteratura italiana* (Torino: Einaudi, 1967).

13. Edward Said, *Culture and Imperialism* (New York: Knopf, 1993), p. 129.

14. Josephine Gattuso Hendin, *The Right Thing to Do* (New York: Feminist Press, 1999); Flavia Alaya, *Under the Rose* (New York: Feminist Press, 2001).

15. Diane Di Prima, *Recollections of My Life as a Woman: The New York Years* (New York: Viking, 2001), p. 6.

16. Hans Busch, coll. and trans., *Verdi's Aida: The History of an Opera in Letters and Documents* (Minneapolis: University of Minnesota Press, 1978), p. 55.

17. John Dizikes, *Opera in America: A Cultural History* (New Haven, Conn.: Yale University Press, 1993), p. 317.

18. Donna Gabaccia, *Italy's Many Diasporas* (Seattle: University of Washington Press, 1999), pp. 179, 180.

19. See Robert Viscusi, "'*Ritorna vincitor*'!: Packaging and Repackaging in the Italian Trade Network," in *Italian Cultural Studies 2001,* ed. Ben Lawton, Graziella Parati, Miriam Suennen Ruthenberg, and Anthony Tamburri (Boca Raton, Fla.: Bordighera, 2004), 199–211.

20. See Soprintendenza per i Beni Ambientali e Architettonici di Roma, *Il vittoriano: 2 giugno 2002* (Roma: Ministero per i Beni e le Attività Culturali, 2002), pp. 1–11.

21. Chris Messenger, The Godfather *and American Culture,* pp. 173–298 (see chap. 2, n. 21).

22. See Luigi Bonaffini, ed. *Dialect Poetry of Southern Italy: Texts and Criticism: A Trilingual Anthology* (New York: Legas, 1997), pp. 501–6; and Luigi Bonaffini and Achille Serrao, eds. *Dialect Poetry of Northern and Central Italy: Texts and Criticism: A Trilingual Anthology* (New York: Legas, 2001), pp. 664–67.

23. Joseph.Kerman, *Opera as Drama* (New York: Knopf, 1956), p. 166.

24. Jay Parini, "The Cultural Work of *The Sopranos*" in *A Sitdown with* The Sopranos: *Watching Italian American Culture on TV's Most Talked-about Series,* ed. Regina Barreca (New York: Palgrave, 2002), pp. 75–87.

Chapter 5. The Text in the Dust

1. The Admiral of the Ocean Sea had a labile imagination easily excited by coastlines. One of the most brilliant works to appear in the quincentenary year, Valerie I. J. Flint, *The Imaginative Landscape of Christopher Columbus* (Princeton, N.J.: Princeton University Press, 1992), intricately outlines how both reading and hearsay had shaped Columbus's conclusions about what met his eyes in the various places he paused in his travels:

> To the end of his life Columbus maintained that he had reached the "Indies" he set out to find. He had landed on islands close to Cipangu, and on the mainland of Cathay. He had skirted the coasts of Marco Polo's Mangi, and been only leagues away from the domains of the Great Khan himself. He had constantly heard tell of the accessibility of what he took to be the "Aurea Chersonese" or "Patalis regio," (the modern Malay Peninsula), with all its fabled gold. He had traveled along the pearl coasts bordering the Indies, and had come within an hair's-breadth of the strait leading from Cathay to India itself. He had visited many of those islands of which earlier travelers had told. He had gazed upon lands close to the Terrestrial Paradise, as some of the travelers had too, and he had discovered a great southern continent, previously unknown. (p. 115)

2. Luciano Formisano, "Introduction," in *Letters from a New World: Amerigo Vespucci's Discovery of America,* ed. Luciano Formisano, trans. David Jacobson (New York: Marsilio, 1992), p. xxi. "*Mundus Novus,*" Formisano continues, "met with particular success in the German-speaking countries, where there was no lack of commercial enterprises directly interested

in the recent discoveries. The Augsburg edition of 1504, the first to bear a date, was followed by those of Cologne, Nuremberg, Strasbourg, Rostock, and translations into German (Nuremberg, 1515) and Flemish (Antwerp, 1506–1508?)."

3.

Ciò che mi ricordavo, però soprattutto, di essere straniero in uno città straniera, erano i nomi delle strade e il loro disegno. La graticola ad angolo retto delle avenues e delle streets, ciascuna numerata come uno scaffale in un grande magazzino o un deposito all'aria aperta, sembrava trasformasse la città non più in una cosa viva, che era andata crescendo spontaneamente secondo le proprie leggi, ma in una invenzione arida di geometri e ingegneri. (What I remember above all about being a foreigner in a strange city was the names of the streets and how they were laid out. The rectangular grid of avenues and streets, each one numbered like a shelf in a huge department store or an open-air warehouse, seemed to reshape the city: it was no longer something living, growing spontaneously according to its own laws, but a sterile invention of surveyors and engineers.)

The whole of Barzini's essay, *"La mia New York,"* in *American Review*, reprinted in Galpin et al., eds., *Beginning Readings in Italian* (London: Macmillan, 1966), pp. 232–38, makes an excellent introduction to the perceptual difficulties of Italians, even sophisticated and literate ones such as Barzini, upon their arrival in America.

4. Lucia Perillo, "The Oldest Map with the Name America," in *The Oldest Map with the Name America: New and Selected Poems* (New York: Random House, 1999), p. 119.

5. O. E. Rolväag, *Giants in the Earth*, trans. Lincoln Concord and O. E. Rolväag (1927; repr. New York: Harper and Row, Perennial Library, 1965).

6. This is a widely deployed theme in American literary history, but see especially Perry Miller, *Errand into the Wilderness* (Cambridge, Mass.: Harvard University Press, 1956).

7. On the continuities between Puritan discourse and subsequent American literature see Sacvan Berovitch, *The Puritan Origins of the American Self* (New Haven, Conn.: Yale University Press, 1975).

8. Anzia Yezierska, *Bread Givers* (1925; repr. New York: Persa, 1975).

9. Henry Roth, *Call It Sleep* (1934; repr. New York: Cooper Square, 1965).

10. On Whitman's body as an inscription, see John T. Irwin, *American Hieroglyphics: The Symbol of the Egyptian Hieroglyphics in the American Renaissance* (New Haven, Conn.: Yale University Press, 1980), p. 98.

11. Vespucci, along with Giannotto Berardi, was part of the Medici bank that financed Columbus's first voyage. Formisano, pp. xxxv-xxxvi, writes,

By 10 March 1492 Vespucci has already traveled to Seville, assigned the task of overseeing the management of the bank of Lorenzo di Pierfrancesco de' Medici, newly headed by Giannotto Berardi. As a merchant and outfitter of Atlantic fleets for the Crown, Berardi forms a partnership with Columbus, whose first expedition he finances. The company is gradually expanded to include Vespucci himself.

See Consuelo Varela, *Colón y los florentinos* (Madrid: Alianza Editorial, 1988).

12. All Vespucci's published letters on this subject were written in Italian to Florentines. The Latin text of *Mundus Novus* is based on a letter to his employer Lorenzo di Pierfrancesco de' Medici and the later *Lettera di Amerigo Vespucci delle isole nuovamente trovate in quattro suoi viaggi* (first published in Florence in 1505) on a letter to the chief magistrate of the Comune di Firenze, Piero di Tommaso Soderini.

13. Among histories of Italian Americans, the one that most fully explores the background of political fragmentation in Italy that produces the endlessly varied usurpation of Italian power in the United States is Alexander De Conde, *Half-Bitter, Half-Sweet: An Excursion into Italian-American History* (New York: Scribner's, 1971); the diffidence in De Conde's subtitle should not mislead investigators of this theme: no one has written with a fuller appreciation of the shifting diplomatic substructure of Italian America than has De Conde. For analysis of more recent cultural politics between Italy and America, see R. Viscusi, "The Mind / Body Problem," *Italian Journal* V, no. 2 (1991): 53–56.

14. The narratives in Michael La Sorte, *La Merica*, for example (see Intro., n. 5), or Marie Hall Ets, *Rosa: The Life of an Italian Immigrant* (Minneapolis: University of Minnesota Press, 1970), or Adria Bernardi, *Houses with Names: The Italian Immigrants of Highwood, Illinois* (Urbana: University of Illinois Press, 1990), or Elizabeth Mathias and Richard Raspi, *Italian Folktales in America* (Detroit: Wayne State University Press, 1985) do not, any of them, keep secret how painful an experience was the migration.

15. See Richard Gambino, *Vendetta*; see also Matthew Frye Jacobson, *Whiteness of a Different Color: European Immigrants and the Alchemy of Race* (Cambridge, Mass.: Harvard University Press, 1999), pp. 52–62.

16. See Humbert S. Nelli, *The Italians in Chicago, 1880–1930: A Study in Ethnic Mobility* (New York: Oxford University Press, 1970), p. 118, for Wilson's oft-quoted slurs.

17. For a discussion of this work, see also Rose Basile Green, *The Italian-American Novel* (see chap. 2, n. 21, herein), pp. 74–79: Martino Marazzi, "I due re di Harlem," *Belfagor*, 58, 347 (quinto fascicolo), (30 Settembre 2003): 533–50.

18. Raymond Chandler's detective-hero Philip Marlowe shuttles between this vast *lumpen*-Los Angeles, which he inhabits, and the posh, pointless suburbs that carry much of that city's life; see works such as *The Lady in the Lake* (New York: Knopf, 1943) and *The Long Goodbye* (Cambridge, Mass.: Houghton Mifflin, 1954).

19. Nathaniel West, *Miss Lonelyhearts* (New York: New Directions, 1933) and Gary Wolf, *Who Censored Roger Rabbit?* (1981; New York: Ballan-

tine Books, 1982) are the bookends of this string of mythic geographies, which includes many a hardboiled-mystery and many a first-rate B movie or soap opera.

20. John Fante, *Ask the Dust* (New York: Stackpole Sons, 1939). Citations from *Ask the Dust* are from the edition currently in print (Santa Barbara, Calif.: Black Sparrow, 1980); this edition contains a preface (pp. 5–7) by Charles Bukowski, which offers a good sample of Fante's impact on other writers; see also Green, pp. 157–63; Stephen Cooper and David Fine, eds., *John Fante: A Critical Gathering* (Madison, N.J.: Fairleigh Dickinson University Press, 1999); Stephen Cooper, *Full of Life: A Biography of John Fante* (New York: Farrar Straus and Giroux, 2000); Richard Collins, *John Fante: A Literary Portrait* (Toronto: Guernica, 2000).

21. John Fante, *Wait Until Spring, Bandini* (New York: Stackpole Sons, 1938).

22. The full flavor of the Novice/Superior relationship suffuses the pages of *John Fante and H. L. Mencken: A Personal Correspondence, 1930–1952*, ed. Michael Moreau, consulting ed. Joyce Fante (Santa Rosa, Calif.: Black Sparrow, 1989).

23. Lou D'Angelo, *A Circle of Friends* (Garden City, N.Y.: Doubleday, 1977); Pietro di Donato, *Three Circles of Light* (New York: Julian Messner, 1960).

Chapter 6. The Semiology of Semen

1. These two novels are studied together in Jean Béranger, "Italian American Identity: The Masks of Religious Difference in the Novels of John Fante and Pietro DiDonato," in *The Columbus People*, ed. Lydio F. Tomasi, Piero Gastaldo, and Thomas Row (New York: Center for Migration Studies, 1994), pp. 58–78.

2. Leonard Covello, *The Social Background of the Italo-American Schoolchild* (Leith, Netherlands: Brill, 1967). See also Vito Perrone, *Teacher with a Heart: Reflections on Leonard Covello and Community* (New York: Teachers College Press, 1998), for a study of Covello's contributions to educational theory and practice.

3. Edward M. Cifelli, *John Ciardi: A Biography* (Fayetteville: University of Arkansas Press, 1997), pp. 438–39. See also above, pp. 179–81.

4. Jerre Mangione and Ben Morreale, *La Storia: Five Centuries of the Italian American Experience* (New York: HarperCollins, 1992), was first announced by Jerre Mangione in 1980. It was conceived as a *summa* of Italian American historical scholarship, a step forward in the collective self-awareness of Italian Americans, and it aimed to make this step by summarizing the vast consensus that Italian American scholars had produced after the middle 1960s. This consensus owed a great deal to foundational scholars such as Leonard Covello and Gianni Schiavo, but it offered itself as coming from the other side

of popular forgetting. This consensus had a passion for remembering things people had long considered eminently forgettable. Mangione used to compare his project with that of Irving Howe in *The World of Our Fathers*. In the event, it came to resemble more a large-scale work of civil engineering, a coordination of many divergent vectors and interests. No one had ever done what Mangione here attempted, and he found himself unable to finish it without the help of a coauthor. Mangione and Morreale produced a highly readable summary of a generation of scholarship. Its long-range importance to the development of Italian American self-awareness is substantial.

5. Mangione and Morreale's acknowledgement of the institutional support that they had in producing *La Storia* during in the nineteen-eighties is as follows:

> So ambitious a project as La Storia, which has been in the making for more than a decade, could not have been initiated without the sponsorship of the University of Pennsylvania during the tenure of Provost Vartan Gregorian and the award of two consecutive grants by the National Endowment for the Humanities. The grants enabled the University to provide us with a team of research assistants and the full-time services of Elaine Pascu, the chief researcher, to whom we are grateful for her intelligence and skills. Another N.E.H. grant enabled us to take part in an Ethnic Studies seminar at the University of California at Santa Barbara directed by the noted Anthropologist Paul Bohannon. Throughout the decade our research efforts were greatly facilitated by the University's Van Pelt Library, especially in the person of its liaison officer, Hilda H. Pring. (p. ix)

6. I use myself as informant here: *informant* (also *native informant*), n., a person traveling between both sides of the divide that separates the life of tribe from the life of the university museum with its departments of anthropology and police methods. I was one of the scholars in Mangione and Morreale's list. (My name appears at the end of the fifth among the nine paragraphs of acknowledgements in *La Storia*, a member in good standing at the university corporation.) On the other hand, through my parents and their siblings, I was still an active participant in clan and tribal networks, which meant participating in their numerous periodic ritual observances—life cycle rituals such as confirmation, weddings, first communions, baptisms, and funerals; calendar cycle rituals such as birthdays, anniversaries, feast-specific saints' days; and seasonal holidays such as Christmas and Easter.

7. Letter from Mr. and Mrs. Joseph Viscusi, February 1979.

8. I attended this event. It was organized by my brilliant uncle Eugene Di Rocco, who died in June 1987 at the premature age of fifty-nine.

9. Pietro di Donato, "The First Time," *Oui* 5, no. 9 (September 1976), pp. 42–44.

10. My direct knowledge of di Donato comes from meetings between 1979 and 1991; he died January 19, 1992. Many of our meetings took place at lectures, classes, conferences, and other university ritual observances. We also visited in one another's homes in the company of our wives and my children.

11. I have heard di Donato tell this story to several groups of students on different occasions.

12. We should remember that the power of intellectual fashions in the highly politicized left of the 1930s could have brutal force. Di Donato was not the only one who had a hard time on account of Odets's sudden fame and trendiness. Jerre Mangione, *An Ethnic at Large: A Memoir of America in the Thirties and Forties* (1978; 2nd ed. Philadelphia: University of Pennsylvania Press, 1983), p. 126, writes

> [in 1935] . . . when Clifford Odets rocketed to fame with the production of three plays, I displeased the strict party liners again with a *Daily Worker* review of *Paradise Lost* that found it inferior to Odets' *Awake and Sing*. This time no one spoke to me about my review, but shortly after its publication, the *Daily Worker* published a second review of the play which praised it lavishly. To make certain the second review would have the effect of canceling out the first, the review was assigned to a writer for the theater who was far better known than I, the playwright John Howard Lawson. Apparently, the party did not want to risk alienating as successful a left-wing playwright as Odets.
>
> It was the last review I wrote for the *Daily Worker.*

13. For a discussion of this psalm in its relation to psychoanalytic and literary theory, see Robert Viscusi, "The Other Speaking: Allegory and Lacan," in *The Writer's Mind: Writing as a Mode of Thinking*, ed. Janice Hayes et al. (Urbana, Ill.: National Council of Teachers of English, 1984), pp. 231–38.

14. Pietro di Donato, conversation with the author, East Setauket, September 1981.

15. The old-fashioned Freudian furniture of Poe's works is very fully surveyed in Marie Bonaparte, *The Life and Works of Edgar Allan Poe*, trans. John Rodker (London: Imago, 1949).

16. Pietro di Donato, *This Woman* (New York: Ballantine Books, 1958).

17. In the last years of his life, Mr. di Donato kindly allowed me to study this manuscript, which remains unpublished.

18. Pietro di Donato, *Immigrant Saint* (New York: McGraw-Hill, 1962).

19 Pietro di Donato, *The Pentinent* (New York: Englewood Cliffs, N.J.: Hawthorne, 1960).

20. Pietro di Donato, *Three Circles of Light* (New York: Messner, 1960).

21. Indeed, Eric Bentley uses the expression "the fool in Christ" to explain the career of George Bernard Shaw, an earlier Leftist Christian Nietzsche, in *Bernard Shaw, 1856–1950*, amended edition (New York: New Directions, 1957), pp. 183–219.

22. *The Venus Odyssey*, unpublished manuscript, p. 109.

23. Mangione and Morreale reflect a consensus widespread among scholars during the 1970s and 1980s when they write, "The most powerful of all the novels published about Italian Americans, *Christ in Concrete* is written with a

Joycean flow of diction and cadence to suggest the sonority of the Italian language. . ." (p. 367).

24. The elderly di Donato was at his best in a class of undergraduates. I brought him twice to Brooklyn College and once to New York University as part of courses in Italian American fiction that I gave between 1979 and 1981. Di Donato could hold such a class spellbound for hours. He had the range and freedom of conversation that comes to a person only after giving a lifetime to reading, writing, conversation, and moral passion, without ever having so far forgotten himself as to enter polite society, or to suppose that he would like it if he did.

25. Tom Johnson, Interview with Pietro di Donato, Summer 1985, cited, p. 58, in Tom Johnson, "Pietro DiDonato: *Il professore dei lavoratori*," *VIA: Voices in Italian Americana*, 2, no. 2 (Fall 1991): 51–58.

Chapter 7. Circles of the Cyclopes

1. Walter Pater, "Style," in *Appreciations, with an Essay on Style* (London: Macmillan, 1908), p. 10.

2. Mary Louise Pratt, *Imperial Eyes: Travel Writing and Transculturation* (New York: Routledge, 1992), provides interesting models for thinking about interactions of languages in contact zones; Werner Sollers, ed., *Multilingual America: Transnationalism, Ethnicity, and the Languages of American Literature* (New York: New York University Press, 1998), introduces the large-scale study of many of these issues.

3. William Boelhower, *Immigrant Autobiography in the United States* (see chap. 4, n. 6, herein), certainly accepts "many a neology" "as actually expressive." Boelhower's use of the coinages of Mikhail Bakhtin is both surprising and valuable. In such later works as *Through a Glass Darkly: Ethnic Semiosis in Italian American Literature* (New York: Oxford University Press, 1986) and *Autobiographical Transactions in Modernist America: The Immigrant, The Architect, The Artist, The Citizen* (Udine: Del Bianco, 1992), Boelhower occupies so richly elaborated an intellectual space, deploys the fruits of so wide a reading career, that knowing exactly where he derives his use of concepts or determining whether the new words belong to him or to his interlocutors is often impossible. Boelhower the literary geographer is himself an originator of very considerable poetic power.

4. *Heteroglossolalia* is a typical coinage on a Bakhtinian model. Bakhtin's term *polyglossia* refers to the presence in the community of two or more languages; it is defined in "From the Prehistory of Novelistic Discourse," in *The Dialogic Imagination: Four Essays of Mikhail Bakhtin*, trans. Carl Emerson and Michael Holquist (Austin: University of Texas Press, 1981), pp. 50–51; Bakhtin's term *heteroglossia* refers to the "diversity of social speech types which

constitutes novelistic discourse," and is defined in "Discourse in the Novel," in *The Dialogic Imagination*, pp. 262–63. Both of these concepts underlie my notion of *heteroglossolalia*, which also employs the term *glossolalia*, familiar from the New Testament as the name for would-be-significant nonsense. The joining of these three concepts is meant to specify the particular problem of a minority discourse attempting to create a literary tradition in a majority language. *Heteroglossalalia* should be distinguished from *xenoglossia*, a subset of *glossalalia*, in which a person speaks a foreign language that he or she has never learned. In *heteroglossalalia*, one uses foreign words within one's own language but does not know what they mean.

5. Of twenty New York professionals questioned, all but two recognized this as the name of a Chinese dish; four knew it contained chicken; two added vegetables; but none was more precise than that. I myself, though I have eaten it on several occasions, remember *moo goo gai pan* as a nonsense phrase that sounds like baby talk in English, rather than as a particular dish, whose contents must always be explained to me again every time I think of ordering it.

6. (Los Angeles: Price/Stern/Sloan, 1968).

7. On schema theory, see John R. Anderson, *Language, Memory, and Thought* (Hillsdale, N.J.: Lawrence Erlbaum Associates, 1976), and *Cognitive Psychology* (San Francisco: Freeman, 1980), pp. 128–60.

8. Homer, *The Odyssey*, trans. Samuel Butler (Chicago: Encyclopedia Britania, 1952), pp. IX, 111–16.

9. *Odyssey*, IX, 367. See, also George E. Dimock Jr., "The Name of Odysseus," in *Essays on the Odyssey*, ed. Charles H. Taylor Jr. (Bloomington: Indiana University Press, 1969), pp. 54–72, for a survey of the linguistic play around the hero's name, which does not, however, include the pun discussed here, despite the currency given by it by the Jesuitical James Joyce; see Richard Ellmann, *Ulysses on the Liffey* (1972; New York: Oxford University Press, 1979), p. 112.

10. *Aeneid*, VIII, *ll.* 625–731. A very full discussion of the social, political, and theological aspects of this passage is Philip R. Hardie, *Virgil's* Aeneid: *Cosmos and Imperium* (Oxford: Clarendon Press, 1986).

11. This plan gave Roman history a kind of coherence that, factitious as it may have been, has never stopped attracting the imaginations of the ambitious. In the course of time, even the center was duplicated when the empire was divided into East and West. This was the beginning of the end for Rome, although not for the empire, which survived this division by more than a thousand years.

12. H. W. Fowler, *A Dictionary of Modern English Usage*, 2nd ed., rev. and ed. by Sir Ernest Gowers (Oxford: Oxford University Press, 1965), pp. 447–48.

13. See Pierre Grimal, *Roman Cities,* trans. and ed. G. Michael Woloch (Madison: University of Wisconsin Press, 1983).

14. Lou D'Angelo, *What the Ancients Said* (see chap. 2, n. 7, herein), pp. 11, 14. D'Angelo, p. 14, translates the last of these, "Michelune left it said: Who does good is damned."

15. (Garden City, N.Y.: Doubleday, 1977).

16. A comprehensive account of Acconci's early years as poet and performance artist is Mario Diacono, *Vito Acconci: Dal testo-azione al corpo come testo* (New York: Out of London Press, 1974). As Diacono's subtitle indicates, he fully documents Acconci's career as a writer and shows how it prefigures and informs his career as a body-artist and performer. "Seedbed" is documented, pp. 168–70.

17. Vito Acconci, *Pulse (for My Mother)* (Paris: Durant, 1973).

18. On the interdependence of sense and nonsense and the boundary conditions that define them, see Susan Stewart, *Nonsense: Aspects of Intertextuality in Folklore Literature* (Baltimore, Md.: Johns Hopkins University Press, 1978).

19. Desiderius Erasmus of Rotterdam (1469–1536) in 1515 published *De Copia*, a work that teaches all the ways that a person may achieve an "abundant" style. Periphrasis is among his favorite figures, and he writes pages of example of how one might say "your letter pleased me greatly" and "always, as long as I live, I shall remember you." See Desiderius Erasmus, *On Copia of Words and Ideas (De utraque verborum ac rerum copia)*, trans. Donald B. King and H. David Rix (Milwaukee, Wisc.: Marquette University Press, 1963).

20. Jerre Mangione, *Mount Allegro: A Memoir of Italian American Life* (1942; New York: Columbia University Press, 1981). *Mount Allegro* has been through several editions since its first publication in 1942; the Columbia edition most fully represents the author's textual intentions and includes a valuable epilogue ("Finale," pp. 287–309), written in 1981.

21. *Mount Allegro*, p. 24.

22. *Mount Allegro*, p. 287. William Boelhower, "A New Version of the American Self," in *Immigrant Autobiography*, pp. 179–218, argues that Mangione achieves a "transindividual subject," writing, in effect, the "autobiography . . . of the group's collective consciousness" (p. 217). Such a merging of narrator and group seems to Boelhower necessary if Mangione is not "to be caught in cross purposes" (p. 185), because the narrator's path of "mobility and acculturation" differs radically from the group's "folkloric world view." It is true that these are "cross purposes"; but it is equally true that Mangione manages both of them without confusing their identities, producing a narrative considerably more intricate and ironic than Boelhower's (nonetheless very ingenious and useful) account suggests. Boelhower underlines the ambition of this kind of writing.

23. (Boston: Houghton Mifflin, 1980).

24. (New York: Morrow, 1968).

25. (New York: Putnam's Sons, 1978).

26. (New York: Dutton, 1928).

27. The Church calendar displays a geological stratification: its chief Jewish feasts (Easter, Pentecost, Ascension) all recur according to the Jewish lunar calendar, whereas its Roman feasts (Christmas in the New Testament is a Roman feast that has for its frame the word that "went out from Augustus Caesar" [*Tiberius* to Suetonius and to us] declaring a census) recur on the Roman Solar calendar. The liturgical calendar, accordingly, recurs on both solar and lunar patterns. Christmas always falls directly after the Winter Solstice. On the night of Holy Thursday, once the first night of Passover, the moon is always full.

28. In a footnote to his diary entry for September 2, 1981, concerning his speech that day at the New York State Fair in Syracuse, Mario M. Cuomo, *Diaries of Mario M. Cuomo: The Campaign for Governor* (New York: Random House, 1984), p. 91, n. 1, recalls that he "first referred to the 'family' of New York State." That New York State Fair speech, reprinted in *Diaries*, pp. 406–12, gives the fullest outline of Cuomo's theories. Response to it was so good that he made Government as Family the theme of his campaign. After his victory, in the transcript of Governor Cuomo's Inauguration Address at the Empire State Plaza, *New York Times*, January 2, 1983, B-19, we read how from the arrival of his mother, "alone and afraid" at Ellis Island, and his father's pre-arrival "looking for work," Cuomo was able to draw a direct line to "what our imperfect but peerless system of government has done for those two frightened immigrants from Europe," and he drew this moral: "Those who made our history taught us, above all things, the idea of family mutuality, the sharing of benefits and burdens fairly for the good of all. . . . We must be the family of New York."

29. The crucial importance of the Cyclopean image, as well as the implicit consequences of speech and law in Western tradition from Socrates to Marcuse, is the subject of an excellent essay by James L. Kinnevy, "Restoring the Humanities: The Return of Rhetoric from Exile," in *The Rhetorical Tradition and Modern Writing*, ed. James J. Murphy (New York: Modern Language Association of America, 1982), pp. 19–30.

30. Mario M. Cuomo, *Forest Hills Diary* (New York: Vintage, 1974), pp. 6–7.

31. Frank J. Cavaioli, "Returning to Corona's Little Italy," *Italian Americana: Cultural and Historical Review* XV, no. 1 (Winter 1997): 41; Cavaioli discusses this same passage from Cuomo's *Forest Hills Diary* in the context of a reconsideration of Corona's history, pp. 31–50.

32. "Address to the Fordham Law Alumni Association," March 5, 1982, cited in "Mario Cuomo: Advocatus Advocatorum," *Fordham* 16, no. 4 (July 1983): 18.

33. Jimmy Breslin, "Preface," *Forest Hills Diary*, p. vii (see chap. 9, n. 30).

34. Tina De Rosa, *Paper Fish* (1980; New York: Feminist Press of the City University of New York, 1996), p. 59.

35 Edvige Giunta, "Afterword," in *Paper Fish*, p. 127, writes that "De Rosa views the family as a homeland that can be revisited only through writ-

ing," and, p. 128, cites De Rosa's essay "Career Choices Come from Listening to the Heart," *Fra Noi* (October 1985), p. 9, which sets forth the author's motives for writing about her family members: "I wanted them to be eternal. I wanted the brief, daily lives they lived never to end."

Chapter 8. A Literature Considering Itself

1. *Important archives*: Center for Migration Studies, Staten Island, N.Y.; Immigration History Research Center, University of Minnesota, Minneapolis; Balch Institute for Ethnic Studies, Philadelphia. Bibliographies continue to appear but can hardly keep up with the flood of material coming into print in recent years. Among those that are especially useful are the following: Raffaele Cocchi, "Selected Bibliography of Italian American Poetry," *Italian Americana* X, no. 2 (Spring/Summer 1992): 242–62; Fred L. Gardaphe, *The ItalianAmerican Writer: An Essay and Annotated Checklist* (Spencertown, N.Y.: Forkroads Press, 1995); Anthony Julian Tamburri, Fred L. Gardaphé, Edvige Giunta, and Mary Jo Bona, *Italian/American Literature and Film: A Select Critical Bibliography* (West Lafayette, Ind.: Bordighera, 1997); Fred L. Gardaphe and James J. Periconi, *The IAWA Bibliography of the Italian American Book* (New York: Italian American Writers Association, 2000); James J. Periconi and Steven Boatti, *The IAWA Bibliography of the Italian American Book,* online edition, 2004: www.iawa.net The online bibliography is the most complete listing of Italian American books and is regularly updated.

2. Boelhower's work stands firmly on this article of faith in American literary historiography.

3. The subtitle of Green's study points precisely to this sort of interaction. In fact, we should not speak of relations between two (or three or thirty) cultures, but rather between two *groups of languages,* anglophone and italophone, whose interweaving produces the Italian American intertext.

4. Nicholas of Lyra, *Patrologia Latina,* cited in William F. Lynch, *Christ and Apollo* (New York: Mentor, 1963), p. 229. "The letter teaches the story of what has been done, the allegory what you should believe, the moral what you should do, the anagogy where you should aim to go."

5. Vittorio Nardi, "All'Italia," in *Poeti italo-americani: Italian American Poets,* ed. and trans. F. Alfonsi (Catanzaro: Antonio Carelli editori, 1985), pp. 304–7.

6. For example, consider Dante: *"In vesta di pastor lupi rapaci / si veggon di qua sù per tutti paschi: / o difesa di Dio, perché pur giaci?" Paradiso,* XXVII (   ): 56–58. "Rapacious wolves, in shepherd's garb, are seen from here above in all the pastures. O defense of God, wherefore dost thou yet lie still?" (Singleton)

7. The Coalition of Italo-American Associations of New York prints on its stationery the slogan "'America'—A Beautiful Italian Name." Italian Heritage and Culture Month in New York City announced as its theme for October 2004 "Amerigo Vespucci: An Italian Name for America the Beautiful."

8. Emanuel Carnevali, *The Autobiography of Emanuel Carnevali*, ed. Kay Boyle (New York: Horizon Press, 1967), p. 201.

9. See Antonio Gramsci, *The South*, trans. Pasquale Verdicchio, VIA Folios, 5 (West Lafayette, Ind.: Bordighera, 1996).

10. See Richard Gambino, *Blood of My Blood, passim,* as well as Nathan Glazer and Daniel Patrick Moynihan, *Beyond the Melting Pot: The Negroes, Jews, Italians, and Irish of New York City* (Cambridge, Mass.: MIT Press, 1970), and Thomas Kessner, *The Golden Door: Italian and Jewish Immigrant Mobility in New York City, 1880–1915* (New York: Oxford University Press, 1977), for informed comparative discussion of the social necessities confronted by these various groups in the United States.

11. Robert Orsi, *The Madonna of 115th Street: faith and Community in Italian harlem, 1880–1950* (New Haven, Conn.: Yale University Press, 1985).

12. So argues Marianna De Marco Torgovnik, "*The Godfather* as the World's Most Typical Novel," *South Atlantic Quarterly* 87, no. 2 (Spring 1988): 329–53, implicitly reviving Basile Green's argument.

13. Daniel Gabriel, *Sacco and Vanzetti: A Narrative Longpoem* (Brooklyn, N.Y/: Gull Books, 1983), pp. 74–76.

14. Anthony Valerio, *Valentino and the Great Italians, According to Anthony Valerio* (1986; Toronto: Guernica, 1994).

15. Robert Viscusi, *Astoria* (Toronto: Guernica, 1995), pp. 260–64, has a paragraph representing the phenomenology of broken statues as it acquires its place in the narrator's growing awareness of what it means to be an Italian from the United States.

16. In Helen Barolini, *The Dream Book: An Anthology of Writings by Italian American Women* (New York: Schocken Books, 1985), p. 306.

17. Don DeLillo, *Underworld* (New York: Scribner, 1997), p. 207.

18. See Joseph Papaleo, *All the Comforts* (Boston: Little, Brown, 1967), *Out of Place* and (Boston: Little, Brown, 1970); and Gene Mirabelli, *The World at Noon* (Toronto: Guernica, 1994) is a recent reexamination of the possibilities for Italian American families in the United States.

19. The Italian American family, as befits the widespread faith it has inspired, has stimulated considerable historiographic and critical industry. Three titles stand out as especially influential: Richard Gambino, *Blood of My Blood,* (see chap. 2, n. 20), Virginia Yans-McLoughlin, *Family and Community: Italian Immigrants in Buffalo, 1880–1930* (Ithaca, N.Y.: Cornell University Press, 1977); Donna R. Gabaccia, *From Sicily to Elizabeth Street: Housing and Social Change among Italian Immigrants, 1880–1930* (Albany: State University of New York Press, 1984).

20. English has been spoken in Tuscany more or less continuously since the sixteenth century and is indeed so widely spoken in Italy as to have become, from the Italian point of view and without having lost its distinctive English-ness, a branch of the Italian language.

21. Bill Tonelli, *The Amazing Story of the Tonelli Family in America* (see Introduction, n. 1), paints a portrait of the Italian American mind after three

generations forming its notions of itself more through trips to the mall and to the Sunbelt than to Rome or to the library.

22. Carole Maso, *Ghost Dance* (San Francisco: North Point Press, 1986), p. 224.

23. Joseph Capobianco was Registrar, Queens College, City University of New York, when I heard him say this in a meeting of the Italian American Faculty and Staff Advisory Council. He later became Registrar of Columbia University and then of St. John's University, both in New York City.

24. Gay Talese, "Where Are the Italian American Novelists?" *New York Times Book Review,* March 14, 1993, pp. 1, 23, 25, 29.

25. Gay Talese, "Frank Sinatra Has a Cold," *The Gay Talese Reader: Portraits and Encounters* (New York: Walker, 2003), pp. 18–63. This portrait, first published in *Esquire* in April 1966, was reprinted in the magazine's 70th anniversary issue in October 2003 and celebrated as the best story *Esquire* had ever published.

26. Gay Talese, *The Kingdom and the Power* (New York: World, 1967), p. 7

Chapter 9. The Italian American Sign

1. Marvin Carlson, *The Italian Shakespeareans: Performances by Ristori, Salvini, and Rossi in England and America* (Washington, D.C.: Folger Books, 1985), provides a richly detailed history of this remarkable phenomenon.

2. Murray J. Levith, *Shakespeare's Italian Settings and Plays* (London: Macmillan, 1989), is a comprehensive survey.

3. George Pettie, *The Civile Conversation of M. Steeven Guazzo,* vol. 1 (New York: Knopf, 1927), p. 27. John Leon Lievsay, *Stefano Guazzo and the English Renaissance, 1575–1675* (Chapel Hill: University of North Carolina Press, 1961) is a very thorough study of the influence on English culture of this remarkable writer's work.

4. Sacvan Bercovitch outlines the persistence of this narrative in *The American Jeremiad* (Madison: University of Wisconsin Press, 1978). See also Ellwood Johnson, *The Pursuit of Power: Studies in the Vocabulary of Puritanism* (New York: Lang, 1995), and Michael Kammen, *Mystic Chords of Memory: The Transformation of Tradition in American Culture* (New York: Vintage, 1993).

5. Jean Baudrillard, *For a Critique of the Political Economy of the Sign,* trans. Charles Levin (St. Louis: Telos Press, 1981), introduces the practice of treating the Saussurean sign as operating with social, political, and economic geography.

6. Federico Chabod, *Italian Foreign Policy: The Statecraft of the Founders,* trans. William McCuaig (Princeton, N.J.: Princeton University Press, 1996).

7. On the relationship between post-Risorgimento *grandezza*, such as it was, and the Italians of the diaspora, see Robert Viscusi, "Making Italy Little," in *Social Pluralism and Literary History: The Literature of the Italian Emigration*, ed. Francesco Loriggio (Toronto: Guernica, 1996), pp. 61–90.

8. This economy is the theme of John Paul Russo's classic article, "From Italophilia to Italophobia: Representations of Italians in the Early Gilded Age," *Differentia: Review of Italian Thought* 6–7 (Spring 1994): 45–75.

9. I use this term predominantly here in its reference to architecture and material culture. See Richard Guy Wilson, Diane Pilgrim, and Richard Murray, *The American Renaissance, 1876–1917* (New York: Pantheon, 1979). But the importance of the term *Renaissance* in American cultural and intellectual history goes beyond any single kind of manifestation and is best signaled by the variety of uses to which it has been turned. In literary study, it usually refers to the period between 1830 and 1860, when many of the best-known masterpieces of American literature were published. F. O. Matthiessen, who gave this usage its perennial currency, wrote in his definitive work *American Renaissance: Art and Expression in the Age of Emerson and Whitman* (New York: Oxford University Press, 1941), p. vii, "It may not seem precisely accurate to refer to our mid-nineteenth century as a *re-birth;* but that was how the writers themselves judged it. Not as a re-birth of values that had existed previously in American, but as America's way of producing a renaissance, by coming to its first maturity and affirming its rightful heritage in the whole expanse of art and culture." Summary of reasoning: "The American Renaissance is a Renaissance because we say it is." Matthiessen's desire to assimilate the Transcendentalists to the Renaissance is itself so implausible as to suggest the power of the term *Renaissance*, its generic ability to signify for an American in the mid-twentieth century "the whole expanse of art and culture." Indeed, critics continue to employ the term, even those whose purposes distinctly contest Matthiessen's, such as David S. Reynolds, *Beneath the American Renaissance: The Subversive Imagination in the Age of Emerson and Melville* (Cambridge, Mass.: Harvard University Press, 1988), or the critics collected in Walter Benn Michaels and Donald Pease, eds., *The American Renaissance Reconsidered* (Baltimore, Md.: Johns Hopkins University Press, 1985).

10. Mariana Griswold Van Rensselaer, "The Triumph of the Fair Builders," *Forum* 14 (December 1892): 527–40, repr. in David Gebhard, ed., Mariana Griswold Van Rensselaer, *Accents as Well as Broad Effects: Writings on Architecture, Landscape, and the Environment, 1876–1925* (Berkeley: University of California Press, 1996), p. 69.

11. Ilaria Serra, *Immagini di un immaginario: L'Emigrazione italiana negli Stati Uniti fra I due secoli* (1890–1924) (Verona: Cierre, 1997), pp. 39–160, gives a comprehensive survey of how the United States regarded the Italian immigrants, with particular attention (pp. 58–97) to how The *New York Times* saw the immigrants in the early years, even in the 1870s, well before the massive inflows of the decades that followed.

12. For a full account of Ciambelli's work, see Franca Bernabei, "Little Italy's Eugene Sue," in *Adjusting Sites: New Essays in Italian American Studies,* ed. William Boelower and Rocco Pallone (Center for Italian Studies, SUNY Stony Brook: Fililibrary, 1999), pp. 3–56. See also Martino Marazzi, *Misteri di Little Italy: Storie e testi della letteratura italoamericana* (Milan: Franco Angeli, 2001).

13. Many of the Italophone writers anthologized in Francesco Durante, ed., *Italo Americana: Storia e letteratura degli italiani negli Stati Uniti 1776–1880* (Milano: Mondadori, 2001), retain a vivid connection with the ideological and political concerns that dominate discourse in Rome and Milan, rather than with the conditions and challenges of life in the United States.

14. William Shakespeare, *The Tempest,* ed. Frank Kermode (cambridge, Mass.: harvard University Press, 1954), I, ii, 366–67.

15. Arturo Giovannitti, "To the English Language," in *The Collected Poems of Arturo Giovannitti* (Chicago: Clemente, 1962), p. 110.

16. Bartolomeo Vanzetti, letter to his father, October 1, 1920, in *Justice Crucified: The Story of Sacco and Vanzetti,* ed. Roberta Strauss Feuerlicht, trans. Victor Kostka (New York: McGraw-Hill, 1977), p. 187.

17. Philip D. Stong, "The Last Days of Sacco and Vanzetti," cited in Feuerlicht, p. 344. Feuerlicht, p. 345, reports that the scholar Robert D'Attilio has cast doubt on the authenticity of this speech.

18. Bartolomeo Vanzetti, speech before being sentenced, cited in Louis Joughin and Edmund M. Morgan, *The Legacy of Sacco and Vanzetti* (1948; repr. Princeton, N.J.: Princeton University Press, 1978), p. 500.

19. Europeans since De Tocqueville have engaged in this project with varying degrees of respect and attention. The case of twentieth century Italian writers has its own distinct aspects, and these are well-covered in Martino Marazzi, *Little America: Gli Stati Uniti e gli scrittori italiani del Novecento* (Milano: Marcos y Marcos, 1998).

20. Emanuel Carnevali, in *The Autobiography of Emanuel Carnevali,* ed. Kay Boyle (New York: Horizon Press, 1967), pp. 179–80.

21. Elias Boudinot, *An Address to the Whites, Delivered in the First Presbyterian Church on the 26th of May, 1826* (Philadelphia: Geddes, 1826), cited in *The Heath Anthology of American Literature,* ed. Paul Lauter. 4th ed. (Boston: Houghton Mifflin, 2002), p. I, 1411.

22. John Ciardi, "Foreword to the Reader of (Some) General Culture," *Live Another Day* (New York: Twayne, 1949), p. ii.

23. Archibald MacLeish to John Ciardi, September 1972, cited in *John Ciardi: A Biography,* ed. Edward M. Cifelli (Fayetteville: University of Arkansas Press, 1997), p. 335.

24. Cited in Cifelli, p. 438.

25. John Ciardi, "S.P.Q.R. A Letter from Rome," in *The Collected Poems of John Ciardi,* ed. Edward M. Cifelli (Fayetteville: University of Arkansas Press, 1997), pp. 217–19.

26. Fred Gardaphe, *Italian Signs, American Streets*, p. 13 (see chap. 2, n. 21).

27. William Boelhower, *Immigrant Autobiography in the United States* (see chap. 4, n. 6); *Through a Glass Darkly* (see chap. 7, n. 3); *Autobiographical Transactions in Modernist America* (see chap. 7, n. 3).

28. Constantine Panunzio, *The Soul of an Immigrant* (New York: Macmillan, 1928).

29. Louise De Salvo, "A Portrait of the *Puttana* as a Middle-Aged Woolf Scholar," in *The Dream Book: An Anthology of Writings by Italian American Women*, ed. Helen Barolini (1895; repr. Syracuse, N.Y.: Syracuse University Press, 2000), pp. 93–100.

30. Mariana De Marco Torgovnick, *Crossing Ocean Parkway: Readings by an Italian American Daughter* (see chap. 1, n. 18).

31. Robert A. Orsi, *The Madonna of 115th Street* (see chap 8, n. 11).

32. Kenneth Ciongoli and Jay Parini, eds., *Beyond the Godfather; Italian American Writers on the Real Italian American Experience* (Hanover, N.H.: University Press of New England, 1997).

33. Pellegrino D'Acierno, "Cinema Paradiso," in Pellegrino D'Acierno, ed., *The Italian American Heritage: A Companion to Literature and Arts* (New York: Garland, 1999), p. 619, writes that "perceived as atavistic Whites—people of the (blue-collar) body, the last White ethnics, what the playwright Albert Innaurato calls 'nigger-Italians'—they function as 'floating signifiers' for the majority culture, which voices its discontents through the mouthpiece of their stereotypes, all of those things that it has repressed in the name of political correctness."

34. Tina De Rosa, *Paper Fish* (Chicago: The Wine Press, 1980).

35. Don DeLillo, *Underworld* (see chap. 8, n. 17).

36. Anthony Julian Tamburri, *A Semiotic of Ethnicity: In (Re)cognition of the Italian/American Writer* (Albany: State University of New York Press, 1997), pp. 77–78.

37. Pierre Bourdieu, *The Logic of Practice*, trans. Richard Nice (Stanford: Stanford, Calif. University Press), p. 56.

Chapter 10. The Imperial Sopranos

1. George Meredith, "Love in the Valley," in *The Poems of George Meredith*, ed. Patricia B. Barrett (New Haven, Conn.: Yale University Press, 1978), I, p. 256, l. 184.

2. Jesse Green, "Her Stage Mother, Herself," *New York Times*, Sunday, April 27, 2003, Arts and Leisure, p. 1. The relationship between Italian American women and their patronyms is a subject that many writers have addressed, particularly Helen Barolini, in "How I Learned to Speak Italian," *Chiaroscuro* (West Lafayette, Ind.: Bordighera, 1997), pp. 1–13, and Maria Mazziotti Gillan, *Taking Back My Name* (San Francisco: malafemmina press, 1991).

3. Sandra M. Gilbert and Susan Gubar, *The Madwoman in the Attic: The Woman Writer and the Nineteenth-Century Literary Imagination* (New Haven, Conn.: Yale University Press, 1979).

4. Curt Schleier, "The Many Faces of Evan Hunter," *Ironminds http:// www.ironminds.com/ironminds/issues/010110/hunter.shtml*, downloaded July 6, 2003.

5. Alex Witchel, "The Son Who Created a Hit, 'The Sopranos,'" *New York Times,* June 6, 1999, rpt in *The New York Times on* The Sopranos (New York: ibooks, 2000), pp. 43–53, writes "[Chase] says it was his paternal grandfather who changed the family name from De Cesare to Chase, but he won't say why. 'It was a situation of l'amour fou,' is as far as he'll go, worried that relatives will get angry if he divulges more" (p. 47).

6. *The Sopranos,* Brad Grey Television (HBO Home Video DVD). Complete first four seasons. Referred to herein by season and episode number.

7. See for example, Glen O. Gabbard, M.D., *The Psychology of* The Sopranos: *Love, Death, Desire, and Betrayal in America's Favorite Gangster Family* (New York: Basic Books: 2002); Marice Yacowar, The Sopranos *on the Couch: Analyzing Television's Greatest Series* (New York: Continuum, 2003); Michael Flamini, "Pa cent'anni, Dr. Melfi," in *A Sitdown with the Sopranos: Watching Italian American Culture on T.V.'s Most Talked-About Series,* ed. Regina Barreca (New York: Palgrave, 2002), pp. 113–127; Ellen Willis, "Our Gangsters, Ourselves," in *This Thing of Ours: Investigating* The Sopranos, ed. David Lavery (New York: Columbia University Press, 2002), pp. 2–10.

8. Dr Melfi reminds him, "In your worst dreams, a duck flies off with your penis" (I, 10).

9. W. R. Burnett, *Little Caesar,* 2nd edition (New York: Dial Press, 1958); Mervyn LeRoy, director, *Little Caesar* (Warner Brothers, 1930); Paulie Walnuts cries out, "Mother of Mercy, could this be the end of Rico?" when Christopher turns down an evening with prostitutes to keep a date with Adriana (I, 10).

10. The best treatment of this subject is Philip V. Cannistraro, *Blackshirts in Little Italy: Italian Americans and Fascism 1921–29,* VIA Folios 17 (West Lafayette, Ind.: Bordighera, 1999).

11. Ronald G. Musto, *Apocalypse in Rome: Cola di Rienzo and the Politics of the New Age* (Berkeley: University of California Press, 2003), pp. 344–47.

12. François Lafitte, *The Internment of Aliens,* new ed. (London: Libris, 1988), p. xiv. Terri Colpi, *The Italian Factor,* pp. 99–129 (see chap. 2, n. 10), tells the story of the internment and deportation of Italians in Great Britain during World War II. See also P. Gillman and L. Gillman, *Collar the Lot: How Britain Interned Its Wartime Refugees* (London: Quartet Books, 1980).

13. Colpi, pp, 114–21, recounts the events surrounding the sinking of the *Arandora Star* and pp. 217–78, provides a list of passengers lost on the ship. See also, Pietro Zorza, *Arandora Star,* supplement to *Italiani in Scozia,* Glasgow, 1985.

14. Rose D. Scherini, "When Italian Americans Were 'Enemy Aliens,'" in *Una storia segreta*, pp. 10–31 (see Intro., n. 9).

15. Gay Talese, *Unto the Sons* (New York: Knopf, 1992), p. 94.

16. Roy Palmer Domenico, *Italian Fascists on Trial, 1943–1948* (Chapel Hill: University of North Carolina Press, 1991), p. 148.

17. See Intro., n. 3.

18. Thomas Carlyle, *The French Revolution: A History* (New York: A. L. Burt, n.d.), I, p. 95.

19. Edward Alsworth Ross, "Italians in America," *Century Magazine* 87 (July 1914): 443–45. Cited in Salvatore J. La Gumina, *Wop! A Documentary History of Anti-Italian Discrimination* (Toronto: Guernica, 1999), p. 138.

20. Edward Alsworth Ross, "Italians in America," cited in La Gumina, *Wop!*, p. 140.

21. James Goode, *Wiretap: Listening in on America's Mafia* (New York: Simon and Schuster, 1988), pp. 13–14. The degree of surveillance is hard to overestimate. In the investigation of the famous "Pizza Connection" case alone, for example, Robert J. Kelly, in *The Upperworld and the Underworld: Case Studies of Racketeering and Business Infiltrations in the United States* (New York: Kluwer, 1999), p. 125, writes,

> In 1982, Italian and American law enforcement agencies began to cooperate and exchange information, which eventuated in parallel investigations in the United States and Italy. Electronic surveillance was authorized at numerous business locations and establishments where suspects gathered. Through wiretaps, physical and electronic surveillance, law enforcement agents were able to identify the roles played by participants in the drug conspiracy. Within 2 years, the drug routes, delivery points, cash flows, distributors, collectors, and leaders of the conspiracy had been identified. Police in Brazil and Spain cooperated in making arrests and these were coordinated with arrests in New York, New Jersey, Wisconsin, Michigan, Philadelphia, Brooklyn and Queens, New York City, where homes and businesses of Pizza Connection conspirators were raided.

22. Joseph F. O'Brien and Andris Kurins, *Boss of Bosses, The Fall of the Godfather: The FBI and Paul Castellano* (New York: Simon and Schuster, 1991), p. 127.

23. Google search on October 14, 2003.

24. A good introduction to the subject is Sarah Bradford, *Cesare Borgia: His Life and Times* (London: Weidenfeld and Nicholson, 1976).

25. Niccolò Machiavelli, *The Prince,* trans. George Bull, rev. ed. (New York: Penguin, 2003), p. 25. See also, Wayne A. Rebhorn, "Spectacles of Violence and the Memory of Fear," in *Foxes and Lions: Machiavelli's Confidence Man* (Ithaca, N.Y.: Cornell University Press, 1988), pp. 86–154.

26. Carol Gino, "Afterword, " in Mario Puzo, *The Family*, completed by Carol Gino (New York: Avon, 2001), p. 415.

27. Richard A. Levin, *Shakespeare's Secret Schemers: The Study of an Early Modern Dramatic Device* (Newark: University of Delaware Press, 2001), p. 18.

28. Nicholas Pileggi, *Wiseguy: Life in a Mafia Family* (New York: Pocket Books, 1985), pp. 13, 36–37.

29. Gramsci, *Selections*, p. 219.

30. Julia Kristeva, *Powers of Horror: An Essay on Abjection*, trans. Leon S. Roudiez (New York: Columbia University Press, 1982), studies the relationship between identity and the power of the things one must reject. John Limon, *Stand-up Comedy in Theory, or, Abjection in America* (Durham, N.C.: Duke University Press, 2000), p. 4., calls the focus "a psychic worrying of those aspects of oneself that one cannot be rid of, that seem, but are not quite, alienable—for example, urine, feces, nails, and the corpse." This intrapsychic process has an obvious application as a social model; Karen Shimakawa, *National Abjection: The Asian American Body Onstage* (Durham, N.C.: Duke University Press, 2002) coins the expression "national abjection," using it to define the relationship between Asian Americans and U.S. Americanness, and offering "this paradigm as a descriptive model of the particular forms of racial, cultural, and often sexual abjection that (partially) construct 'minority' and 'dominant' cultures in the United States" (p. 165, n. 5).

31. Robert Venturi, Denise Scott Brown, and Steven Izenour, *Learning from Las Vegas*, rev. ed. (Cambridge, Mass.: MIT Press, 1991), pp. 18–19, find Rome in Las Vegas, with particular reference to Caesars Palace, though not only to that.

32. Martin Spevack, ed., *Julius Caesar* (Cambridge, England: Cambridge University Press, 1988), p. 55, in a note to 1.2.3, cites "Stevens' comments on the spellings 'Antonio,' 'Octavio,' 'Flavio': 'The players were more accustomed to Italian than Roman terminations, on account of the many versions from Italian novels, and the many Italian characters in dramatic pieces formed from the same originals.'"

33. Herbert Wise, director, *I, Claudius*, TV mini-series in 13 episodes (London: British Broadcasting Corporation, 1976), shown on American television by Masterpiece Theater, Public Broadcasting System.

34. Michael Parenti, *The Assassination of Julius Caesar: A People's History of Ancient Rome* (New York: New Press, 2003), places Julius Caesar firmly in the tradition of *populares*, or aristocrats who built their strength on sensible representation of the needs of ordinary Roman citizens rather than only those of their own class. Roosevelt and Kennedy, among U.S. presidents, have received the most frequent criticism from other millionaires as "traitors to their class."

35. Don DeLillo, *The Names* (New York: Vintage, 1983), p. 202.

36. Don DeLillo, *Underworld* (New York: Scribner's, 1997). Few of DeLillo's critics have seen how his work functions in the Italian American intertext. Fred Gardaphe, *Italian Signs, American Streets*, pp. 172–92 (see chap. 2, n. 21), published a few years before *Underworld,* does an excellent job of reading DeLillo's earlier works from this point of view, and provides a theoretical and cultural grounding for reading DeLillo's subsequent, more openly Italian American, work. *Underworld* has inspired a number of commentaries specifically focused on this aspect of the work: James Periconi, "DeLillo's *Underworld*: Toward a New Beginning for the Italian American Novel," *VIA: Voices in*

Italian Americana XI, no. 1 (Spring 2000): 141–58; John Paul Russo, "DeLillo: Italian American Catholic Writer," *Altreitalie* 25 (2002): 4–29; "Little Italy and Technology in DeLillo's *Underworld,* Proceedings of the Conference, "Culture e contatto nelle Americhe," Univerity of Salerno, Salerno, Italy, December 2000, forthcoming; "Technology and the Mediterranean in DeLillo's Underworld," in *America and the Mediterranean. Proceedings of the Sixteenth Biennial International Conference,* ed. Massimo Bacigalupo and Pierangelo Castagneto (Torino: Otto editore, 2003), pp. 187–96.

37. Tony's career as a critique of American culture is the theme of two essays in Regina Barreca, ed., *A Sitdown with* The Sopranos: Jay Parini, "The Cultural Work of *The Sopranos,*" pp. 75–88 (see chap. 4, n. 24), and Fred Gardaphe, "Fresh Garbage," pp. 89–111. The gangster myth functions this way according to Chris Messenger, The Godfather *and American Culture: How the Corleones Became "Our Gang"* (See chapter 2, n. 21).

Index

"Introduction," *in Letters from a New World: Amerigo Vespucci's Discovery of America*, 229n2

Fowler, H. W., 117, 236n11; *A Dictionary of Modern English*, 236n11

France, 7, 86, 194, 205; French, 2, 7, 11, 28, 31, 32, 34, 42, 101, 161, 194, 195, 216, 227n6, 246n18

Franzina, Emilio, xx

Fratelli d'Italia: La vera storia dell'inno di Mameli, 220n4

Freud, Sigmund, 60; Freudian, 103, 127, 226n5, 234n15; Freudianized immigrant, 226n5

From the Margin: Writings in Italian Americana, xxi, xxii, 224n4

Frost, Robert, 179

Fucillo, Vincent, xx

Fumento, Rocco, 49, 153, 224n15; *Tree of Dark Reflection*, 49, 224n16

funeral(s), 64, 97, 108, 149, 196, 208–9, 233n6

futurism, 107, 172

Gabaccia, Donna, 228n18, 240n19; *Italy's Many Diasporas*, 228n18; *From Sicily to Elizabeth Street: Housing and Social Change among Italian Immigrants, 1880–1930*, 240n19

Gabbard, Glen O., 245n7; *The Psychology of* The Sopranos: *Love, Death, Desire, and Betrayal in America's Favorite Gangster Family*, 245n7

Gabriel, Dariel, xx, 150, 240n13; *Sacco and Vanzetti: A Narrative Longpoem*, 150, 240n13

Galante, Carmine, 203

Gallagher, Dorothy, 225n22; *All the Right Enemies: The Life and Murder of Carlo Tresca*, 225n22

Gallo, Joey, 203, 207

Gambino, Richard, xx, 96, 220n2, 224n20, 231n15, 240n10, 240n19; *Vendetta: The True Story of the Largest Lynching in U.S. History*; 220n2, 231n15; *Blood of My Blood: The Dilemma of the Italian Americans*, 224n20, 240n10

gangster(s), ix, 3, 22–23, 79, 152, 185–86, 190–93, 197–200, 205, 207, 210, 214–15, 217, 245n7, 248n37; as military leaders, 192–93; as subaltern force, 192–93

Garcia, Magdelibia, xxi

Gardaphe, Fred, ii, xvi, xvi, xxi, xxii, 41, 72, 77, 152, 178–79, 181–83, 186, 224n4, 225n21, 239n1, 244n26, 247n36, 248n37; *Italian Signs, American Streets: The Evolution of Italian American Narrative*, xxii, 186, 225n21, 244n26, 247n26; *Dagoes Read: Tradition and the Italian American Writer*, xxii; *Leaving Little Italy: Essaying Italian American Culture*, xxii; "Mora Amore," 224n4; *The ItalianAmerican Writer: An Essay and Annotated Checklist*, 239n1; *The IAWA Bibliography of the Italian American Book*, 239n1, "Fresh Garbage," 248n37

Gardiner, Eileen, xx

Gardner, Isabella Stewart, 165

Gastaldo, Piero, 232n1, *The Columbus People*, 232n1

Genealogy, 21, 193; genealogical, 21, 43

Gershwin, George, 125

Gestures, 9, 38, 53, 85, 101, 106, 126, 217

Ghislanzoni, Antonio, 228n10

Gilbert, Sandra M., 178, 189, 245n3; *The Madwoman in the Attic: The Woman Writer and the Nineteenth-Century Literary Imagination*, 245n3

Gillan, Maria Mazziotti, xx, 25, 158, 215, 221n1, 221n3, 244n2; "Growing Up Italian," 221n3; "Public School No. 18: Paterson, New Jersey," 221n1; *Where I Come From: Selected and New Poems*, 221n1; *Where I Come From*, 221n3; *Taking Back My Name*, 244n2

Gillman, P. and L. Gillman, 245n12; *Collar the Lot: How Britain Interned Its Wartime Refugees*, 245n12

Gino, Carol, 204, 246n26; "Afterword, " in Mario Puzo, *The Family*, 204, 246n26

Ginzburg, Natalia, 222n7; *La famiglia Manzoni*, 222n7; *The Manzoni Family*, 222n7

national enemies, 20
national heroes, 20, 74
nationalist, 9, 12–13, 15, 17, 33, 35, 42, 74–75, 85, 186; ideology, 15
national imaginary, 19, 31
National Italian American Foundation (NIAF), 184–85, 223n15; *Beyond the Godfather; Italian American Writers on the Real Italian American Experience*, 185, 244n32
nationalization, 20, 74–75
national languages, xiii, 17, 25, 31–33, 35, 78, 178, 222n7
national literatures, xiii, xvii
national Italian, 26, 31–34, 37, 194–85, 221n10, 222n7
national standard Italian, 25
Neapolitan(s), 11, 14, 52, 70, 89, 132, 134, 153, 198–200
Nelli, Humbert S., 231n16; *The Italians in Chicago, 1880–1930: A Study in Ethnic Mobility*, 231n16
Nero, Claudius Caesar Drusus, 158
neurotic disturbance, 122
neurotic "solutions," xii, xiii
New England, 84, 86, 194, 244n32
New Jersey, 76, 170, 194, 221n1, 246; Edgewater, 76; Ocean City, 194; Paterson, 170, 221n1; North Caldwell, 190, 200
New Orleans, 88, 194, 231n15
New Republic, The, 95
New World, The, 20, 44, 45, 63, 67, 81, 82, 142, 144, 146, 151, 164, 217, 229n2
New Yorker, The, 158
New York Times Book Review, The, 157
Nicholas of Lyra, 141, 239n4
Nicknames(s), 44, 55, 57
Nietzsche, Friedrich, 92, 107, 153, 234n21
Nocerino, Kathryn, xx
nonsense, 111, 113, 115, 118–19, 122–23, 128–30, 134–35, 236n4–5, 237n18
Norton, Charles Eliot, 164
notion of an Italian American as an Italian export, 154
Nowell, Geoffrey, 220n6

O'Brien Joseph F., 201, 246n22; *Boss of Bosses, The Fall of the Godfather: The*

FBI and Paul Castellano, 200–1, 246n22
obsessional neurosis, 60
Odet, Clifford, 99, 234n12; *Awake and Sing*, 99–100, 234n12
Oedipus, 61, 104
Old World, 63, 142, 146, 164
Onomatomania, 190
opera, 2–3, 10, 16, 20, 23, 62, 65, 72, 74–76, 126, 141, 162, 164–65, 191, 195, 203, 228n17, 229n23, 232n19
Origen, 141
originary solitude, 110
Origo, Iris, 38
Orsi, Robert A., 147–8, 184, 240n11, 244n31; *The Madonna of 115th Street: faith and Community in Italian Harlem, 1880–1950*, 147–48, 184, 240n11
Orsini, Daniel, 225n24; "Rehabilitating diDonato: A Phonocentric Novelist," 225n24
Oscan, 34
O'Shea, Nancy, xxi
Ossoli, Margaret Fuller, 38
Ovid (P. Ovidius Naso),7

paesani, 8, 14, 101, 122, 124, 127–29, 228n5
paese, 65, 78, 89
Painter, William, 205; *The Palace of Pleasure*, 205
Paglia, Camille, 37, 153, 185
Palazzo Adriani, 46
Palazzo di Giustizia, 164
Palestine, 16
Palladio, Andres, 165
Pallitto, Elizabeth, xx
Pallone, Rocco, xx, 243n12; *Adjusting Sites: New Essays in Italian American Studies,* 243n12
Palma, Michael, xx
Pane, Josephine, and Remigion Pane, xx
Panetta, George, 215, 225n28; *We Ride a White Donkey*, 225n28
Pankiewicz, Flavia, xx
Pantheon, 7, 73, 242n9
Panunzio, Constantine, 184, 244n29; *The Soul of an Immigrant*, 184, 244n29
Paolucci, Anne, xx

worker Christ, 105–6
working class culture, 105–6
World's Columbian Exposition 1893,
    156–66
World market, 29
World War I, 12–13, 67
World War II, xxi, 3, 13, 78, 96, 105, 107,
    110, 173, 200, 219n1, 245n12
Wright, Richard, 100
writers, 1, 5, 13, 15–18, 21–23, 31, 37,
    39–40, 42–46, 49, 53, 58–59, 77–78,
    87, 105, 126–27, 130, 155, 157–59,
    161, 169, 173–74, 178–79, 181–82,
    184–86, 201, 215, 220n8, 221n8,
    222n11, 232n20, 239n1, 242n9,
    243n13, 244n32, 244n2
Wyatt, Sir Thomas, 38, 223n17

xenoglossia, 236n4
Xiques, Donez, xx

Yacowar, Marice, 245n7; The Sopranos on
    the Couch: Analyzing Television's Great-
    est Series, 245n7
Yale Italian Studies, xxi
Yale University, 41, 86
Yans-McLoughlin, Virginia, 240n19;
    Family and Community: Italian Immi-
    grants in Buffalo, 1880–1930, 240n19
Yezierska, Anzia, 84, 230n8; Bread
    Givers, 84, 230n8

Zanderer, Leo, xx
Zegna, Ermenegildo, 37
Zukin, Sharon, xx